MW01101146

For Katherine
with best wishes
David Dollenmayer

Childhood

JUDAIC TRADITIONS IN LITERATURE, MUSIC, AND ART
Ken Frieden *and* Harold Bloom, *Series Editors*

Other titles in Judaic Traditions in Literature, Music, and Art

Facing the Fires: Conversations with A. B. Yehoshua
Bernard Horn

Finding the Jewish Shakespeare: The Life and Legacy of Jacob Gordin
Beth Kaplan

A House with Seven Windows: Short Stories
Kadya Molodowsky; Leah Schoolnik, trans.

In Lieu of Memory: Contemporary Jewish Writing in France
Thomas Nolden

The Jewish Book of Fables: Selected Works
Eliezer Shtaynbarg; Curt Leviant, trans. & ed.

Nathan and His Wives: A Novel
Miron C. Izakson; Betsy Rosenberg, trans.; Ken Frieden, ed.

Polish-Jewish Literature in the Interwar Years
Eugenia Prokop-Janiec; Abe Shenitzer, trans.

Representing the Immigrant Experience: Morris Rosenfeld and the Emergence of Yiddish Literature in America
Marc Miller

Songs from Bialik: Selected Poems of Hayim Nahman Bialik
Atar Hadari, trans.

Who Will Say Kaddish? A Search for Jewish Identity in Contemporary Poland
Larry Mayer, text; Gary Gelb, photographs

CHILDHOOD

◆ ◆ ◆ *An Autobiographical Fragment* ◆ ◆ ◆

Moses Rosenkranz

Translated from the German by David Dollenmayer
With an Introductory Essay by Matthias Huff

SYRACUSE UNIVERSITY PRESS

First Edition 2007
07 08 09 10 11 12 6 5 4 3 2 1

Originally published in German as *Kindheit: Fragment einer Autobiographie* (Aachen: Rimbaud Verlag, 2003).

This book was published with the assistance of the Office of the Provost, Worcester Polytechnic Institute.

The paper used in this publication meets the minimum requirements of American National Standard for Information Sciences—Permanence of Paper for Printed Library Materials, ANSI Z39.48-1984.∞™

For a listing of books published and distributed by Syracuse University Press, visit our Web site at SyracuseUniversityPress.syr.edu.

ISBN-13: 978-0-8156-3178-1 ISBN-10: 0-8156-3178-2

Library of Congress Cataloging-in-Publication Data

Rosenkranz, Moses.
[Kindheit. English]
Childhood : an autobiographical fragment / Moses Rosenkranz ; translated from the German by David Dollenmayer ; with an introductory essay by Matthias Huff. — 1st ed.
p. cm.
Includes bibliographical references.
ISBN-13: 978-0-8156-3178-1 (cloth : alk. paper)
1. Rosenkranz, Moses—Childhood and youth. 2. Authors, German—20th century—Biography. I. Dollenmayer, David B. II. Title.

PT2678.O7585Z46 2007
830.9'00914—dc22 2007028528

Manufactured in the United States of America

• • •

Contents

MOSES ROSENKRANZ was born in the Austro-Hungarian province of Bucovina in 1904. His first volume of poetry was published in Czernowitz in 1930. During the Second World War, he was interned in a Romanian fascist labor camp, escaped in 1944, was arrested by the Soviets in Bucharest in 1947, and spent ten years in the Gulag. In 1961, he fled Romania and settled in West Germany, where he died in 2003.

◆ ◆ ◆

DAVID DOLLENMAYER, professor of German at the Worcester Polytechnic Institute, is the author of *The Berlin Novels of Alfred Döblin* (University of California, 1988) and has translated works by Bertolt Brecht, Michael Kleeberg, Anna Mitgutsch, and Perikles Monioudis.

◆ ◆ ◆

Translator's Note

MOSES ROSENKRANZ (1904–2003) was above all a lyric poet. As he makes clear in *Childhood*, the poems he quotes were youthful experiments, but several examples of his mature work can be found in Matthias Huff's introductory essay.

In translating the poetry, which is almost always rhymed, I have abandoned rhyme and hewed closely to the sense of the German, while retaining as much of the strong rhythmic pulse as possible. For comparison, the German originals are reproduced in the notes.

The original manuscript has no chapter divisions, so I have created them and added titles (in square brackets).

My deepest thanks go to the poet's widow and coeditor of *Kindheit*, Frau Doris Rosenkranz, for her invaluable assistance, advice, and encouragement.

◆ ◆ ◆

"I Carried My Villages Within Me . . ."

Reflections on Moses Rosenkranz's Autobiographical Fragment *Childhood*

MATTHIAS HUFF

THIS WORK IS A MEMOIR written in a void, an extraordinary temporal and spatial vacuum. It conjures up a world, but not just for the reader. In Bucharest in 1958, at the age of fifty-four, Moses Rosenkranz re-created the story of his childhood and thereby re-created himself as well.

In 1957, Rosenkranz had returned to Bucharest after ten years in the Gulag Archipelago. Between him and his childhood in the Bucovina lay thirty-eight years and several lifetimes. The childhood he describes in his memoir ended in 1919. In the decade that followed, Moses Rosenkranz would eke out a living as a porter, apprentice printer, private German tutor, factory worker, graphologist, and translator, among other things. In Alsatia and Paris, he experienced the lot of an underpaid migrant worker. From 1927 to 1930, he served in the Romanian army. Friends and patrons persuaded him to publish his first volume of poetry, *Leben in Versen* (Life [or Living] in verses, Czernowitz, 1930). In it and in the subsequent volumes *Gemalte Fensterscheiben* (Painted windowpanes, 1936) and *Die*

Tafeln (The tablets, 1940), Rosenkranz proved himself one of the outstanding German poets of the Bucovina, although he lived mostly in Bucharest, far from the literary salons of Czernowitz (today, the Ukrainian city of Chernivtsi). There he associated with Romanian politicians, journalists, and artists. He translated Romanian folk songs and poetry, worked for the Romanian Foreign Ministry, and was the private secretary of the politician and writer Ion Pillat. He prepared graphological analyses for a newspaper. The queen of Romania was so impressed by his analysis of an anonymous sample of her handwriting that she hired him on the spot to ghostwrite the German version of her autobiography.[1] After the Germans invaded the Bucovina, Rosenkranz spent the years from 1942 to 1944 in a Romanian fascist work camp, from which he managed to escape in 1944. When the war ended, he worked for the International Red Cross, fell out of favor for aiding ethnic Germans, was abducted by the Russian secret service in 1947, and spent ten years in the Gulag, mostly in the northernmost camp Norilsk and often in extreme deprivation.

In 1958, although he survived the camps, he had not yet really returned and was still a nonperson. Two poems from that year bear the titles "Der Gemiedene" and "Der Erledigte": "Shunned" and "Discarded."

Discarded

No one comes to visit me,
no one awaits me anymore:
whom life has crossed out in its book
to him the world denies return.

The world's done crying over me,
has laid upon me its last word;

who cares to see, when sunlight shines,
that a dead man is drawing nigh?

And that is me. The world denies
that I have risen from the grave,
have taken back my erstwhile face,
and come back down the mountain slope.

Whom life has crossed out in its book
to him the world denies return:
no one comes to visit me,
no one awaits me anymore.[2]

The poems in which Rosenkranz laconically articulates his experience, capturing what is happening to him with lyrical concision, are directly accessible to contemporary readers and certain to gain our sympathy. This is neither the poet's only nor even his original style. It began to appear as the Shoah was reaching the Bucovina, and it became his means of survival in the Gulag, for those were ten years of not just physical suffering. Moses Rosenkranz was not able to write because it was strictly forbidden to possess writing implements. Instead, he memorized his poems, including such icily comic ones as "Der Kuss" and wrote them down only much later:

The Kiss

The white light from the watch tower
flows down upon those squatting
on the plank in the Black Storm
and letting fall some dollops

The guards are standing close at hand
pointing rifles at them

so they can see officially
the movement in the rear

And that two faces, heedlessly,
dare to approach each other
causes one of the watchmen
to take a look from the front

And as he pulled his trigger
two mouths were in his sights
the kiss hung long in the frosty air
only the faces fell[3]

Moses Rosenkranz loves the laconic, the sensuous, the concrete. He is capable of writing about a romance between a tractor and a cow.[4] But his determination to poeticize, to speak in long lyrical lines, to reach out beyond his own life reasserts itself, in spite of everything militating against it.

Even from his years on the shore of the Arctic Ocean, there are paeans to the landscape. For Rosenkranz, nearness to the forces of nature was also an aide to survival.

Arctic Landscape

I walk upon Siberia's white map
where in the north it meets the Arctic Sea
the moon stands in the peacock's tail of northern lights
that shine down crackling on the tundra

From icy gorge Creation's storms drive mountains
of primeval, crystal snow before their blast
only large rivers reach the coast at last,
beneath the ice are wedded to the sea

Here ice-age glacier strangles still the soil,
in purest hardness glitters here the snow
upon it, as if cut from snow appears
the white bear and like a dream the deer

Against the black sky jangles a white pennant
brandished by invisible spirit's hand,
a triangle of geese and this portends
that Helios now recalls this land as well[5]

But in his Bucharest isolation of 1958, having been cut off from politics, history, and culture for ten years, Rosenkranz lacked all prerequisites for such poetry. At heart a political man, he must have been tortured by his inability to participate in society and public affairs.

In these circumstances, Rosenkranz began to write the first part of his autobiography. It was not really his genre; his life had been the source, not the subject, of his poetry. After two subsequent drafts of *Kindheit* and one entitled *Jugend* (Youth), he abandoned the project.[6] Rosenkranz published none of these drafts himself. He lost his eyesight in 1999 and approved but did not participate in the publication of *Kindheit* in 2003. The impetus came from the publisher, Rimbaud Verlag. For Rosenkranz, the poetry took precedence.

But the first version of *Kindheit*, written in 1958, published in 2003, and now translated into English, is a self-contained world. From its beginning—a series of unadorned facts, as if graven in stone—to its lapidary end, where Rosenkranz's gaze opens out into the world through the stories he hears, one can feel his gravity, vehemence, and poetic power. Through sheer willpower, the poet re-creates with his own hand the story of his life. Moses Rosenkranz applies to himself the procedure that characterizes his poetry, the turn downward and back to the past:

Prelude

In the downfall of poetry
with ear to shoulder blade
I discovered my direction
by taking backward steps.

I moved in my own heritage
where there's a German part as well
I started humming German
to heal my riven breast

From suffering's flames I salvaged
the word's pervading light
and thus armed found my way . . .
my way to poetry[7]

Rosenkranz chose this poem as a motto for the 1986 volume *Im Untergang.* In *Childhood,* this son of an eastern European Jewish peasant tells of his extraordinary recourse to German poetry and the genesis of his turn toward the past: "I began to perceive my family as a crumbling shell and inwardly tried to struggle my way down toward my ancestors. I felt their vigorous presence deep within me and hoped it would accrue to me, cushioning the collapse of the world around me" (p. 98). This turn to the past, a past lying not behind but beneath him, is fundamental to Moses Rosenkranz. Is it nostalgic, backward, out of date? The least one can say is that here the individual does not automatically find security in tradition, nor is the relationship to the past easy or unproblematic. The image of the individual consciously aiming to "accrue" the vigor of his ancestors is a modern one, perhaps more modern than Rosenkranz would have liked. To be sure, whoever engages with Rosenkranz soon learns that "modern" is not necessarily a positive attribute. But his modernity is an attempt to salvage both the individual within the tradition and the tradition by way of the individual who passes it on. Tradition becomes a weapon against the deficiencies of the present. If this turn downward does not necessarily represent progress, it always represents liberation:

Simile

Low-hung eaves and narrow walls
cruelly restrict his growth
force his green hands, against
their nature, to sink downwards

But the soil that gave him birth
is not indifferent to his pain
nourishes him with the full
richness of its pasturage

For one day he'll surely burst
what restricts him, cast abroad
that which has accrued to him
from the secrets of the earth[8]

Recourse to his roots is not just a matter of where he comes from or of survival, but of growth.

◆ ◆ ◆

The opening sentences of the memoir set the tone: "At the time of my birth in the fourth year of the new century, my mother was in the thirty-second year of her life. Father was ten years older." Here is someone exerting himself to the utmost to rebuild himself and his world with no cheap wallowing in memories. His powers of recall are neither problematic nor cause for celebration. The writer is happy with whatever he can rescue from oblivion: facts, memories, feelings, thoughts. He is no psychologist, but rather a sculptor, an architect, or a mason. Behind Rosenkranz's characterization of his mother as a raconteur, one can sense an entire theory of narration, or at least a narrative ideal: "Her subject matter was only what had really happened in her life, and yet, in sentences nourished by humor and irony and so precisely constructed that each word fit like a brick in a wall, she conjured up images of life beyond which one's ear always caught the distant rustle of the landscape of eternity, the spirit of the Seven Days of Creation" (p. 104).

If the narration is successful, then its significance will become clear. Nothing is forced. And when experience becomes insight, it still remains close to the experience that produced it rather than unraveling and destroying it:

> This is how a good soul like my mother could be lured into misdeeds by allowing herself to be guided by her speculative intellect.
>
> It wasn't that we were mistreated by her family, only that we suffered the same plight that was grinding them down. (p. 9)

Perhaps the attitude here is unmodern; certainly it is free of vanity. The narrator directs our attention to what is being narrated, not to the narration itself. If anything feels forced, it is the consciously understated gesture, the lack of sentimentality typical of Moses Rosenkranz:

> A book of human realities,
> no revelations, just report:
> its pages tempered with my sweat,
> in which the blood weaves images[9]

And about his Shoah poems, he said, "These poems are demonstrations of human possibilities. There's no lamentation, no weeping, just description."[10]

This memoir romanticizes nothing—not his poverty, not his family, not village life or homeland or east European Jewry, not the Bucovina. It never becomes cozy or anecdotal. Unbelievably moving events such as being taken prisoner by the Russians, flight, and exile are narrated so casually they may appear almost too matter-of-fact to contemporary readers, so that it takes us a little while before we realize their strange and extraordinary character:

> Father was the eighth of . . . eleven children, and after the Passover celebration in the tenth year of his life, he was given some polenta and a piece of cheese wrapped in a red handkerchief, summarily ejected from the cottage at the edge of Tlumacz, and sent out into the world like the four brothers who had preceded him. The outcast lad found shelter and work on the estate of a count, where, beginning as a stable boy, he worked his way up to tenant farmer by the time of my birth. (p. 2)

His father's life in two sentences, the fate of a child abandoned because of poverty. Rosenkranz's gesture: that's how it was. But also: it wasn't good and didn't have to be that way. What at first seems like tradition proves later to be individual guilt for which his grandfather, "who, by God's will, was our begetter but, through his own wickedness, not our provider" (p. 35), asks his sons' forgiveness.

Everything is seen from the pragmatic perspective of a peasant. Poverty is not idealized. The appropriate attitude toward it is not acceptance, but the effort to escape it, typical of his parents' lives. They treat the break with agricultural tradition in the same way. Education for the children loses or gains in value depending on how useful it promises to be and how endangered their agricultural existence is. Even during the family's farming life, however, education and literature play a role through his grandmother's poems, his sister's stories, and the ever-present question of schooling. Rosenkranz does not neglect these things in the interest of some false naïveté.

This memoir is especially valuable because of its authentic picture of peasant life. The narration is truly not just "about" the lower classes, but comes from below, a rare thing in German literature. Neither is it pseudonaïve, nor does it represent the yearning for authenticity of an intellectual who sees only himself when he looks into the depths. Moses Rosenkranz is a profound thinker, but neither an intellectual nor an academic. He is one of the few poets from the Bucovina—indeed, one of the few German poets at all—not subject to the leveling effect of a middle-class education that turns one's origins and homeland into mere random facts or picturesque themes. By leaving school at fifteen, having completed only the third year of gymnasium, Rosenkranz denied himself precisely this abstract and universal education. He became an autodidact in the best sense of the word, supplying himself with the knowledge he needed and could absorb:

School

Knowledge so they taught was power
I thought that over carefully
and I left the school[11]

These recollections are written by a person forced to leave his village, someone who has been around, who has seen much but still looks at and judges everything primarily from the point of view of the village: "I didn't possess or even know about the skills needed here: erudition, above all, and a quick tongue. Not that I thought any less of myself for all that. I carried my villages within me, and they lent even my silence weight and significance.

At least, that's how it seemed to me" (p. 94). And so the world of the village, far from any cultural center, is seen from a perspective distanced enough to allow one to see it whole—including its dependence on external forces—but also near enough to comprehend it as well.

Moses Rosenkranz was no peasant-poet, but his peasant origins put a decisive stamp on him and his work. He looked at everything from ground level. His whole life long, he judged situations first and foremost by what they offered in terms of room and board. In the Romanian army, for instance, he appreciated the food and his own bed: "I joined the army. For the first time in my life I got some good coffee. For the first time in my life I was surrounded by people who were gentle and didn't curse at me. For the first time in my life I had a bed, a place to sleep with a warm blanket, and at night I noticed that someone pulled it back over my feet."[12] The consistent starting point in the sensuously concrete, the practical, the physical is one of the most important characteristics of his poetry.

This look at his origins has nothing to do with romantic sentimentality. His villages have no superficial wholesomeness, nor is he seamlessly integrated into them. As the child of poor, non-Orthodox Jewish parents, this schoolboy was already falling between all possible stools.[13] Indeed, it is almost astonishing how badly villages and their inhabitants come off and how little their lives are portrayed as idyllic in the memoir of such a decisive partisan of the village and village life. In the village, nature, human nature, and God are closer than anywhere else, but that doesn't mean that everything is natural, humane, and divine. An adequate portrayal requires the poet and the poem:

The Village

First comes the crust
of sunburned, blackened moorland

a tangled mass
and reed stems shrilly whistling

And then the bodies
mysteriously emerging
as woman, man
from swamp's buffooneries

Such grimaces
play too across brash faces
coyly sly
hidden in pipe smoke

And bustling women
hounded by their chores
who dare to snatch
a momentary love

It's peat, that's all
remnant of worlds primeval
that in the village
gives its best to life[14]

The poet gives voice to the village: taciturn, precise, forceful, every word primordial, close to the phenomenon, expressing it seemingly for the first time and for all time. Poems like this have a tone unique in German literature. They attempt to grasp the world in its essence, without intermediaries. They are the work of an individual acting alone, standing completely outside the literary establishment for his entire life, someone without extensive schooling or university study who spent his first fifty-seven years not surrounded by the language of his poetry.

◆ ◆ ◆

One can sense throughout this memoir how Moses Rosenkranz is reconstructing not just his past, but the German language as well. Every word is tested, weighed, sometimes stroked against the grain. Literal meanings are uncovered and exploited. This German takes nothing for granted and is free of platitudes and clichés. The language is sometimes arduous, more often provocative. I have the impression that the recollections and the language that carries them emerged simultaneously, reinforcing each other. The language is the distant goal on the horizon of the memoirs, if they can be said to have a goal at all.

Moses Rosenkranz's decision to write in German is even more remarkable than it was for the other poets of the Bucovina who wrote in it. For them, German was simply the language of the upper class, the standard language of family life, the salons, the gymnasium, and the university. But Rosenkranz's home was a babel of Polish, Ruthenian, German, and Yiddish. German was only one option, although probably favored by his mother to facilitate the advancement of her children in society. It was not a foreign language for Rosenkranz, but neither was it his mother tongue. Until 1961, it was neither necessary nor even obvious that he write in German. If other Bucovina poets were wedded to German for social or practical reasons, Rosenkranz married it out of love: "My relationship with the German language is like a relationship with a—lost lover. Originally, my attitude toward Germany and its language was idealistic. I revered the Germans and loved the German language. Well, you know how that turned out, and that had consequences in my life as well."[15]

Bucovinian's Vision of Imperial Germany

Only known to me through hearsay
and the works your hands have fashioned
Land whose gleam I glimpse through fog
legendary and yet real

In fall when herons in migration
turn their flight in your direction
realm of poetry: my eye
follows from my heart their wake

But from afar I want to see you
lovely Germany in the distance
terrible they say is beauty[16]

When Rosenkranz wrote the memoir of his childhood in 1958, the final disappointment was still in store for him. He was writing a different kind of poetry in German at this point and not just in the poems directly related to the Shoah, such as "Der Weg zur Brause" (The path to the showers) or "Die Moritat vom entflogenen Sintiknaben" (The ballad of the Gypsy boy who flew away).[17] One can still sense the hope that the land of his poetic language, which he originally had no strong desire to see, might have something to offer him now: hardly a new homeland, but perhaps a refuge and a new audience. Three years later, however, when Rosenkranz fled to the Federal Republic of Germany, his hope for an audience would be bitterly disappointed. The threat that he might be indicted again had driven him from Romania, not any yearning for the West, and visa problems at the border were the handwriting on the wall:

At the German Border

My folk hangs from gallows
my village is burned
I've come to your country
on the sound of its word

My teeth held it tightly
I've guarded it well

in tears of defiance
for this day I've saved it

It belongs to your people
I held it in pledge
to me you will open
the gate to your land

. . . shut tight is the entry
no hearing I find;
have German words ceased
to have currency here?[18]

In the Federal Republic, the year 1961 was a very bad time for Moses Rosenkranz. He fit no category, belonged politically to neither the conservative nor the progressive camp, and the literary landscape was dominated by an extremely narrow modernism. University departments of German and the literary scene, bent on repressing the recent past in the interest of a lifeless, antiseptic hermeticism, had neutralized many opportunities for a lyric poetry already suppressed by the Nazis. Rosenkranz had no chance to be heard in this Germany.

The Federal Republic is thus a priori "your land," not his. It would not and could not become his homeland, but he surely expected his works to have a certain echo. He withdrew to the mountains of the Black Forest, forgotten by and too proud to force himself onto the literary establishment. He published the poems in the volumes *Im Untergang* (1986) and *Im Untergang II* (1988) on his own initiative. They were followed by *Bukowina: Gedichte 1920–1997* in 1998, a collection of thematically related poems published by Rimbaud Verlag.

Rosenkranz worked on old and new poems, was engaged by current events, and spoke out against both alienation from nature and environmental destruction—a spurned ally of the Green

Party, as it were. Without any hope of being heard, he wrote a kind of German exile literature within a Germany that could not possibly become his homeland:

The Reflection

Look into Lake Constance
gaze into the Rhine
into your dreams
spy out Germany

Nowhere you find yourself
everywhere see
vaguely a stranger's face
with mark of Cain

No water heals this hurt
no dream the pain
not from Lake Constance
not from the Rhine[19]

Moses Rosenkranz and Germany—a curious, dramatic story, and for Germany a shameful one. But to treat Rosenkranz's life and work only as a particularly egregious case of the German-Jewish identity crisis would be to diminish them unacceptably. Rosenkranz was justifiably bitter at being used and misused by German public opinion as a mere witness to history and at having his poems read narrowly only as images of the fate he suffered. We can be led astray by sympathy for someone who has been dealt an unbelievably harsh blow by fate. Rosenkranz's life was neither simply a destiny imposed by forces beyond his control nor a path leading straight to the final goal of civilized comfort in western Europe, vouchsafed to him only late in life. The horizon of his life and work extends far beyond the context of German-Jewish relations.

◆ ◆ ◆

Leben in Versen, Rosenkranz's first collection, could have no better title. He experienced both senses of *Leben.* Often enough there was nothing else he could do but *live*—and survive—in his verses. But he never abandoned the claim also to be capturing *life* in his verses.

The basic assumption of modern academic poetry—that only the hermetic, ideally empty poem is the appropriate counterpart to a modern reality that is inhumane and void of meaning—was as foreign to Rosenkranz as it could possibly be, and he suffered the consequences. His conception of language is more mature, more rich: "Language for me is a collection of everything that mankind has been through. And one has only to tap into it anywhere, in the right way, for it to come bubbling out."[20] Thus, language becomes the royal road leading backwards and downwards, making accessible those experiences that far transcend the individual.

Rosenkranz's literary ideal is formulated in the impression that the Grimm brothers' tales made on him as a child: "In the words of these stories . . . the real landscape and my place in it pulsated like a wave in a river, and this harmonious accommodation of reality within imagination, of nature within the spirit of art, delighted and enraptured me. It made more sense to me than anything had before" (p. 147). But in the twentieth century, it was not possible for Rosenkranz to be this ideal poet. What he creates as a poet of nature automatically acquires a different, rebellious character. At the age of eighty-nine, he described his path to literature:

> For me it was the feeling of being a stranger, alone—in the village community and even within my own large family—that led me to poetry. Isolated in this way, I preferred to wander the forest or spend time along the banks

> of the Pruth and the Czeremosch. I conversed with trees and waves and discovered that each of their movements possessed an inherent rhythm all its own. When I began to write poems, I tried to reproduce this rhythm in the melodies of my verses. I even thought I could hear this rhythm during my deportation, whether in the work camps in Moldavian villages or during my Siberian incarceration in the roar of the Russian winter gales. This is the explanation of the "miracle."[21] In other words, my poems are self-contained, like a group of marching men. They are disciplined and keep in step—in rhythm. They point to existing conditions but have an undertone of rebellion. They demonstrate things in a civilized way, and as a consequence they should be read with restraint but animation, within the context of a well-ordered freedom.[22]

Writing has to do a priori with isolation. Moses Rosenkranz's ideal poet is not a working farmer who writes poetry intuitively, in his spare time, so to speak. The poet is a stranger who nevertheless lives among his people, someone who puts up with his isolation rather than celebrates it:[23] "Playing a little higher than my brothers, / Off to one side, and yet the same as they."[24] Wandering around by himself, humming half-understood German—thus Rosenkranz began to write poems. The rhythm of life observed in nature, which he considers part of his heritage[25] and is still present in folk poetry, is the starting point for the rhythm and rhyme of his poems. Something of this determination to poeticize is preserved in all his poetic forms, even when in his later work the powerful tension between form and content sometimes almost reaches the point of parody.

What the poet learned from the natural world becomes a form of rebellion in the context of his life and times. To tell the truth, however, Rosenkranz's poetry does not support these starkly opposing fronts. If poetry's sole aim were to protect and preserve humanity and meaning, it would be hopelessly overburdened. That goes for the individual poet as well. The last thing Rosenkranz hoped for and dreamed of was to live only in his verses. If he later wrote, "To escape death in the snow / I hid myself in words,"[26] this personal motivation was never his ultimate goal.[27] The counterbalance to this burden is Rosenkranz's periodic disregard for all literature and for his own poetry.

The role of poet from necessity, of frustrated peasant,[28] is also—but not exclusively—an impressive pose. It is a response to the eccentric and isolated situation of a man whose poetry is not aiming for isolation. It comes from the awareness that poetry cannot actually be written under such circumstances, but that no other option is available to the poet.

Moses Rosenkranz never wrote in complete harmony with his times. His recourse to the past or to transcendence was also a challenge to present conditions. In this connection, the rhythms of the natural world acquire an even stronger "undertone of rebellion." The turn downwards and toward the past becomes a survival strategy for both the poet and his poetry. Rosenkranz is the singer of lost villages, and he places them, precisely in their lostness, in opposition to a world intent on doing away with death, transience, and aberrance.

My Villages

My villages resemble wary dogs
lying blind in blackness of their moors
lying sick and licking at their wounds
lying lost and hidden from the world

Years are passing and go by unheeded
death arrives his stretcher full of bones

Winter comes and with it storms of white
throttles them within its endless nights
locks them up within its freezing towers
they lie as if in vaults of expiation

Filling their souls with nothing, only darkness
they huddle in the coldness, seeking sleep

Spring arrives, unlocking grip of frost
and waters, liberated, take their huts
and sweep them off like leaky kegs, that bump
hollowly on the river's broken banks

Summer comes and dries them in its fires
Autumn hides them behind veils of rain

My villages resemble wary dogs
lying blind in blackness of their moors
lying sick and licking at their wounds
lying lost and hidden from the world

Years are passing and go by unheeded
death arrives his stretcher full of bones[29]

Moses Rosenkranz becomes the "terror from the swamps."[30] He contrasts our era to other, greater ones. He reminds an intellectually arrogant humankind of its animal nature[31] (frightening only if suppressed) and cuts its vaulting and destructive ambition down to size:

Reminder

We attempt to steal our way to heaven
advancing toward the stars and toward the angels

What fools we are when to our soles our souls
still clings the moor . . . [32]

In western Europe of the 1960s, one might have expected more understanding of Rosenkranz's critique of the illusion of absolute freedom and rationality. But this critique, too, met with blind incomprehension from the believers in continuous progress, to whom a bard of a lost homeland was deeply suspect. Perhaps today the bankruptcy of all grandiose notions of historical progress has freed us to really see Moses Rosenkranz. Of course, given the conditions of our times, it is a bold claim that one can still give rhythm to existence, can find poetry through recourse to something other than the badness of the present, and can use it to combat that badness. But even today the attempt to empower language not just to speak, but also to sing, is more poetically honorable and more exciting than seeking refuge in the arms of academic commentators in literature seminars.

And so Moses Rosenkranz remains a centaur who has strayed into the city:

The Centaur in the City

An anger drove him out from chasm, forest
once home to gods, and blew him here to us
his beard fantastically ringleted
he trots forlorn across the asphalt streets

Blind from loneliness and traffic lights
he treads upon our autos' beetle roofs
and innocently, gently, picks his way
through roadblocks like the wind in spring

He cannot find the way back to his grove
and our day takes the dancing from his hoof

the curl from his beard and the shining from his eye
and lays about his neck an old hack's noose[33]

It would be another misunderstanding to take the Centaur as just a rhetorical figure, to read Rosenkranz's work only as a critique of the present and a witness to its downfall. Much more fruitful is to pay attention to the wisdom, experience, and memory of other worlds that he brings to ours.

Translated by David Dollenmayer

Childhood

◆ ◆ ◆

[Berhometh, 1904–1909]

AT THE TIME OF MY BIRTH in the fourth year of the new century, my mother was in the thirty-second year of her life. Father was ten years older. I was their seventh child and the fourth in the male line. My parents' house stood in a meadow on the Pruth River outside the village of Berhometh, beside the emperor's road, which stretched from Vienna to the Russian border. Its roof sheltered our living quarters, stables for the animals, and a tavern dispensing alcoholic beverages.

My mother had sprung from the loins of the spiritual couple Faibisch and Rifka Hefter. Her father cheerfully lived his life in voluntary poverty in the little East Galician town of Stanislau and enjoyed the reputation of a Socrates of the Jewish alleys, though without thereby losing his sense of self-irony. His round-eyed wife drafted poems in Hebrew between the columns of figures in an immense account ledger she had salvaged from the collapse of the family fortune. The modest housekeeping chores were left to my mother's two younger sisters, who, despite crowns of raven black hair and huge swallow eyes in their sweet doll faces, remained long in the nest, for their pride and poverty frightened away suitors.

My father belonged to a family of onetime Frankists. At the end of the eighteenth century, during the reign of the second Joseph from the House of Habsburg-Lorraine, they had followed the pseudomessianic Jakob Frank to the Catholic baptismal font, but later returned to the synagogue. Only once, in my earliest childhood, did I catch sight of Father's progenitor striding past. He was an itinerant carpenter and preacher of Jewish law. His mighty form, shod in tall boots, was topped by a prophet's head of curly hair, with the beard of a Moses and the forehead of a steer. Father was the eighth of his eleven children, and after the Passover celebration in the tenth year of his life, he was given some polenta and a piece of cheese wrapped in a red handkerchief, summarily ejected from the cottage at the edge of Tlumacz, and sent out into the world like the four brothers who had preceded him. The outcast lad found shelter and work on the estate of a count, where, beginning as a stable boy, he worked his way up to tenant farmer by the time of my birth.

In addition to caring for the family, my mother saw to the running of the household, which included the inn and its tavern, the stable with four cows and two horses, a creamery, poultry yard, vegetable garden, and forty plum trees. Her only assistant in this work was a servant girl, although her children who were already able to do so lent a hand, too. Father and Sigmund, the eldest of his brood, were in charge of the leasehold that lay thirty kilometers away on the forested eastern slope of the Carpathians. There, with the help of some hired hands, they worked forty-five hectares of land, which had to feed, in addition to all of us, fifty head of cattle, eight work horses, and all the animals who shared our roof.

Without exception, my older siblings as well as the two brothers born after me were nursed at our mother's breast, some of them even into their second and third years. Why I alone did not partake of this good fortune I don't know. Nevertheless, I too prospered on the whole milk (watered down for my human digestion) from the most magnificent of our domestic cows, and to this very day I retain a childlike gratitude toward that Finnish cow and all her woolly browed siblings. The first years of my life are enshrined in family tradition as those of an angel, although the death of my next oldest brother, falling in my third and his fourth year, dimmed the impression of my radiance. In whispers, the tragedy was chalked up to the power of my other-worldliness to clear a path for itself. Father spent his brief respites from work behind the pass-through to the tavern, and there he had probably bounced me high on his knee once too often; the envy and jealousy of my siblings had developed into a grudge against me. And so one day something unusual occurred.

It was in the seventh year of the century and the third of my existence, late in the summer and late in the day. Autumn and evening were already gaining upon the light. The plum trees had been relieved of their sweet burden, which was being boiled to jam in large copper kettles over two fire pits among the trees. We children stood around the big-bellied cauldrons of bubbling syrup. As the sun was setting, wooden rods were passed through the pot handles, and the pots were carried into the house. We knelt down at the edge of the larger pit, our gaze drawn into its depths by the spectacle of the dying fire. I was the youngest of the little company, clad only in a shirt. The red, flickering element below seemed to me alive, and I fed it by pushing in more twigs with my bare feet. "What if we pushed you in?" my second oldest brother, six-year-old Arnold, is supposed to have said, and then I was shoved from behind and fell into the pit. Besides my two brothers, my sisters Tylka, Susi, and Pepi—ages nine, twelve, and fifteen—were also present. Seventeen-year-old Sigmund, the eldest, was busy with the harvest on the leasehold. Once I arrived at the bottom of the pit and it had grown dark and silent down there, the malefactors and the girls who had watched without intervening are said to have been swept up and scattered off under the trees by the power of their terror. Finally, after a considerable time, my sister Pepi led a rescue party to return and recover the victim. The story goes that when they pulled me from the ashes, I was silent and motionless but still breathing, my shirt and curly hair smoldering. They wrapped me in a wet sheet and hid me on the beaten earth floor under one of the brass beds in my parents' bedroom.

My mother didn't discover my absence until an hour later. She was scattering corn to lure in the poultry so she could count them over before locking them into the henhouse, an evening activity I never failed to join. If at first she was only perplexed by my absence, she grew uneasy after calling my name into the twilight and receiving no answer. And finally, when none of my siblings showed up either, she was seized by panic. They all were crouching in their hiding places, guilt lying heavy on their silent mouths. Once my mother had ferreted out her older children in the search for her youngest and read calamity in their faces, she forced them to confess, and, led by Pepi, she found me at last. So the family story goes.

I myself have no memory of the time between the moment I fell into the brush-fire pit and the moment my mother's blessed hands applied the first poultices of alcohol and sour milk. For several days thereafter, I had to lie motionless in my mother's bed and was blissful right into the evening, when the object of my worship joined me after her day's work and I fell asleep.

Around this time, the daughter of one of my father's sisters showed up at our house. Relly hailed from the forests of Galicia, and our little ten-year-old visitor—like my father, his entire clan, as well as his children, starting with his youngest daughter, Tylka—was rosy complexioned, blue eyed, and flaxen haired. She was tall and slender with long legs, her swanlike neck a stem supporting her little budding head. In beauty and physical grace Relly was in no way inferior to us, her cousins, something that could not be said of any other child for miles around. Convalescing, I lay on my back in a wheeled laundry basket, and it was this Relly who pushed me across the pastures. For days on end, I saw her face above me, while beyond it cloud formations and Vs of migrating birds floated in an upside-down autumnal sea.

About this time, my brother Samuel was born. I can still hear in my ear the soulful voice of my mother, forbidding those gathered around her bed for the newborn's bris to awaken the invalid lying beside her, since when I awoke, it was only to more suffering. I wasn't sleeping, however, just persisting in the motionless state my burns had earned me and in which I thereafter loved to conceal myself—at any time, but especially in large gatherings of people. My mother's words symbolize for me even now the benefit I have derived from this habit throughout my life.

By the time the first snow fell, I had recovered, with only very faint traces of the flame's kisses left on my body. Now I really became Father's favorite. However, I would have preferred to see Arnold be favored, or at least not neglected. That beautiful, shy lad who must once have been the favorite himself seemed unable to get over losing the place of honor in the paternal heart. Arnold had not observed—as I had—our father's behavior toward Samuel, the next in line: it pleased our great begetter, irrespective of who the little person was, always to set only the youngest upon his knee. For my part, I tried to keep a hold on my mother's billowing skirt as she was driven mercilessly about the house by her countless obligations. How often did I hear her banish me from her presence with an exclamation whose angry condemnation was softened only by her replacement of the little word *black* in front of the Jewish synonym for Satan. *"Gey tsim gitn riekh!"*—Go to the good spirit!—were her exact words, for all too often I got in her way.

My parents spoke Yiddish with each other to express the yearnings of their hearts. They spoke German to us children; Ruthenish to the servant girl, the farmhands on the freehold, and the villagers; Polish to the local estate owners; and whichever of these was called for to the travelers visiting their tavern. They may not have had perfect command of any of them, but they seemed to use each in an agreeable, imaginative way since everyone always listened to them with pleasure and interest. To be sure, the linguistic atmosphere surrounding my mother's childhood in the little town of Stanislau had been Polish, and she had even read the classic works in that tongue. She had not actually studied it, however, any more than she had the Yiddish that had rung in her ears at home or the German to whose greater powers of flight her affable father usually entrusted his thoughts. And she hadn't begun to learn Ruthenish until she followed her husband into rural Bucovina to become his partner as an estate manager. Father, on the other hand, had not been able to acquire any learning at all in his own parents' house. By the age of five, he was already at least partly earning his own keep by tending the geese of his native village, which promoted learning about life, but not languages. And when my father was thrust willy-nilly into the world in his tenth year, he got nothing from his parents but what he had inherited naturally by way of their seed. This was apparently not an inconsiderable amount, however, for he not only possessed a healthy, strong, and attractive exterior, but also a rich and generously endowed mind, capable of great thoughts, and his endeavors to express them as precisely as possible in four different languages fell on receptive ears.

But I felt quite ill at ease in this Babel of incompletely mastered languages echoing through my immediate surroundings, and I did my best to withdraw from the confusion by seldom opening my little mouth to speak. I was at pains to shelter even my unspoken perceptions, feelings, and thoughts from my unreliable knowledge of these idioms, and so I learned to experience the motions of my inner life in a mute and pure form, devising even at that early age an immaterialized intellectual sphere.

• • •

[*Stanislau, 1909–1910*]

IN MY SIXTH YEAR, Father made the decision to move thirty kilometers toward the southwest down that same emperor's road and pitch his tents by the village of Berbeschti, where a narrow country road empties into the broad imperial artery, overlooking the picturesque valley of the Pruth and Czeremosch Rivers. From the counts of Delascala, he had leased the estate of Kalineschti in the Carpathians above Berbeschti and planned to move his household in the fall of 1909. Beforehand, however, my brother Arnold and I were taken to my mother's parents in Stanislau, so we did not participate in the patriarchal cavalcade of herds, children, and hay carts in the dust of the autumnal countryside. Of our wagon journey to Stanislau, sixty kilometers away on the other side of the Pruth, with Father himself as coachman and me sitting on the box beside that awe-inspiring driver, what seems to me worth mention is that, although out of the corners of my eyes I must have perceived the landscape on both sides of the white ribbon of road, I'm ashamed to say that my gaze was focused on the tantalizing flanks of the horses, which looked appetizing enough to kiss.

My grandparents lived with their marriageable daughters Regina and Etka in a cottage made of clay brick, whose beaten clay floor lay a third of the house's height below ground level, so it was always dark and cold and damp inside. My uncles, Osias and Chaim, had already moved out and founded their own families. The former, the older of the two, was a tailor in Vienna, the younger a brushmaker in Stanislau. Like their father, they wanted no part of commercial machinations and financial speculations. Grandfather, after deliberately bringing about the collapse of the business he had inherited, sought to earn his dry bread as a watchmaker. Grandmother sat on a swivel chair at a prayer-house lectern, constantly bent over folios, reading or writing. I never saw her do anything else. Her slim figure, straight as a candle, was always clothed in a high-necked silk dress whose black luster was no match for the bluish sheen of the crown of hair that seemed too heavy for her small white countenance with its pouting mouth beneath an aquiline nose. A lorgnette lay suspended from a white cord on her girlishly swelling breast, but its function must have been purely decorative because whenever I saw the lady's close-set dark eyes, they were sparkling without its help.

Based on later experience, I now surmise that Mother sent eight-year-old Arnold and me to her parents' house—heedless of the consequences for our development—in order to make the aid she was sending them more palatable since what they actually gave to us boys of the cash and generous payments in kind she sent for our board and room was, to the total, like a paper bag to a flour sack. My mother, a keen observer thoroughly acquainted with her clan and the circumstances of their existence (her impoverished sisters, badly paid seamstresses and lovelorn housekeepers dreaming of being abducted, set the tone of misery)—my mother, I say, could have been in no doubt that our sojourn in that sunken cottage of clay, in that family impoverished by its spirituality and only half-armed against the damages deprivation can cause to human character, would be unhealthy and damaging to her children. If she nevertheless hazarded the sacrifice of her own flesh and blood, she did it not so much for the sake of the parents who had borne her—for she had already distanced herself from them with knowing disdain—but rather in rational consideration of the probable fate of her sisters. The overpayment for us was intended to give Aunt Regina and Aunt Etka a chance to fill their empty dowries. This is how a good soul like my mother could be lured into misdeeds by allowing herself to be guided by her speculative intellect.

It wasn't that we were mistreated by her family, only that we suffered the same plight that was grinding them down. Arnold and I slept side by side under an old coat on kitchen chairs pushed together, with only a threadbare wool blanket to protect us from their hardness and the icy wind that blew along the floor. We were constantly hungry, and at the sparse morning and evening meals—not eaten at the table with the family since they ate only one meal a day—my fast-eating brother was so skillful in inventing jokes to tickle my funny bone that I laughed so hard I couldn't get down a bite or a swallow and usually ended up tipping most of my portion into his bowl. My poor brother needed it more than I did, too, for he had shot up in height, with an unnatural bluish translucence to his flesh, while the fire of life shone only from his great bright eyes. More bothersome was that he wet the bed every night and then lay on top of me to keep himself dry. I began to suffer toothaches and chilblains on my hands and feet. After several appeals for help went unanswered, I resolved to meet these pains by pulling myself together and suffering them with dignity.

The German-language public school was unwilling to admit a five-year-old, so I was enrolled in a Polish private school. My first encounter with the faculty of that educational institution took place among glass cases filled with glittering minerals and stuffed animals. There I had my first conscious experience of beauty. It revealed itself to me as an immediate physical unity of mystery, peace, and stringency of form. It seems to me that, down to the present day, I have never seen anything so beautiful as that divinely created, oval, upright, softly golden vase with hooded eyes. I'm talking about the barn owl I saw there for the first time, whose image has defined my soul's sense of taste ever since.

I was not only the youngest in my class, but also the smallest, and they put me in the first row. Our teacher, a full-figured woman whose bare arms, thick as thighs, emerged from a yellow blouse trimmed with chalk white lace, stood at the blackboard, writing and explaining. I summoned up inner strength to sharpen my eyes and try to distinguish the marks rapidly following one another onto the black rectangle—it was hopeless. I propped open my eyes with my thumbs and forefingers in order to see better—to no avail. I held my hands telescope-wise before my eyes—it didn't help. I perceived only chalky sequences on the board without being able to distinguish their individual components. Finally, my eyes started to tear up; I had to close them and perk up my ears. I heard the tender music of the foreign language, but couldn't even tell the vowels from the consonants. The woman on the podium turned her motherly gaze toward me and said something in German. I stared at the movement of her pleasant mouth from which issued these melodious sounds, but understood nothing. Thus, I had the sense that I was both nearsighted and hard of hearing and was incapable of following her instruction. That I nevertheless kept up my end when tests were given was the result of the autodidactic diligence to which, by the light of a tallow candle, I sacrificed hours of the sound sleep I enjoyed despite everything.

My brother Arnold, my companion in misery, had already learned German and arithmetic in the Hebrew school of our native village and now easily passed the entrance examination for the third grade of the public school in Stanislau, where he quickly became a star pupil. The poor fellow was becoming visibly taller and thinner and bluer, and to his weak bladder was now added a chest cough that, especially at night, seemed intent on tearing his skinny young body apart. Sometimes, if he had forgotten to make me laugh during a meal and I had emptied my little bowl all by myself, I suffered all the more remorse at his subsequent coughing fit and at the next meal gave Arnold my portion even without laughing. That's how things were with us, but to whom could we have complained about our deprivations? Mother was far away, Grandfather tried to help us over these terrible conditions just by being cheerful, and Grandmother remained bent over her folios on the prayer-house lectern—motionless, mysterious, and stern.

I'd rather not even mention my aunts. Thanks to their nubile femininity, they probably only metaphorically appeared to be in better shape than we were. What help could they have been to us? They didn't go out until after dark because they owned nothing presentable to wear, and when they returned, they spent half the night talking, painting a mental picture of the man whose footsteps had followed them right up to the front door. No, we were on our own with our torments, and each of us had to figure out how to survive them. Arnold seemed not to have accepted the challenge and simply tried to snatch from life as much as he could grab, like a person whose time on earth is short. His brain devoured the insipid lessons in school just as ravenously as his mouth the dry crusts at table. Forced by suffering into premature bloom, his spirit longed for love; stirred up by deprivation, his flesh longed for pleasure. He found neither and was in constant, unremitting search for them. In form and feature, he was assuredly beautiful and was, moreover, transfigured by spiritual radiance—whether despite or on account of his sickliness I can't say—so I suspect that the unkindness Arnold encountered at every turn came from his overintense, too obvious appeal for its opposite. The boy poignantly concealed his disappointment—it must have felt like a defeat—beneath a shell of coarseness, and his search for love began to display a prickly aspect.

To my sorrow, I was already discovering that the only thing people find attractive is a carefree manner. I, who lived a more withdrawn life and encountered others with more equanimity, was besieged on all sides by their importunate mouths. Even Grandmother's veiled eyes would light up with little flickers of laughter as soon as she caught sight of me. I was shamed by this affection, for I could respond only with a thin smile. I had withdrawn and mustered all my powers of love around my inner being in order to mount a stout defense against the evils that besieged it. I was incapable of trusting the benevolence of a world that had poured cold into my veins, night into my eyes, and lead into my ears. I was ignorant enough to feel embarrassed by my mistrust, but not so foolish as to cast caution to the winds for the doubtful benefit of the pleasure people took in me. At this point, I must declare that I undertook all of this neither consciously nor un- or subconsciously. Instead, it was something that happened to me, like my physical growth, which, by the way, came to a halt right then in order to regroup its existing forces in anticipation of further assaults. I was six, yet it would have taken almost two of me to measure out Arnold's height, though he was only three years older. That's how little I wanted to grow up in a world that was already weighing oppressively on my half-pint head. In fact, I even wished I could regress and, while retaining my intellectual dimensions, end up displacing no more air than, say, a fly at rest.

In the afternoons, we went to a teacher of the Mosaic religion. Physically he was a Goliath of a man, and thirty pupils of our age sat on tiny benches in a vaulted cellar, clustered around three miniature tables, literally at his feet. Clad in tall boots and a black kaftan, he habitually stood among the tables, his booming voice instructing us in God's opinions, while his bamboo cane glided like a finger over the folios of Scripture open before us. His head atop its long neck was so small that, in the twilight permeating the cellar, I could discern it only by way of the crackling red apostolic beard with whose flame he often wiped dry his sweaty countenance. It was this man who told us of the great and powerful judge and king Samson in the land of Judah, on the frontier with the Philistines. While this hero lay on his back, staring dreamily into the starry heavens, a knight in armor could ride beneath his bent knees without having to lower his fixed lance. Who could have doubted the truth of this tale in view of the lofty mouth from which it issued? If anyone did dare to question his pronouncements, he cried out like a demigod, and his hands fumbled blindly down among us, seeking the malefactor. Terrified, we fled into the corners of the cellar, palely heckling the enraged man. At the end of the school year, however, he sat right down on the floorboards, stretched his legs out under the three tables that had been pushed together for the purpose, knit his bristling eyebrows, and proceeded to decorate the borders of green sheets of paper with red, gold, and silver embellishments that wound around lions' heads and menorahs, in the midst of which he then drew up for each of us, in ornamented Hebrew script, the certificates of our accomplishments. Like the others, my diploma was a work of art that acknowledged my ability and seemed to me a worthy reward. Since I was able to hold it very close to my face, this was the first time I experienced the marvel of bright colors. All other, more distant visible phenomena appeared to me muted and dull by comparison.

Unfortunately, I was unable to store my diploma safely among my possessions. It had a larger format than my school books, and besides, even for them I had no special place, not even a cardboard box. One night, in desperation, I stuck it secretly into the poetical ledger on my grandmother's lectern. Arnold pinned his to the wall with a thumbtack he had found. He was more inventive and daring than I, devoted to the world with all his senses and willing to display his treasure, while I hid mine jealously. Nor did he care when mold attacked the white menorahs between the lions' claws and cockroaches moved into their lifelessly laughing mouths. He didn't object to these phenomena and was indifferent when their swarms overran the bounds of civilized cleanliness. Ah, it was only because I loved him that

I made an exception for him among the other inhabitants of that clay hut, whom I despised although they glossed over their manginess with cheery wisdom and entered poems into account books. Deep in the night, when my homework was finished and everyone was asleep, I got up with my little tallow candle and went to the lectern to immerse myself secretly in the bright colors of my treasure. But the source of my secret pleasure was soon taken from me. One night I searched in vain for my diploma between the ledger pages. In the nights that followed, I leafed through the whole book, page by page. My weak eyes became ensnared by the sober columns of the familiar ornamented Hebrew letters, flanked by Arabic numerals and standing on the large pages like resounding pillars. I had already learned enough from my fiery-bearded Goliath to easily extract their sound from the mysterious symbols, but not as yet their meaning. The more practiced I became at this, the more powerfully my narrow chest expanded. Then one night I forgot myself completely, awakening the sleepers in the house with my rhyming song. After that, I never saw the book on the lectern again except when its severe mistress was bent over it.

More than the loss of my decorated diploma, I mourned the sequences of sound I had so briefly enjoyed. Today they still fill my memory with great music. I regarded my grandmother in a new light from then on. Into the sober cordons of numbers standing loyal guard over the vanity of worldly riches, her writing hand led the advance of the resounding hosts of the spirit. It was a triumph of lasting values over the ruins of transience. How mighty was that old woman with her huge book! Only my spectral owl could adequately serve as her symbol. Once I learned to see this poetic woman in her true light and began to understand that the bounds of civilization enclose the entire universe and are able, in the form of love, to embrace all phenomena without exception, I repented of my childishly judgmental feelings. But that happened only much later, at a time when my grandmother had long since merged with the spirit whose individual manifestations she once evoked with her calligraphy, and I had already set out unheralded on the trail she had blazed. I caught sight of my diploma weeks after its disappearance, being used as a pot lid. I felt a twinge in my heart, but I left it to its fate. After what had happened, no diploma could ever again captivate my feelings.

If my grandmother's spirit reveled in the book, that of her wise spouse reveled in life. To stroll through the little town with him was as jolly as it was instructive. From beneath a furrowed brow, his eyes surveyed everything and sparkled with the most serene irony. "My spit and image," he might address me, letting go of my hand to remove his round velvet hat and, with a snap of his middle finger, flick off some garbage that had come flying down out of an upper-story window, "my *Ebenbild,* are we and the cats not better humanitarians since we eat up our garbage ourselves rather than throw it onto the heads of innocent passers-by?" He always spoke German to me. I'm convinced that he, unlike my mother, who would always slip from German into Yiddish, would have spoken it even in anger—that is, if he had ever forgotten himself so far as to get angry. But even when the Dual Monarchy[1] and its ancient kaiser were being denounced—most often by Slavs—he would parry their thrusts with eyes laughing behind his shiny spectacles, although the thin blond brows above them remained severe. He called the Austro-Hungarian state the boarding school of nations, with a Habsburg headmaster, and considered it an honorable cultural necessity, in contrast to its neighboring Slavic empire, which he referred to in hushed tones as the prison house of nations. Three years later I would hear Russians stopping by my parents' inn use the same words to describe their fatherland, while calling our splendid Austrian regime, with amazed envy, "positively paternal."

In this regard, the weekend verbal duels Grandfather was accustomed to engage in on Saturday nights in the prayer house were instructive. There were always Russian merchants overnighting in

Stanislau. One could recognize them by their little peaked caps, strong-smelling boots of Russian leather, and the vests they pulled down over their waists, halfway between cap and boots. The Jews among them dressed the same way, and I could always pick out several of them on prayer-house weekends, when we schoolboys did duty as errand boys. In those years, the Jew, by definition a man without a country, was quite well suited to represent the interests of foreign lands. That was doubly true for the Jews among the Great Russians because the latter had a latent inferiority complex and always delegated the representation of their interests to others, especially when it came to verbal propaganda beyond their borders. Such have always been the preliminary tactics of barbarian regimes bent on conquest. I mention this to suggest that these guests at our prayer-house festivities were quite possibly propagandists. That would explain but not excuse their zealous defense of the "prison house of nations" in which their tribe, too, was being tormented. It was against these men that Grandfather entered the lists.

This took place only after the actual ritualistic solemnities that brought the week to a close. The shouting, stamping Torah dance had thrice circled the long table with its hastily emptied fish platters, and the profane festivities could begin. Reb Beyreschl, the dwarflike, redheaded beggar with his goatee and bulbous blue nose between runny eyes, would begin to sing and wave his glass. Putting his arm around the copious waist of the factory owner Motl, he danced the light fantastic. The women stood on the wooden balcony up near the ceiling of the room, clapping the beat with their soft hands, while their bearded menfolk below also clapped softly, crying, *"pleska, pleska!"*—clap, clap—all the while. And so the religious ecstasy in which they had danced the round, clutching beneath their beards the decorated Torah scrolls, passed over into an alcoholic exuberance of voices and limbs whose fantastic gestures were magnified by flying coattails and fur hats. During this second part of the program, I was always amused at the way the dancers, hopping in circles, simultaneously spun on their own axes. Grandfather always referred to it as the circuit of the stars and encouragingly called each of the participants by the name of one of those shining similes of the nighttime sky.

Grandfather's assimilating intellect would not allow his delicate body to expend itself in ecstatic motion. Instead, he sat in observant enjoyment, a smile in the mottled mustache that formed a delta with the two creases descending obliquely from his lively nostrils. At its clean-shaven base, shimmering rows of teeth were visible in his small mouth. My usual place was between his knees, while Arnold and the other boys took part in the general merrymaking. As the dancers towered over them, they either hopped along with them or played practical jokes, sticking a foot between their legs or catching their feet in snares fashioned of long hemp strings. From time to time, Grandfather would awaken me from my deep reverie by drawing my jug ear to his mouth and letting an order fall into it. *"Ebenbild,"* he would say, "refill little Sirius's glass before his star grows cold and falls from its orbit." Little Sirius was Reb Beyreschl, the blue bulb of his nose in a copper-red face. The fat rabbi with pouting lips in a white face was the sun. I had to protect them from Arnold's ambushes; he had already lost most of his respect for these lights of the faith. I didn't like the cruel pranks of my poor brother and his companions, but I was also oppressed by the knowledge that they were mostly acts of revenge for how he had been treated. It was Arnold above all who suffered from the intolerance of these bigoted, mistrustful men. His devoutness was somewhat in doubt, and they took every opportunity to question it. They wouldn't let him get away with anything during prayers—neither skipping over texts nor stuffing snacks into his skinny cheeks. He reviled them as God's policemen and sought to get back at them in his childishly impish way.

In the intermissions, when everyone crowded around my grandfather and even the rabbi came over to sit beside him, the

Russians would throw down their verbal gauntlet. "So, Reb Faivele," they would say, "what's your Kire Wedel been up to?" (That is to say, "King Wag.") "Protecting us from the mad fits of Red Nicholas," was the answer, alluding to the bloody coronation of the Russian ruler and his government's pan-Slavic craving for Habsburg lands. There followed a mutual denigration of each other's fatherlands, segueing into an antiphonal apologia for one's own, after which they clinked glasses in toasts to their fatherlands and dynasties, still not reconciled, to be sure, but united in their wish for peace and prosperity for all good Jews. These debates were carried on at the tops of their voices, so I was able to follow them and discern through my grandfather's colorful and lively imagery, as in a dream, the two fateful empires of my world. From then on, I trembled for my beloved Austria and her legendary kaiser and shuddered at mysterious Russia and her ethnic ferment.

◆ ◆ ◆

[*Tlumacz and Berbeschti,* 1910–1913]

EXACTLY ONE YEAR after Father had deposited us with my grandparents, he reappeared at the cottage that was sunken almost up to its windows in loess. At the sight of us, the tall, narrow-faced man sucked his lips between his long teeth, picked up each one of us in a powerful arm, and loaded us onto the hay wagon he had brought to fetch us home. Having learned the state of our health from Grandfather, he decided the only way we could survive the journey to Tlumacz, where he was taking us to one of his sisters, was if we lay down. Back then, I was heedless of the features of both the time and the space I inhabited. During my recovery from the fire pit, while my cousin Relly wheeled me across the pastures of Berhometh, that meadow with its single tree—a willow—and a stray cloud in the sky above had become ingrained in me. For years, they were my only reference points in the spaces through which I moved, and, except for bodies of water, I refused to perceive any others. I say this by way of explanation for why I am unable to describe the village of Tlumacz. I can still clearly recall what I sensed, felt, and thought there, and can also remember what occasioned those thoughts and feelings—especially when they had to do with people, animals, or the effects of light. I am still able to describe the farmyard, the farmhouse, and the room that were my immediate surroundings. But I have no idea about the location of the town or the surrounding country, for while there I paid as little attention to them as a lover does to a face near that of his beloved. To me, that meadow with its tree and cloud stood for all the landscapes of the world. It left no room for any others.

Father's sister was waiting for us at the gate of her farmyard. She was older than he, a widow and the mother of children who had flown far away across the sea. She was a blonde, tall and rangy like her brother, with the measured dignity of a woman who owned and ran her own farm. She was as taciturn as a pine tree when the night wind rustles through it. That is to say, she stood there in front of her house (the night wind was indeed blowing) and gave off creaking sounds. In the six weeks of our sojourn there, I heard not one word from her austere mouth. Nevertheless, every day she dispensed the morning and evening meal to me just as she did to the geese she was fattening. She held them pressed against her left thigh and stuffed them with cornmeal dumplings until they almost choked to death. But whereas she gave the geese a contemptuous kick toward the watering trough once they were full to bursting, she laid me gently down among the big pillows on my cot and spooned herbal tea into my mouth. She'd concluded that my brother had no need of such care. She laid platefuls of food onto the table for him and didn't seem to notice that by the second week more and more of it remained uneaten. Restless flames flickered in the depths of his blue-black eyes, and though he was free to choose how much to eat, he ate less than I. When I think about the relationship between what I consumed and my physical appearance, I recall a saying of my mother's from a later, more impoverished time: *"Di fresst, in der Rich esst dich"*—You gorge, and the devil eats you.

During our last months in Stanislau, Arnold had already begun to come home only for meals, and this continued in Tlumacz. The rest of the day and deep into the night he followed his unquenchable lust for life. He had a need to be everywhere, see everything, and pitch in wherever work was being done—except in his own family. But how bitterly he always returned, empty-handed. Why did no one love him, when he was so lovable and so deeply in need of love? He was prickly—of course he was—but only because he thirsted for love and strove to capture it. On nights when Arnold had not yet come home although the moon was already shining into our room, I would leave my bed and go outside to wait for him by the farmyard gate. How I worried about him! I saw him threatened by a thousand dangers! How I trembled for him! How many prayers for his safe return did I send out into the rustling stillness of the night! When he finally appeared, my breast was so overwhelmed with relief that I didn't even perceive the look of antipathy, mockery, and contempt he shot me as he strode past, whistling, into the house. In Stanislau, my concern for him had given wings to my heels, and I trotted after him everywhere. But that only lasted until the incident with the bull. After that, the wings that had carried me behind him fell from my heels, and I let him go, despite the worry I still felt. The bull had been housed in one of the long public stables at the big cattle market on the edge of town. Arnold, with me right behind him, was just walking across the large sandy square that shortly before had been refreshed by a passing shower. Suddenly I saw people on the square crouch forward and flee with outstretched arms into the surrounding buildings, hats and kerchiefs fluttering off their heads. My brother seized my hand. I felt a mighty tug, then I fell. Looking up, I saw him rush away, leaping like a dancer. Only then did I hear people cry out in fear, and in the very next moment the animal was standing over me. I saw the longish scrotum between his flat legs and felt his moist mouth on my face. The terrifying beast gave a short bellow and trotted away. I had to laugh to myself, for he looked like he was walking on eggs. Before I could pick myself up and continue our interrupted walk, they laid me on a stretcher and carried me home. On the way, and especially once we reached home, I read on the faces bent over me the danger I had been in. A female shaman was sent for, and she tore off my clothes and tossed them into the fire. Pouring molten lead onto a brick, she espied the steer in its cooling shape and threw it into a bucket of water. I was wrapped in a burlap charcoal bag after its black contents had been shaken out over my head. Thus encased, I was carried seven times around the house by the sorceress while whispered words issued from her lips. Only then was I entrusted to my aunts, who washed and kissed me. Then Grandmother herself put me into her bed and thought to beam strength into my breast with a concentrated stare. All this hullabaloo was in response to my pale face and my silence, although both had been present long before the runaway bull stood over me and brought them to everyone's attention. Only when they made so much fuss over me and Arnold, shamefacedly, came home very late did I realize that I had been touched by something truly terrifying at the cattle market and that my brother was not completely without blame in the matter. The experience cost me the wings on my heels and much worry about the brother whom I no longer followed protectively.

At the end of our convalescence in Tlumacz, our aunt drove us to the Kolomea station in her little cart. Arnold was in charge of the trip from Kolomea to Berbeschti, our parents' new home. From the bridge near Nepolokautz, I saw how the Pruth River—which up to this point flows placidly through the valley it shares with the Czeremosch—anticipates the narrowing of the valley farther downstream and trips up its little brother, so to speak, who then falls into it and disappears. Not that the larger river becomes malicious or sly in its dilemma; its mass simply tips the balance in its favor. With great circumspection, Arnold oversaw our transfer in Nepolokautz to a train on the branch line Nepolokautz-Wischnitz, on which lay Berbeschti. I marveled at him and knew that I would never be so worldly-wise. It was nine-year-old Arnold who asked the red-capped station guard when the little spur train was scheduled to depart. Learning we had an hour and fourteen minutes to wait, he carefully deposited me in the waiting room and, with his own share of the candy money that Father had divided evenly between us, gallantly purchased for me a packet of caramels from a dispenser of the Stollwerck candy company. I had already invested my share of the money in Kolomea—Arnold had helped me while shaking his head in disapproval—in little gifts for our siblings and Relly, who were awaiting our arrival at home. But once he had pressed the candy into my hand, my beloved Arnold disappeared, and I was alone in the brownish, echoing room with its long benches, now worried not just for him, but for myself as well. But, amazingly, just at the last moment, he stuck his head through the door and squinted up at the pedestal clock in the waiting room. God knows how, but he could read the time from the face of that clock, which for me was merely filled with mysterious intimations. Before shoving me into one of the narrow compartments, he weighed us on a penny scale, again with his own money. I weighed forty pounds, he fifty-one. I came just up to his shoulder and was skinnier, too. How could our considerable difference in girth amount to only eleven pounds? I wondered. I decided Arnold was too light. In Tlumacz, however, he had gotten rid of his cough and recovered from his bladder problems. He abandoned me again in the compartment and didn't leap aboard, out of breath, until the train was already moving.

The Berbeschti station was located on the Kalahura, two or three kilometers from the village farther up, and on the shoulder of a hill overlooking a ravine sloping gently into the valley of the Pruth and Czeremosch Rivers. The emperor's road, down which the colorful Viennese border patrolmen traveled to the Russian frontier, ran straight across the Kalahura. On the southeast side of our new house, a narrow country road crossed the highway and led down the ravine into the valley of the fraternal rivers and, in the opposite direction, up through the village and Father's new leasehold, named Kalineschti, and on into the higher peaks. Strung out along the emperor's road, at considerable distance from each other, stood my parents' house, the office and residence of the postmaster to the northwest, and the house of the railroad inspector. Facing Venderéu's house on the other side of the highway was the red brick station with the residence of Station Master Berger and his family. As we descended from the train into the golden air of a September afternoon, our three sisters and our cousin Relly—her parents had died in the meantime—were standing on the platform. With their long legs below and light summer blouses above, topped by rosy faces framed by heavy brown or golden hair, they looked like a bouquet in motion. Behind them, the station master's three children shone like a nosegay: a boy and two girls, in age between me and Arnold. Off to one side and somehow abashed stood the daughter of the railroad inspector: Aurelzia, in blue, white, and red, with sparkling black eyes, more beautiful than all the rest and the same age as me. If you include our two younger brothers, three-year-old Milku and two-year-old Duziu, and the Bergers' three-year-old Wiliu, the three of whom had not shown up on the platform to greet us, those were all the children of the Kalahura, the society into which we alighted.

The house in Berbeschti was an exact copy of the one we had left in Berhometh: a timber frame filled in with bricks, daubed with clay, and painted blue. Inside the house and in the yard as well, I found everything just as it had been. The same cattle and horses were in the stable, occupying one-fifth of the livable space beneath the roof. The remaining four-fifths were taken up by my parents' bed-sitting room and the kitchen next to it, both separated from the stable by a long corridor. On the other side of the spacious kitchen's southeast wall was the equally roomy tavern. A pass-through window connected the two. Along one side of the tavern and divided from it by a screen and a buffet was the narrow bar, whose redolent kegs bore taps of various colors. Here there was another pass-through into an adjoining guest room reserved for members of the so-called upper classes.

The floors of all the rooms were of compacted clay, and only my parents' room had proper middle-class furniture. We ate in the kitchen, but only when Father was at home did the entire family gather at the same time around the massive oak table. We slept in four groups: the serving girl and the hired man in a partitioned-off stall in the stable, we four boys in the kitchen (three of us on a bench that pulled out into a bed and Duziu, the youngest, in his basket), my three sisters and Relly on two sofas in the guest room, and Mother and Father on two brass beds in their room, except when exhaustion simply felled them in their tracks where they happened to be working. When my oldest brother, Sigmund, came down from the leasehold to spend the night—a rare occurrence—then Tylka and Relly slept on the kitchen table.

In Berbeschti, Mother had to toil even more than in Berhometh, for the costs of feeding and clothing the family as well as the children's educational fees (private tutors had been hired for us) had to be covered by the income from their inn, its guest room, and the bar. Meanwhile, her children had increased in both number and size, as had the taxes. At the same time, my mother—that valiant warrior of everyday life—was making even larger contributions to fill the dowry chests in Stanislau, which had to grow in proportion to their owners' age. It was in those days that I did something I hadn't done for a long time; I stepped into my mother's bustling path to ask her for some relief from the headaches (that's what I thought my eye problems were) that plagued me ceaselessly. She just shoved me aside unsympathetically, however, like some object that had gotten in her way, and, hurrying on, recommended a bandage for my knee to relieve my pain. Dismayed, I withdrew to a corner and bandaged the joint, fervently hoping it would help in order to keep myself from thinking that Mother was mocking my suffering.

Father, meanwhile, was struggling against the flood of simple and compound interest into which he was plunged by the loans he'd taken out to lease, equip, and run the farm. He had pledged himself to fulfill his life's plan, which included finding middle-class husbands for his three daughters and Relly—only possible on the basis of solid dowries—as well as providing each of his five sons with a long runway for their take-off into life and, finally, ensuring himself and his plucky mate a comfortable retirement. Since Father's cardinal principles in business were honesty, reliability, and modest markups, fulfilling this plan meant years of furious work and ceaseless engagement of both mind and hand—and sometimes even teeth—during endless days that swallowed up his nights. That's exactly how both Father and Mother worked, and every one of their children, once we turned seven, became imperceptibly caught up in the same feverish rhythm of toil. Twice since our arrival, the neighborhood children had led us at a run down the three-hundred-meter-long ravine into the valley of the two rivers. By the third time, however, we found our sunset race encumbered by a barrel mounted on two wheels, which we had to fill with water at a spring in the valley because the Kalahura had no well. Only a few days after our arrival, Arnold was already wielding a shovel, pitchfork, and rake in the stable or the field behind the house, mornings and evenings, and it was my job to look after the poultry and keep the farmyard in order and the vegetable garden flourishing with the help of a broom, garden hoe, and watering can. In the time between our busy mornings and evenings, we also ran errands, supplied the whole house with water, and, besides that, had to meet with both our secular and religious teachers in the guest room, where they attempted to teach us the worldly skills of German and arithmetic as well as those skills more pleasing to God, namely Hebrew and prayer. Alas, our tutors—an unemployed bookkeeper's assistant and a would-be Talmud student—were themselves still apprentices in these subjects and, worse luck for us, had remained in their own schools only by seeking to perfect their skills autodidactically. Without a systematic pedagogic plan acquired through advanced study, even an expert in his subject has nothing to offer, except the potential to ruin much for young pupils.

We were also sent to the Ruthenian village school three kilometers from our house. It was there, on a spring day of the year 1911, that, as if by a miracle, I suddenly was able both to hear and to understand completely what the teacher was saying. I was still unable to read the blackboard, however. Thus, it was as if I could see with my mind's eye explanatory texts that simply had blank spaces in them, whereas my fellow pupils, by means of clear images and signs, could enjoy the concrete essence of the lessons, in addition to the teacher's oral presentations.

It was also at that time that my oldest sister, Pepi, began to gather us around the kitchen table on Thursday evenings and tell us fairy tales while she kneaded and braided the *Kolatschen*[1] and cakes to celebrate the end of the week. From her lips, I first heard the artistic beauty of German. Once she recited for us Mörike's poem that begins "Früh, wann die Hähne krähn,"[2] which she claimed was her own composition. On the following Thursday, however, to my great chagrin, Relly accused my sister the muse of plagiarism. Cousin Relly had found the work in a poetical monthly the girls liked to read in secret, and she showed it to all of us in black and white, at which Pepi turned red with shame and burst into tears. Surely the lofty poet himself would not have condemned her spiritual ambition. He would have been happy to accept her deception as a sign of esteem and to reward her for the dissemination of beauty. When I peevishly called my cousin to account for her hardness of heart, the little barbarian annoyed me even more by bursting into sobs and admitting that she had done it only because I hung so dreamily on Pepi's lips. Pepi was the embodiment of poetry, her charm diminished only by seeking poetry somewhere outside herself. I can see from the preceding pages that it is as impossible to describe my fellow men as to fathom them. I will only say this much about my sister Pepi: in my entire life I never saw a girl so beautiful, yet, from the contradictions in her nature, so inscrutable. At Pepi's urging, Mother had subscribed to an illustrated edition of the complete works of Schiller, which were placed with great respect on a shelf in the linen cupboard. Later, they were joined by Goethe's poems. Every month a new issue of the poetic journal fluttered into the house and was carefully hidden from Father. He didn't like books and pursued with special malice the ones that were light and colorful. Mother forced him to accept the two classic authors, insisting they were a necessary part of the girls' intellectual dowries. Pepi was behind this. One could call her the pioneer of culture in our house. Beyond being an active advocate of cleanliness and good manners, however, she expressed her zeal only by speaking German and reading us fairy tales and poems. Where did the nineteen-year-old get this from, a girl who had been in the constant custody of parents for whom *Kultur* meant nothing more than cultivation of the soil? Could it have been the extended visit her Stanislau grandparents had paid during Pepi's childhood? Father often humiliated his stalwart spouse by accusing her parents of windy spiritual aspirations, for even back then Mother was ready to expose her children to her parents' influence without worrying how it might turn their heads. Perhaps Pepi got it from her pedagogical votaries at the local elementary school, the teachers Frunza and Maidan? Or was it simply her innate sensibility for nuance, attuned to the sublimation of the Habsburg Empire, whose expiring breath was in those years animated by the linguistic sorcery of Hofmannsthal, Rilke, and Trakl?[3] I remained enthralled by the magic of the verbal music in Pepi's stories and in her Mörike poem, unable to hear my way through to understand or reflect upon their content. Was their aural machinery so powerful? Was my brain still too small? Or did I simply lack the knowledge to understand the concord of words and phrases?

Yet I not only failed to understand the meaning of literary language, but failed to grasp the forms of life itself. As soon as the light of the sunrise upon my face woke me in the morning, I ran outside. The new day rose up before me like a mesa of music, and I perceived the forms of plants, animals, and men moving on a screen of light, just as if they were the notes of a score on teacher Frunza's music stand, from which, after glancing at his watch, he would read the tune he was playing on the fiddle under his chin.

In one of my dreams back then, I saw a golden pocket watch that began to ring when I touched it. "This is time!" a voice announced. "It lives only if you make it sound." I picked up the golden object, and suddenly a thousand hairy ghost hands were trying to grab it. I put it into my mouth and shut my lips tight. But there the watch emitted ear-splitting chords and began to grow, soon threatening to block off my air. A scream tore my jaws apart, and, waking up, I saved myself from suffocation. Nevertheless, I began looking for the watch. Still under the dream's spell, I ran my hands over the warm bodies and into the open mouths of my nocturnal companions on the pull-out bed, whom my dream cry had already awakened. With hypnotic determination, I searched our bed, the kitchen, and the entire house for my golden dream-treasure. I felt that I had lost an organ and would die without it. I just wasn't sure whether it was my heart, my stomach, or my penis that was missing. Of course, all those parts were still there, but I thought that they were illusory, that only the watch's time was real, and that I must make it sound so that it could live. But I had spit it out in order to breathe. If only I had choked on it! I continued in that state for several days. I strayed from the path on the way to school, searched for the watch in the fields, and regressed into the silence I had maintained after being burned. My lips, like worms that have been disturbed, closed tightly and turned inward. I could hardly get them apart even to take nourishment. My siblings avoided me. Relly drew me into a corner and tried without success to ferret out the reason for this change. When I got in the way of Mother's busy circuit of obligations, she looked me over with ironic concern. I heard her tell Pepi, "Just leave him be; he'll get over it soon enough." And so I did. And quite soon, too. But only when the music of a new dream drowned out the first. This one passed through me like a stream of light, illuminating the landscape of my soul. I was lying beneath the thatched roof of our house and yet could see everything that was happening on top of it. There stood Master Stork in his nest in the sunlight of a Passover morning, surrounded by his family. Standing on one leg, he opened wide his beak and with his free foot drew a fiddle bow across his lower jaw, all the while singing a song. Astonished and happy at the thought that miracles were possible, I felt that what the stork could do, I could do as well. I arose, intent on reaching the nest by climbing up a rope that was hanging down. But as I looked up to measure the distance, the Gypsy Bogdan was standing there with his musicians. They all were playing and singing, as lively and delightful as when they played at the births, marriages, and funerals of the local estate owners. When my covetous gaze froze the kapellmeister's hands, his violin fell from his grasp, and with terror I felt it resting on my collarbone. "Play it better," said the instrument in Relly's throaty voice. But I had no bow and was looking for a way out. All around me, however, stood my maternal grandfather in various shapes that were holding each other by the hand as if ready to dance. "With your arm bone, my *Ebenbild*. Somebody's got to do it. We'd like to have a little dance." As I obeyed, the fiddle became a fire that shot up into my face. Without moving, I opened my eyes and saw above me a glass balloon, held by Arnold and shining in the early sunlight. I was tied up and lying in the farmyard in front of our house, uncovered and exposed to the view of the girls, who were dancing in a wild ring around my naked body. Together they had carried me, sleeping like a log, into the yard, to have some fun and usher in the Passover.

I felt the effect of this dream even more deeply—if such a thing were possible—when Arnold shortly thereafter brought home a fiddle and persuaded teacher Frunza to give him music lessons. During this instruction, which took place by lamplight in the cellar out of fear that Father would find out about it, I stood on a footstool behind Arnold and propped my eyes open with thumb and forefinger to try and discern which notes on the music stand went with which tones from the strings. Every time I came slinking out of the corner where I hid from my brother's hostility while waiting for his violin lesson to begin, I ran up against his intransigent opposition. My presence must have disturbed him. But Frunza the teacher kept a protective hand over me, for in the meantime I had become the messenger of love between him and my sister Susi, the second oldest. After the failure of Frunza's long siege of Pepi, Susi was the new object of sidelong glances from his black eyes. Unfortunately, the catastrophe that Arnold had feared in taking music lessons, the calamity he had tried to forestall by secrecy, found its way to the cellar after all. Whether Father had seen us descending or heard the notes ascending, one evening he appeared in the basement, and a terrible judgment day was at hand. *Terrible* expresses my sense of the event, and *judgment day* Father's understanding, which I herewith emphatically reject by giving voice to the horrified feelings of a child. What he did was a crime masquerading as justice, as always when a superior power resorts to violence. "The horses," hissed the terrifying apparition through his long teeth, "the horses are waiting to be fed and watered, and here you are learning Gypsy tunes! Hand over that foolish contraption this instant." His voice rose as he grasped the fiddle by the neck.

"It belongs to me," said the teacher to prevent the barbaric act threatened by Father's gesture.

"You think you can get away with seducing my children? This time it'll cost you this music box, next time it might be your head. And you, you little beggar," he turned his wrath back onto Arnold. "That's exactly what you are. Just think, at your age I was already earning my own bread on a stranger's farm, and here you still dare to give me a fresh look!"

"I didn't ask anybody for bread. Go ahead and chase me away. I'll gladly leave this prison and never look back. But I'm taking the violin with me." And he reached out his skinny arms in their short velvet sleeves toward his furious parent.

"So, Herr Teacher Frunza was lying! It's yours! Bought with my money!"

"With mine!"

"And who do you belong to, you damned little bastard?!" Briskly he smashed the violin down onto Arnold's tender skull. Blood and splinters showered to the floor. "I'll teach you to fiddle! I'll make your head ring! Now march upstairs and take care of the horses! Herr Frunza, you're welcome in the guest room on the first floor, but you've no business down here. And you, Munkacz," he used a diminutive of Edmund, my given name, as he gently took hold of my wrist, "what are you doing down here?"

"I made them let me stay. Arzin"—our pet name for Arnold—"didn't want me here."

"I see. You're my smart boy; keep your ears open for more serious things. Nobody makes a living from music."

And so the seeds of more serious things were sown in my understanding, in my soul, things that I vowed would not be subject to breakage by Father or anyone else. Arnold protested against Father's act of vandalism by hiding out and not eating for two days. For those two days, I stayed by his side and didn't eat anything either. I couldn't stand to see him suffer alone. But as a form of protest his behavior seemed to me feckless and senseless. I lacked the trust in the moral capacity of man that my brother already seemed to possess to the full. His demonstrative suffering, after all, was meant to call Father to account, or at least to pay him back for his iniquity. On the third day, we resumed our daily schedule of chores and appeared at the lunch table again. Father, however, called loudly over Arnold's head, ordering that no food be brought for the humiliated boy until he had asked forgiveness. My poor brother left the kitchen again. I followed, trying to persuade him to give in. He threw stones at me and ran off across the fields and into the nearby woods on Czortoria Hill. I didn't find him until evening and then brought blankets and food to his new protest hideout. The next day he found his way back into our society. But right up to his premature demise, he often subjected himself to such demonstrations of suffering. He wanted to shock Father and, later, Mother—both of them already pushed to the limit in their struggle for the survival of the entire family. He wanted to lodge a moral protest against their repeated frustration of his attempts to desert the family and follow his inner voice. This raises the question of the imperatives of a combat commander versus the freedom of the individual soldier. The fact that Arnold was still a child back then was of no significance in the world of rural poverty, where the necessity to work began at an early age.

Shortly thereafter, the very boy who had been so barbarically taken to task gave Father an opportunity to demonstrate what supreme exertion he was capable of and how far superior it was, in terms of its moral effect, to any artistic achievement. On an autumnal, fallow field behind our house, a breeding stallion from the leasehold had been tethered to a stake and stood in the moonlight, impatiently awaiting one of his spouses from our stables, who was still out somewhere, being worked late. Arnold, however, had decided to play a joke on the black swain. In preparation, he held an old worn-out doublet underneath a mare who was hitched to a little wagon and had halted in front of our house to make water. After putting on the greenly dripping jacket and tying it tightly around his waist with a string to ensure his freedom of movement, he went out to the waiting black and began to jump around him in a circle, whinnying seductively all the while. The beast, nostrils atremble, snorted the perfume of love, and his body stiffened. His eyes became bloodshot, his penis engorged, and waves of lust tore from his mighty chest in whinnying cascades that seemed to shake the earth. The madcap

Arnold even tickled the horse's abdomen with a willow branch. The stallion, forehooves thrashing, reared back on his pasterns, then threw his full weight onto his tormentor. With a derisive laugh, however, the skinny boy in mare's clothing had jumped sideways and galloped a short distance away on all fours. But the demon was already in the air, leaping over Arnold, and when he landed and didn't find a mare beneath him, he wheeled, mane flying and tail aflame, trailing the snapped tether from his rear leg as a symbol of his unbridled power. God knows what would have become of my brother had not Father at this moment fallen from heaven and landed on the back of the stallion. With this loathsome burden suddenly on his back, the beast stumbled sideways, allowing the object of his pursuit to escape. Father had been sleeping in his room after an exhausting day when the horse's blaring neighs had awakened him with a start, and he had raced into the field in his underwear. I was the only eyewitness to this event and didn't see Father until he was halfway through his mighty leap onto the horse's back. After saving his son, that valiant man had to battle for his own life. He triumphed, literally on his high horse, by staying on the back of the frothing black stallion, its heaving ribs between the white legs of the long johns that encased Father's thighs, one of which—once the battle was over—proved to be fractured. In the meantime, other men had rushed to the scene and put a halter, bit, and chin chain onto the exhausted animal. Father dismounted and called Arnold out of the hiding place from which he'd been watching. He picked the boy up and, limping, carried him into the house. He called for two mugs of mead, gave one to the son he had rescued, clinked glasses, and then sent Arnold to bed, saying as if to himself, "If you're not a mare, don't rile up the stallion."

On a hushed Christmas Eve in the year of these events, 1911, in the ditch beside the emperor's road at the point where the trees of Czortoria Forest petered out toward the Kalahura and not three hundred meters from our house, the lifeless body of our paternal grandfather was discovered. The hungry wolves had not killed him, but they had discovered his body and were the heralds of his death. Hearing their howls, Father had gone to the place with his rifle in hand. After a while, the hired man, whom Mother had awakened and supplied with two torches, hurried after him. Father and he brought the as yet undefiled corpse back to the house on a litter of bare branches. Mother joined them in her long nightshirt. After Father had laid the body down, he handed her a longish wooden tablet he had discovered beneath the mangy cat skin that covered the rigid corpse's hairy chest. By the light of the hired man's torch, Mother read in her rich alto voice the Hebrew characters written on the board. They proclaimed in Yiddish, "My sons! Death is knocking on my front door, so I'm leaving out the back to go into the wide world in search of you. I intend to find you and obtain your forgiveness. For behold, I fear the judgment that awaits me for what I did to you when you were but weak little lads. I found it prudent to drive you out in favor of your more delicate sisters, whom I fed until they had chosen spouses for themselves. But a prudent act in this world is a sin in the next, and now that I feel the wind from above, I grow fearful. I shall hang a tablet around my neck and several more on trees along the road. I ask those who read them to bring word to my sons that they may forgive me expressly and by name. Then I shall find pardon in heaven and after my death can send them my blessing, not my curse. Signed, the third Chaim of the reconverted clan of Guttmann, son of Moische. We hereby declare before the God of Abraham, Isaac, and Jacob that we forgive the aforementioned—who, by God's will, was our begetter but, through his own wickedness, not our provider—that we forgive him with our whole heart before God and mankind. Herewith we declare this and confirm it with the signature of our right hand, while in spirit we lay our left upon his loins." There followed the names of the sons he had banished: Baruch, Mendel, Wolf, Gerson, and Izschok

(Father). It seems that before the God-fearing man died, he had succeeded in finding the three middle sons and personally obtaining their forgiveness. Their signatures—in Father's opinion genuine—stood beside their names at the end of the document. Before the burial, Father was able to locate his eldest brother, who telegraphed authorization to affix his name to the board as well. Not until shortly before the burial, however, after a long and visibly painful struggle with angry childhood memories, did Father draw three Stars of David beneath the words he dictated to Mother to be written in calligraphic script next to his name: "Me too." Under Mother's tutelage, he had made enough progress by then to dispense with the Xs he used to make on secular documents, but not yet with the stars for sacred ones. Father framed the tablet behind glass, like a diploma, and laid it on the breast of the dead man in the coffin.

My soul, but poorly served by my small, deep-set eyes, developed its own capacities for emotional sight. What I saw was comprehended through all the pores of my skin; I attained the most distant things and penetrated the most hidden. It seemed to me that I consisted of a thousand eyes beneath my skin, eyes whose nerves responded not just to the outward appearance of objects and actions, but to their essences, transmitting them to a central point where they were displayed in spiritual reflection. The optics of my soul also enabled me to recognize the indeterminable germs of development, the covert omens of impending events. What I'm describing is neither clairvoyance nor divination nor any sort of telepathic or magnetic sensibility. It's a phenomenon that can best be described as a universal consciousness. At least, that's how I experienced it when its symptoms first appeared at that time, in my ninth year. Of course, their appearance was a purely internal event, a sort of spectral correspondence with the world. Outwardly, meanwhile, I had simply become a little taller and sturdier, remaining otherwise "the angel" with jug ears and a sharply delineated little "kissy mouth." In diametrical opposition to my older brother, I was outwardly obedient and playful, but my inner life was headstrong and defiant.

Arnold had always been "the wild child," but when he was twelve years old, he suddenly began to take after Father, indulging not only in that great role model's somber and willful sternness, but also in Father's measured and dignified gait, and if I dared to laugh at him, I had to endure being punched and rebuked. In the meantime, Arnold had graduated from the fifth grade of the village school and was promoted to a better job at home, advancing from barnhand to the responsible posts of stable supervisor and Mother's aide-de-camp for the entire household. Now it was my turn to muck out between the rails of the seven stalls, lay down fresh straw, fill the cribs with feed and the racks with hay, and perform the daily morning toilet of the huge inhabitants of those stalls, my dear cows and beloved horses, wielding curry combs, felt rags, and hoof scrubbers. In the warm months, I drove the cattle out to pasture before sunrise so that I could bring them back full for the first milking of the day. While I massaged the finger-size teats of the round udder hanging down between a cow's thighs and flanks, I would hear above me its ruminant grinding, and even before enjoying the fresh milk, I was suffused with the corpulent peace that so undemandingly ate and gave of itself.

Like Arnold, I no longer attended the village school, where in three years I had already covered the material of four. My report cards declared me an excellent pupil in all the subjects taught there. The slim hand of Aglaia Mirosch, the teacher who filled them out, was probably guided by sympathy for me, just as my own studiousness was but an homage to that dear young woman. Around that time, we were also liberated from our two inadequate home tutors, a welcome relief for us. Since coming to Berbeschti, I had resolved to serve the world as a farmer, like the Ruthenians around me and Father above me. According to these masters and my own observations, the agricultural arts were best learned by toiling in the fields, not scribbling ink onto paper. And yet I also yearned for an art and a knowledge to be gained neither in the village school nor in the fields. This yearning had long been a part of me. It ran back through the cruel termination of Arnold's violin lessons, the dreams of the Gypsy band on the roof and the ringing pocket watch, Pepi's fairy tales and Mörike's poem, Grandfather's conversation and Grandmother's mysterious meters, the Hebrew school diploma and the sacred tales of the Goliath who taught us there, the owl in the glass case, and all the way back to the meadow in Berhometh with the willow tree and the cloud shimmering above it. Eleven identifiable and who knows how many other unconscious sources, a primal spring at work even before my birth, as I already suspected. So I was not displeased when Pepi tried to convince Mother of the necessity of preparing me for middle school. Unwilling and hesitant, without admitting it to myself, I began to nourish deep within me the hope that this might be the way to attain knowledge of the art that had merely grazed but already bewitched me in dream and reality.

Before departing for Stanislau, Pepi advertised for and hired a student from Czernowitz to be our new tutor. He arrived promptly, but his graying muttonchop whiskers and bald head above a pince-nez unfortunately attested to his status as an old and perhaps even perennial student. I had wished for a young and attractive teacher from whom I could suck knowledge sweetened by my fondness for his person, and I lowered my eyes in shame and sorrow at the sight of this new arrival, who didn't please me. But precisely this man—a bankrupt spice salesman, by the way, who had become a student only out of desperation and until something better came along—was to prove my best pedagogical friend after my grandfather. His teaching took place mostly during long walks on which he recounted his life to me, which contained the requisite amount of arithmetic, Austrian history and geography, and German grammar. I found the act of writing difficult, so it was pleasant that he placed no emphasis on it. In composition and stylistics, I was a quick study, but my large, clumsy hands spattered ink when writing down the letters, which always ended up too large and overshot the lines above and below. The lines oscillated between my fingers and the paper like annoying bars. When it was necessary to write, Kissil Katz—that was my good teacher's name—let me do it with chalk on a slate tablet, where I could delete the irregularities of my idiosyncratic handwriting without a trace and produce an even appearance. The best gift this worthy "pedagogue from necessity" passed on to me was Uhland's poem:

> Bei einem Wirte wundermild,
> da war ich jüngst zu Gaste;
> ein goldner Apfel war sein Schild,
> an einem langen Aste.[4]

I read these strophes and learned them by heart while sitting in the big cherry tree in front of our house. The real landscape and my place in it pulsated in the words of this poem, like a wave in a river, and this harmonious accommodation of reality within imagination, of nature within the spirit of art, delighted and enraptured me. It made more sense to me than anything had before. I experienced the happiness of complete comprehension in language. I ransacked our henhouse for the loveliest eggs for my bearded friend's second breakfast and watched without envy as he slurped them dry, although we children never got a second breakfast and had eggs only at Passover. Unfortunately, our comradeship lasted only a few weeks. It was not a bullet that came flying but a policeman that came riding to snatch him from me[5] and rough him up considerably because he didn't give in to the will of his creditors without a fight. They wanted to be compensated for his violation of their trust. Undoubtedly, the same desperation that led him to become my teacher had led him to steal. Couldn't his extraordinary accomplishments as a pedagogue have compensated for his common crimes elsewhere? Apparently not. In the minds of this world's judges, our acts are not seen in relation to each other. Judges do not see that Veit Stoss the forger is only the mischievous shadow of the creative artist whose honorable cheeks they order punctured.[6]

What was going on? A restlessness had awakened within me. It must have been what suddenly gave me an aural illusion: noises in the air, the clashing of weapons and brazen thunder in the sky above. Nothing of the kind was to be heard far and wide, not even the slightest hint. The cultivated land with its geometry of colorful fields between green borders, light gray roads, hills and houses, wheeled as always beneath the rays of the sun, against which we wore broad-brimmed hats pulled down low over our brows, while we worked, to protect our water blue eyes. Nothing suggested that I was justified in seeing on a rise at the edge of Czortoria Forest men in blue uniforms with white daggers in their hands repelling riders in shaggy fur caps (although it was summer) storming up from below. But I heard it and saw it and kept my secret to myself, for I wasn't able to trust its reality and feared being laughed at.

A little while earlier Pepi had left us. For hours, she and mother had sat together, poring over a letter and the photograph of a young man by the name of Josef Trost with a mustache and starched collar beneath a top hat. As if drawn by the moon, Pepi had then boarded the train for Stanislau, where lived the matchmaker proposing this scheme. A few days later the twenty-two-year-old Sigmund surreptitiously left the leasehold and fled over the border, encouraged by Mother, who also supplied him for the journey. The first word we had came from Dresden, where he had obtained a foothold at a bookkeeper's desk in the Koh-i-noor Pencil Factory and hoped to advance into the urban middle class. I know only by hearsay that the encounter between my parents following this escapade didn't prove quite as idyllic as the one long ago that had led to its occurrence. But it didn't surprise me to learn after the fact that Father was not stingy in his application to us of the phrase "your little bastards." Seeing how things stood, he didn't mean thereby to deny his participation in the organic, but rather, emphatically, in the spiritual begetting of our humble selves. Mother took it that way as well and was ready to make the sacrifices necessary to ensure her spiritual perpetuation in her children, seeking to provide them with the conditions she herself considered conducive to their future well-being, even in the face of Father's opposition. However, her maternal care receded considerably once the paternal blood became dominant in the developmental rhythm of our life's course. Perhaps then the good woman was tempted to speak to her spouse (of whom Arnold and I were the spitting image) of *his* little bastards, if ever she would have dreamed of recriminating with the husband she so admired. But she thought his hand lay too heavy upon us and sought to alleviate its pressure, especially on the heads of her daughters, but also on the coal black, pomaded locks of milk white Sigmund, her favorite.

With the departure of Pepi and Sigmund, the contraction of our household had only just begun. Soon thereafter Susi and Tylka, our next oldest, were sent off to Czernowitz to attend a six-month stenography and typing course and acquire the social graces—that is, learn the secrets of physical attraction—a dancing school had to impart. What had happened? Had the earth buckled beneath our house so that its inhabitants began to tumble off? What whirlwind had touched down in our midst, snatching us up and carrying us away? Weren't the stones perhaps the omens of these events? For in the nights preceding all these departures, stones, fist-size projectiles, came flying from the emperor's road, shattering our windows, wreaking havoc in our china cupboard and engendering fear in our faces. Fear? Yes, certainly. But probably only in those who, under various pretexts, were leaving the place and especially in me, who was remaining. Father, however, set his mouth firmly and picked up a cudgel leaning against the wall, while Arnold, whose habit it was to have these arm extenders ready for use each night, took a smaller one. Quite coolly they stepped out the door. Not until they reached the long road that stretched from Vienna to Russia did they raise their voices and no doubt their arms as well, which held the clubs to drive away the stone throwers. The latter, however, returned again and again.

Deep into the fall of the year 1913, our house overlooking the valley of the two rivers stood with gaping windows, like an abandoned house, a blind man forsaken by the spirits of light. And so it had been. Those who had held high the light within it were gone: Pepi and Sigmund, Susi and Tylka. Beneath our thatched roof, it was they who had represented propriety and the printed word, for Father and Mother had their hands full of tools and bread, with no room for anything else. The exodus, however, continued to run rampant: one morning my wet nurse, Finni, departed, she with the round sunny patch between her horns. Arabella, a Dane who produced thirty-five liters a day, followed on her hooves. They weren't headed for any photographic groom or to dancing school. It was clear that they wouldn't be coming back. Was Father breaking up the household? Did we still have the leasehold, when it came to that? Then one of the long-haired Ruthenians came to fetch away Lisbeth, the gray mare. She was followed by our German shepherd Bodo, head hanging and tail wagging. His big-eared triangular head was bowed down at leaving us, but his rear half was delighted to be following his great lady friend. Arnold whacked him on the rear, annoyed that it wasn't following the dog's head, but going its own way. "As if we men don't go running after our girlfriends in a similar hangdog way," I wanted to tell my stern brother. I had observed such behavior among the young cavaliers lured to our guest room by the girls' fragrance. Apparently Father had observed it as well; that's probably why he had watched without objection as Mother engineered the departure of our belles.

Not long afterwards I would experience it for myself, when Relly began to favor me with her love. She was the only girl left in the house and the unchallenged mistress of the four boyish hearts still inhabiting it. Now she was to sleep by herself in the guest room, but she feared being alone. On the other hand, she didn't want to give up her cozy sofa for the hard tabletop in the kitchen, where our dormitory crew would have welcomed her with open arms. Instead, she asked Mother to assign one of our number as her special nocturnal guardian. When she was given permission to select for herself, her choice fell on me. Although she said she had chosen me as the bravest, it would prove to be really because I was the most discreet, for she initiated me into her virginal school of love, about which, self-evidently, not a word could be uttered. The fact that my lessons in pleasure began just as prematurely as my formal education and that sixteen-year-old Relly thrust into my demure hands what thirteen-year-old Arnold tried in vain to pluck with his own seems to me an indication that the span of all our lives was too short. A compassionate God tossed into the lap of a withdrawn boy like me—much too early—that for which he had matured the organs of my playmates before their time. It was not just Relly and I who had become secret lovers: all the human inhabitants of the Kalahura, from the greatest (who had a bolder look after the act) right down to the lesser and the least who swarmed below them—everyone seemed to be pairing up for the furtive comedy. In this Rubenesque garden party, in fact, only the overeager Arnold was left out, alone and upright. The village farther up the slope seemed to be in the same state of affairs. From behind all the huts and hedges, one could hear the girls singing the brand-new hit, *"Oi, junger Mann, junger Mann; ich rufe dich, komm bloß heran."*[7] At the same time, an irresistible impulse to amuse ourselves led us children on a mad dash through the neighborhood, descending like a plague, while the adults celebrated without good reason and played cards. Only our parents stayed aloof from all this.

• • •

[*The Advent of War,* 1913–1914]

IN THE MIDST of all that joyous delirium, Father sat hunched over the paper, reading news briefs in a low voice. Constable Drelich, whose hippopotamus face was topped by a yellow spiked helmet, clenched his fist, smashed it down on the table, and summed it all up: war was coming! Everyone began to descry signs and wonders, each according to his own horizon. In the tobacco smoke, among the wine red faces in the tavern and guest room where I had to help serve customers in the evenings, there arose an entire hallucinatory fauna of world-historical harbingers of war, from the cross-scaled serpentine comet with the sun in its crocodile jaws to the cattle-devouring cattle that signified not years, but emperors. How could my vision of a battle on Czortoria Hill compete with them? But then again, how could that whole smoky tangle of premonitions compete with the palpable stones landing in our nocturnal rooms, thrown by the very hands that then lifted Father's glasses to our prosperity?

And then von Rotzki, a stout officer from the General Staff, appeared on a chestnut stallion whose fire was somewhat dampened by the weight on its back. The fat-bottomed rider scanned the landscape through his field glasses, and without turning his head to the adjutant behind him, who was mounted on a skittish black horse, he sputtered out a command to see to it that trenches were dug on the slopes of the ravine. "Because he'll be coming through here," he coughed.

"Who's coming?" asked Reverend Melniczink in alarm. This was happening right in front of our house, and that clergyman was standing there with us.

"Eh, not who you're thinking of. Just the enemy."

"Of course, just the enemy, just the enemy," the old priest giggled into his goatee.

"Who did you think I meant?" thundered the officer in his gold-braid collar. And then he lowered his voice: "The enemy in our maneuvers, naturally. In a little while, there are going to be imperial maneuvers here, good people." Now he was speaking to all of us. "Get to work immediately, Becker," he ordered the adjutant, giving spur to his horse. Becker did his duty and excavated the redoubts as ordered in two overtime days, using our shovels and our muscles.

Then the heir apparent and his wife had to die in Sarajevo, where not stones but a bomb was thrown, and Pastor Melniczink was strung up by Lieutenant Becker personally, who was obviously more suited to handling a noose than a shovel. And Father spelled out *"An meine Völker,"*[1] while I reinforced my little group of playmates with boys from the village, appointed Arnold leader of the enemy group, and began prewar maneuvers. It went without saying that it would be a war for kaiser and fatherland, and I would save them both, descending upon Russia from the Czortoria Forest and leading the Austrians to victory, in the rays of whose blood red sun it was then my wish to die. Soldiers passing through on munitions transports tossed me unusable pieces of weaponry, Relly sewed flags for me, and Constable Drelich clapped me on the shoulder: "What a guy! A second Prince Eugene!"[2] I staggered under his heavy hand and had to pull myself together not to belie his words. My earnest, delusional activities, my playacting preparations to defend the fatherland, made me feel exempt from my duties in our shrunken household, although the soldiers passing through kept the tavern very busy. I felt no pangs of conscience in allowing the uncomplaining Arnold to take over all my work, although he already had more than enough to do himself. Such was the consequence of my seismographic sensitivity to the world in those prewar days. The tremors and glowing lava of catastrophe were transmitted directly into my soul.

In the meantime, Pepi paid us a lightning visit one evening in order to obtain our parents' approval to get married and hold the celebration in Stanislau. "How can she?" I thought. "Grandfather is drawing his last breath, and Pepi's going to dance?" And I said as much to her.

She stared open-mouthed at me: "How did you know that, Muniku?" I couldn't explain it, however. "But you just said it."

"So?"

"Don't tell anyone else, because I've got to get married quickly. Grandfather really is dead."

I couldn't grasp what she was telling me. And she kept her secret, took the train back to Stanislau, and danced in her bridal dress on the fresh grave of the Stanislau Socrates who had been our grandfather. Earlier, however, she had sat by his deathbed in an imperial and royal[3] hospice and attended his last words. She was supposed to convey them to our mother, the eldest daughter whose intellect had clashed with his. "Tell Fanny . . . " he smiled with half-closed eyes, "tell her that I passed away in the care of the kaiser, like one of the greatest of the realm, and I was buried at the expense of the state." Much later, when this message finally reached my mother's ears, she took it as a reproach for her lack of involvement at the end of his life. I interpret it as an allusion to the fact that in the end, his poverty, of which she was so critical, came to the same end as the vaulting ambition of the great. This antithesis had been the lifelong debate between father and daughter.

And then one day Arnold left us as well. He was still in the house, but only to eat and sleep. His active intelligence no longer inhabited it. He had become an apprentice in the postal service and left for the office every morning with a pencil behind his ear and a briefcase under his arm. He didn't reappear until lunchtime and seemed very hurried and absentminded. At suppertime, he was more cheerful, but also preoccupied with his own thoughts. He now slept by himself in the kitchen. Meanwhile, the two youngest boys had been assigned to one of the two sofas in the guest room, and I slept on the floor in the same room, next to Relly's sofa. I was glad that Arnold no longer had to work under Father's hand, which all too often had descended upon him in punishment. I was also pleased to see that he was distancing himself from me, for the soul that seemed to weep in his overlarge eyes and gnash its teeth in his sleep awakened feelings in me with which I was unable to cope. Sympathy was the most unendurable of them. How was it that I, the little retarded shrimp, could be so presumptuous? Wasn't Arnold, more than all the others, incomparably more magnificent than I? He was taller and stronger, sharper of eye and keener of ear. He carried himself not like a mollusk in its shell, but rather with every fiber aquiver. He was actively, stubbornly, purposefully alive. And my playmate Loniu—the station master's son and the same age as I—hadn't he passed the entrance examination for gymnasium[4] one fine day and already set off on that great educational path toward which my secret chain of dreams and experiences, my aptitudes and knowledge, were impelling me? And yet I was still tarrying in the twilight of my childishness, merely sentimental and unrealistic, not even man enough to hold onto the girl who had chosen me, even though I was playacting at preparing to fight for the fatherland. It's true—I was pitiful myself and certainly not in a position to look down on Arnold or on other contemporaries even smaller than he. From within me, however, the eyes of my maternal grandfather did look down on them. His presence there was often disconcerting. When I heard news of Loniu's success in school, for instance, tears spurted from my eyes, but the old man in the depths of my soul rubbed them out between his snuff-yellowed fingertips, thus letting me know how pointless it was to cry, but not helping me out of my despondency.

Meanwhile, the siblings who had taken flight began to return, but none of them held an olive branch in their mouths. First came the golden blond Tylka. Hard on her heals came Susi, white as milk, red as blood, and crowned with black hair, like our mother. Pepi was still on her honeymoon, but Sigmund showed up from Dresden, coal black and milk white, the blood of his mother undiluted by that of her father, the grandfather who had once called him Squire Panza without a knight. When his train arrived at the station, he was so handsome the girls tried to kiss him, but he waved them off with his short arms and rebuked them: "*Pfui!* You're all so provincial! Nobody does that in Germany." "But there aren't any girls like this in Germanland, my son," said Father with a straight face. He always said "Germanland, Russianland, Englishland." His notion was that it wasn't the land that was German or Russian, but rather it was the land of the Germans or Russians. But Sigmund hadn't come back to live in the ark. He was all fired up to go to war with our Twenty-second Provincial Infantry Regiment and gain victory by force of arms for a German Mitteleuropa, Europeheart, the heart of Europe. He thwarted Father's attempts to have him declared unfit for duty, nor did he desire to stay behind the lines as a worker indispensable to the war effort. Neither would he allow his manly, patriotic determination to get ensnared in more modest privileges. Like a simple, common field worker, he turned his steps directly from the army physical to his column without bothering to pay a visit to the parental home on the way. "He's such an idealist," the girls said, and in the precipitate events getting under way, droves of idealists passed before my eyes: on horseback, on gun carriages, and on foot, but also on gallows and in chains, waving rifles and crosses, laws and books, bobbing up like swimmers in mountainous waves, then sinking back into the red flood of that time, which now scowls from these pages as a senseless confusion, just as it assaulted my boyhood soul back then.

One morning the hippopotamus face topped by the yellow spiked helmet emerged from the ravine. Behind him came a pair of oxen, chewing at their bits and pulling a little wagon at their tails. Bolt upright in the cart sat a man with a long wrinkled neck topped by a vulture's head and mad eyes. Far below that, a gigantic hand emerging from a sleeve half torn from his sloping shoulder loosely grasped the haft of a forester's ax, its rusty blade buried deep between the breasts of a woman whose turned-up eyes stared at the murderer from a skull thrown back and matted with dirt, hair, and blood. "A patriot," grinned the hippopotamus, pointing over his shoulder. "He felled his trollop when she wouldn't let him go to war." A court-martial acquitted the madman and awarded him the honor of being sent to the front. A Ruthenian teacher whose house was built on the ruins of a steam-driven mill often spent time in his basement, where he grew mushrooms. There he was discovered by a patrol, who reported that he was communicating with the enemy via underground wires and tubes—the remains of the ruined mill. He was taken straight to the gallows. I had others read me the sign around the neck of the hanging man and didn't envy the traitor his pendulous elevation. When autumn storms surged and wailed around the house, they were said to be the souls of hanged men. "So many traitors!" I exclaimed.

"Everybody here is a traitor," said the pipe bowl lid of an officer billeted in our house.

"But whom are they betraying?"

And then everyone crowded around the field glasses of the strategists standing on the edge of the Kalahura observing the movements of the enemy across the valley on the left bank of the Pruth. I couldn't see much beyond the end of my nose and not much more through a pair of binoculars. But when Relly got a look through them, she described the Cossacks for me. "So, up above they have pillars of fur . . . "

"Hm."

"Looks like, say, a bearskin sack, frozen stiff."

"On their faces?"

"What an imagination you've got! Cossacks don't have faces, my friend."

"Right."

"A wolf's muzzle is what they've got: broad above, then narrowing down, and black at the end where they bite. Above the snout, slanting from their ears toward their nostrils, slitted eyes gleaming brightly from under thick eyelids. Their eyebrows are like sewing needles."

"You saw that?"

"Exactly that. Even more terrible is what you can't see or even sense about them."

"They smell?"

"That goes without saying. But they eat people as well."

"People?"

"People!"

"Impossible."

"I'm telling you, they do! Ask the lieutenant!" And we believed what the lieutenants told us. And when a Cossack patrol of fifty men, darkly lustrous in the morning sunshine, came trotting up the emperor's road from Nepolokautz, we dropped everything and fled head over heels, like hares before wolves.

We fled toward the village, running in the ditch beside the road, with Father in front and Mother in the rear, the girls wearing nothing but their nightshirts. The company of local militia assigned to watch over the river valley from the heights of the Kalahura, two hundred men strong, went fluttering up Czortoria Hill and took cover on its wooded summit. Meanwhile, the Cossack patrol had posted a sentry at the top of the ravine and was galloping through the fields toward the village in two groups, one on either side of the road. Just then we were aghast to see two blue uniforms in a hay wagon rolling toward us down the road from the village. Their wearers seemed unaware of the danger they were in. Mother threw herself in front of the vehicle, tore the uniforms from the two young Austrians, and thrust them into the column of her fleeing children. The mounted foreigners seemed not to have noticed this scene or else not understood what it meant, for we all arrived in the village unharmed and took refuge with a farmer who was a friend of ours. We hid the girls especially well. For wasn't it well known that besides watches, the Russians stole girls' breasts? Father and Arnold kept watch through a skylight and reported that some of the black horsemen were on the ridges that surrounded the village. Before evening, it was officially announced that the enemy "squadron" had been "driven back across the Pruth by our heroic militiamen," and we set off for home, where we had plenty of time to prepare for the victory celebration that had been ordered by district headquarters over the telephone because it took quite some time for our troops to return from Czortoria Hill. The Venderéus had not fled their house. The reaction to their report that the Cossacks were harmless (yes, two of them had entered the house after first asking permission, but hadn't even so much as cast a glance at either the watch the railroad inspector had offered them in his initial terror or the taut nipples of his young spouse) was that either these "treacherous Walachians"[5] were spies—otherwise, how would they have dared to stay in their house?—or that those "Asiatics" were so cunning that they planned to lull us into a sense of security with exaggerated politeness so as to lay their hands on everything—watches, breasts, and all—on their very next raid. In any event, not a hair on the head of anyone in the entire area had been harmed, not a shot had been fired, and in his toast at the celebration the captain of the local militia was right to call it a "victory of civilization," but wrong to call it a "debacle for the invaders," to whom he claimed to have "given it." During the following days, we heard the sounds of several skirmishes between patrols, in one of which the militia captured a prisoner and brought him back to the village. We all ran out to look at him, and from close up I was able to determine that Relly's description of Cossacks had been made out of whole cloth. On the other hand, the foreigner returned our looks with a gaze that betrayed that he, too, helped along by our reality, was inwardly wiping cobwebs from his eyes. Then the fighting moved farther away, and its sounds reached us only in the rustle of newspaper pages.

They set up a military hospital in the village, and the wounded brought there were a sign that civilization was now being trampled underfoot. Our girls set off for the village one morning in white caps and aprons and Red Cross armbands. In the evening, they returned exhausted. But at night they lay on the sofas in the guest room (with us boys now lying on government-issue horse blankets in the middle of the floor) and talked long into the night about the young male bodies they had cared for during the day, bodies that were wounded, unfortunately, but all the more reminiscent of the Greek gods one saw in reproductions. They, too, had broken or missing arms and legs and smashed jaws. Meanwhile, my sisters' admirers, the teachers Maidan and Frunza, had also passed their army physicals. Their departure was resoundingly toasted in our tavern; then they took their suitcases and were sent up to the front. Arnold had in the meantime become an important person at the post office and was already receiving a monthly wage. He sat there, bent over the telegraph, and from the paper strips ejected by that nervously vibrating machine he read the news from afar. And when it grew still, he rattled out our news in return. The telegraph was at that time exclusively in the hands of the military command, and my brother was merely the human connection to the wires through which that power moved its pieces from square to square. This impersonal function as a conveyor of information seems to have insulted Arnold's inner self, and, like every functionary, he made a public display of his importance to society, thus compensating for his dehumanized psyche. I felt sorry for him, and when he was watching, I mucked out the half-empty stalls with pretended contrition so as not to arouse his envy.

• • •

[*Flight*, 1914–1916]

ONCE I HAD OBSERVED the incipient war games of the adults for a while, I gave up my own preparations in disgust, amazed that the kaiser had the bad taste to spend his money on such things. Noncommissioned officers passing through our area came in often to get dry and warm themselves with a cup of tea, and from the conversations I overheard, I gathered that "the Old Man in Schönbrunn"[1] had tried to resist this monkey business and had been choking back his tears since the outbreak of war. This corresponded to the image of the kaiser I had from my grandfather, but not to the absolute power attributed to him. So, there were men more powerful than he, compared to whom he was a weakling and had to weep. By the time the noise of battle reached us again, now not just through the newspapers, but crashing about our ears in monstrous, adamantine reality, I was already having to shovel snow from the path to our gate. It was the Russian winter offensive of 1914–1915, and one night we again sprang into the ditch beside the road and fled through the deep snow into the mountains. This time, however, to the right and left of us, the Austrian army, repulsed by the Russians, was fleeing as well, and we were also accompanied by projectiles flying through the air at tremendous speed—although buzzing like slow, heavy insects—until they fell hissing to earth and, as they expired, buried beneath them here a man, there a horse or a case of ammunition that exploded in flames. Father and Mother were carrying our two youngest, seven-year-old Milku and six-year-old Duziu, in baskets strapped to their backs. The boys stood in them, peering over the rims at the catastrophe and whining. We had been snatched from our beds and forced to flee, and Father had barely had time to shout to the hired man that he should stay and look after the house. Once Father had looked at the road, he gave up the idea of hitching the horse to the sleigh to escape more easily. This wintry white artery seemed almost to shudder beneath the ponderous load of a world war arsenal in retreat, with unwieldy artillery, overloaded baggage trains, frustrated cavalrymen, and exhausted foot soldiers. In the rear, cartloads of wounded were crawling along, heads and limbs hanging over the side, and behind them came herds of cattle and the fleeing populace. And the whole thing seemed not to be moving on wheels or feet, but on sticky disks, like a caterpillar. To my near-sighted eyes, it made the impression of an immovable mass on a slowly rolling belt. Down in the ditch, we were of course able to make better time into the hinterland. Indeed, our pace was accelerated even more by the cold, for above our booted feet we were covered by little more than our terror; just as we were about to empty our clothes cupboard, a piece of shrapnel had landed in it. As we ran through the village, friendly farmers threw sheepskins over our shoulders.

Just as the December sunrise snarled at us from its house of cold mist, we reached the village of Kalineschti, eight kilometers higher up the mountain. Father still worked half of this leasehold, and he hitched the four horses we had there to two sleighs, in which we continued our flight, wrapped in blankets and bedded in hay, with Father and Arnold driving. Now that the sluggish mass of the military disaster was far behind and out of sight, we detoured silently around the market town of Staneschti and, after climbing for ten more kilometers, reached the village of Upper Staneschti. There we rested, crawling out from under the blankets and laying them over the steaming horses. In the hospitable house of German friends, we dried out our shoes and drank hot milk. Our hosts were Swabians and spoke a dialect that sounded purer to me than the German I had learned up to then. After this way station, we abandoned the main road for a farm track. The powerful horses had to pull us even higher into the mountains. The sleighs' runners sank deep into the glittering snow. From a distance, we must have looked as if we were sitting upon little rafts on their way to heaven. The abstractly shining sun was at its zenith by the time we reached the mountain village of Schadowa. We drove through a forest of bare, frost-covered trees humming like tuning forks at the touch of the icy wind. Beyond the forest, a rounded mountaintop rose before us, which we had to climb along a series of switchbacks. Now both pairs of horses had to pull a single sleigh in which all nine of us sat cozily crowded together. Our shadow on the snowy slope beside us grew longer and longer. By the time its blue silhouette was darkening the mountainside all the way to the top, we could look down on the other side and see the copper red ball of the sun roll behind a chain of peaks below us. The full moon had begun its watch when we stopped again beneath an overhanging ledge and climbed down from the wagon behind a natural balustrade. After we had walked up and down a while to loosen our stiff joints and get our sluggish blood flowing again, Father led us over to the edge and showed us the little valley of Costeschti far, far below. In the middle of its basin, a few smoking chimneys rose out of the mist like pieces of firewood stood up on end. That was the goal of our flight. I thought all I would have to do was sit down on my tailbone for a smooth slide all the way to the bottom and was quite disappointed when Father informed us we still had a two- or three-hour walk ahead of us. After Arnold had helped him unhitch the horses, turn the sleigh around, and hitch them up again, Father impressed upon us the need for caution and secrecy and appointed Arnold leader of our moonlight march.

Then he had a long whispered conversation with Mother. Before he climbed onto the sleigh, he wrapped his powerful arms around that brave woman, and she stood on tiptoe to lay her swallow-eyed head on his breast. It was the first time I had seen my parents in such a tender embrace, and I felt it was more a show of unity against the powers of fate forcing them apart than an expression of love. But isn't the full measure of love already contained in the will to unite with another person? I heard Father's melodious call to the horses and watched as he glided resolutely back down into danger. At that moment, I felt with special force that this great man, tireless in his concern for our welfare, was the god of our house and that my own worth depended wholly on his regard for me.

Arnold guided us down a narrow track that led abruptly into a jumble of rocks and became an echoing path between high, jagged peaks. All the way into the higher mountains beyond Upper Staneschti, I had been inwardly trembling like a frightened little bird, but now, as the landscape rose even higher, I felt my fear fall away. Although up to that point my inner voice had unceasingly stammered "Never again!" under the impressions of being pursued, of everything being in flight, of bullets above and cold below, now I began to sing quietly to myself as we wandered among the peaks. The mountains lifted both body and spirit above the misery. Of course, our spatial removal from the crushing disaster down below contributed to my feeling of well-being, but it seems to me that if the same disaster had occurred up there on the mountain, it would have been less nightmarish. Is it by preventing us from gazing off into the distance that mountain walls concentrate our inner selves and distill to a new purity the vital, imprisoned urge for freedom? Isn't that the origin of the greater strength and moral character of mountain dwellers compared to those who live on the plains below? Surely it's not by chance that the cowardly ostrich and the reprobate jackal are creatures of the plains, whereas the eagle and the chamois are animals of the heights. Opticians and physicists will have a different explanation than I do for the fact that my sight proved to be less dull up there and I could see farther than I could down below, and I allow that their knowledge may complement my own. On the basis of Father's thorough description of the area, Arnold led us unerringly through the twilit mountains. I was sorry that such a heavy responsibility should be laid on his thin shoulders, but I was full of admiration for the manly way he bore it. The air grew cold as night settled fully upon us, but the luminous antiphony between the full moon in the sky and the snow on the ground prevented the darkness from getting a word in edgewise. When, after maneuvering our way through the mountains, we finally set foot onto the valley Father had shown us, the little houses in its middle stood bathed in the concentrated shimmer from below and above, like porcelain figurines under a bell jar. We made a large and stealthy detour around the settlement, our presence betrayed only by dogs barking in the courtyards, and ducked into a pass so narrow that its walls scraped our sheepskins. The path sloped gently upward, and after two curves we found ourselves on the threshold of a rocky enclosure of cyclopean structure. In one corner of the irregular space stood a hut like a dollhouse in a giant's nursery. Here at last, in this snug refuge, our flight came to rest.

The hut's owner, a thickset man in green hunting garb, admitted us with a friendly greeting. Big blue eyes framed by long black hair were the only animated thing in his flat face, from which protruded a brown pipe. Having kissed the hand of his tall, skinny wife, I decided to call her Pump Handle to myself. She was always stooped forward, a little bucket dangling from her hand. Her place was in the kitchen by the stove, and she left it only to go to the goat shed, the well next to it, or the pots of flowers in the parlor, which was now given over to us. The man of the house took care of all other household business. Once a week he went down to Costeschti and brought back supplies for us as well. It was not until the afternoon of the day after we arrived that I opened my eyes again, and my first thought was to call our dog, Muschka, whose absence I had only just noticed. I loved her dainty little body on its thin legs. She had short, light brown hair with white cuffs above her forepaws. A white stripe also ran between the spirited, bright brown eyes in her soulful little face. She had special feelings for each one of us and always knew how to express them clearly. Toward Father and Arnold she always displayed a fearless but loving reserve. She followed Mother with moist eyes but didn't run after her. Me she didn't take seriously and only out of politeness allowed me to pet her. But she encompassed all of us in her love and concern, and we felt it. Along with the cows, she was for me an emotional substitute for my mother, who withheld herself in this regard, even though the dog paid me as little heed as she did. But Muschka was not there. We had forgotten her. "My fault!" I cried, "my fault!" And I lashed myself with all the scourges of repentance for this terrible betrayal.

In his conversation with Mother, Father had said he would return to us on the second day after we arrived, but he didn't come back until the third day. In the daylight hours between when he said he would come and when he actually appeared, I sat on one of the ridges of our wall of stone, driven there when I sensed Mother's unvoiced worry about the tardiness of our protector. I stared in the direction I thought he would be coming, sending him protective prayers as I had done so often for my brother in Tlumacz. My disquiet and concern were justified in both cases because both there and here, brother and Father moved among violent animals and men: Arnold among bears and Ruthenians, Father among Ruthenians and wolves. And now there were the Russian invaders as well. While I stood on my ridge and prayed, I could see the foreign warriors—more in my mind than in actuality—riding across the distant mountain crests and springing over the peaks in great leaps like giant fleas. When I returned to the house long after the sun had gone down and stepped into the parlor, there was the returnee, already sitting at the table surrounded by Mother, Arnold, and the girls, drinking tea and eating caramels. Standing on the threshold, I greeted him with a bow and approached shyly to kiss his proffered hand. While he offered me a brown caramel and then the hot mug of tea with his other hand, he said with the glint of a smile in his steel blue eyes, "Warm yourself up, my guardian. I saw you from down below, but I thought you were a giant mushroom." I never had anything against being the butt of a joke. This time I was positively happy, for Father hadn't been so affable in years. It was the first time I saw Arnold permitted to sit beside Father, and this filled me with great satisfaction. On that evening as well, Father spoke more than was his custom, turning to all who were present. Up to then, he had usually addressed only Mother, even when the whole clan was assembled.

A new era had begun in the way Father ran the family. Up to that time, our progenitor, provider, and ruler had been unapproachable behind the veil of constant concern for our welfare. Now he found conviviality in the bosom of his family. His face, previously always preoccupied and uncommunicative, now turned a softer aspect toward us. His tense, easily irritated body, its resilient limbs not infrequently at the service of violent outbursts, now dispensed happy caresses to all of us, not just to the youngest. He could be seen taking Susi's face between his large hands as if enfolding it with wings and immersing his blue eyes in her dark ones. Our ecstatic laughter resounded like Easter organ pipes as we watched him readily accept Arnold's audacious challenge to arm wrestle on the table. That was the utter limit of this affectionate thaw in his demeanor. Father seemed transformed, as if he had finally lifted his gaze above the heavy burden of his cares and caught sight of their object—namely, us. Now that precious man was always in our midst. He ate with us, and we watched him chew; he spoke to us, and we hung on his words. We honored his sleep with silence and delighted in his lonely prayers. In sleep and in prayer, his vermilion face acquired an even deeper red and shone with a relaxed, quiet masculinity. Since he now overlooked all the things that used to annoy him, we strove to please him, and our life together in that dollhouse in its rocky enclosure became a pure idyll. Mother now moved among us with affection, humming Polish songs. She was like a busy bee, golden and sweet, although she was really milk white and coal black, with dark, wise, childlike eyes from which Muschka had learned her own moist gaze. In the evenings, after we had eaten our polenta with milk, there were always intimate conversations, mostly among Mother and the three girls. On Saturday evening, however, after Arnold had announced the appearance of the evening star in the sky, Father would proceed to the symbolic burning of the week gone by. He poured alcohol from a silver goblet onto an exposed corner of the table and lit the volatile liquid while saying a blessing. In the darkened room, we chased after the blue flame to grab a fistful and stuff it in our pockets. After that, Father and Mother sang some religious songs, and from the common platter we all ate a trout Mother had been given by our German host, who claimed to be a Pole. Then the lowest of the three candles in the silver candelabra was lit, and everyone was served a tulip glass of cherry juice and a slice of white bread. Father, who had not observed the rituals back home and was mockingly called a "Jewish goy" or a "German" by his fellow Jews, permitted himself this spiritual relief in our hideout and no longer made an embarrassed face on Friday evenings when Mother got herself and us all dressed up and set the table just like at home. Then she would rest her face between her hands, purse her mouth like a bird's beak, and bless the flames in the candlesticks; spreading her arms like wings, she seemed to be on the verge of pressing them all to her necklace-bedecked bosom. We had not brought along the silver utensils used in these devotions. Only after my parents had been "back down the mountain" again did those things reappear in our refuge. Until then, we had to make do with objects of glass and wood. Days like this concluded with saying the evening prayer with our parents, then one after the other, from the eldest to the youngest, we bent over their outstretched hands and pressed them to our lips. My mother was usually the first person in the house to get up and welcome each morning, whispering prayers and getting breakfast ready while it was still dark.

We had secretly received a terrifying piece of news that made us never again light a lamp in the little house as long as we remained hidden there. Indeed, even the days were darkened in the friendly cottage once we piled snow against the windows, leaving only a small space at the top of each one. The entire house took on the appearance of a hillock. I can't remember anymore what clever thing Arnold had thought up to make even the smoke from the chimney invisible. These and other precautions were taken so as not to tempt spies or wayfarers looking for a reward to stop by the lonely house and search for Father. It was him they were looking for because the Russian occupation authority had set a price of five thousand rubles on his head and had published wanted posters. As Mother was giving us this news and then urgently instructing us how to behave from now on, there appeared to me that whole monstrous "prison house of nations" as Grandfather called it and "Russianland" as Father did, a thousand-tentacled octopus, insatiably devouring lands and peoples. "Now it's smacking its suckers over Father," I thought. In those days, I overcame my disgust at the war and decided that if I couldn't become an Austrian soldier because we were cut off from the army, I would go to war against the monster on my own. I began to say special prayers for my brother Sigmund at the front and for the kaiser and his army. Until then, I had merely mentioned them in my three customary daily prayers. Then came the night when I heard Father's voice in a dream saying, "Wake him up, Faizie (Fanny), he must be having a bad dream." In my dream, I felt Mother's hand on my forehead. "The poor child. He's burning up." "Not me, the house!" I said in my dream and looked into the blaze that was consuming our house on the Kalahura. I wanted to go in, but a fat woman with a wildly staring cow's head refused me entry. This unnatural combination filled me with dread. I awoke with my mouth forced open and Mother and Father feeding me some hot liquid drop by drop. For days and days, I lived under the spell of this dream and actually felt relieved when one evening our host brought us the news that our house on the Kalahura had been burned to the ground. For a time, I wallowed in the pangs of a guilty conscience for a crime that I could neither convince myself I had committed, even in thought, nor prevent from weighing upon me, which was the most dreadful mental torture.

"A Ruthenian shiksa just like God makes them!" Father cried in admiration as Mother presented herself for inspection, dressed in peasant garb. It was probably some irresistibly voluptuous memory associated with this costume that prompted his hand to give her a good whack on the behind and then remain there for a while. The colorful, primitive costume showed off that part of the body as well as the bosom in a very appetizing way. Two thick braids of black hair emerged from the green babushka—whose thick knot beneath Mother's chin tilted up her face—and descended like columns on either side of her chest, which rose and fell in the black-and-white embroidered blouse with wide sleeves. A cross of black wood rested against her swelling breasts, suspended from a necklace of red coral by a white, nickel-plated chain. A black shawl with a red border, held together by a yellow belt around her narrow waist, hung down almost to the top of her high yellow boots. In this disguise, supplemented by a sheepskin thrown over her shoulders, Mother had decided to return to the ashes of our house. Father disguised himself in the masculine equivalent. And one evening they set off and went "down the mountain" to recover from the ground on which our house had stood the treasure they had buried there in times of plenty against such black times as had now befallen us. How could Father have dared to take his so temptingly decked-out wife back down into the country said to be crawling with Cossacks? Had he forgotten that they grabbed for women's breasts the same way they did for pocket watches? His silver "horsehead" watch hung on a heavy chain from the wide leather belt holding up his white plissé breeches just as confidently as my mother hung on his arm. He was risking both of them. After the enemy had burned down his house, was he defying them by showing off his most precious possessions? I would sooner have expected something like that from the unthinkingly obstinate Arnold. But from Father, who always acted with great circumspection and never displayed his possessions? I was very alarmed. His plan to move through the Slavic invasion as a Ruthenian was wise and made sense to me. But it was incomprehensible that he undertook it as a rich man, awakening envy with a pocket watch and a female bosom. Was he relying on the Cossack-friendly reports of the Venderéus, on whose bosoms and pocket watches that first patrol had not laid a hand? Had he forgotten what was suggested as the motive for that polite behavior? I still remembered it very well and said it to Relly as loudly as I could—although otherwise I spoke very softly—in order to remind and warn my parents as they were about to depart.

"What's gotten into him?" said my mother with surprise, looking up at Father. Her magnificent getup was covered by the untreated sheepskin, whose white-ringleted twin was already hanging from his shoulders and fitted him like a glove.

"I myshi liudi" (Mice are people, too), said my sister Susi to tease me. Ever since her secret engagement to the teacher Frunza before he left for the front, she liked to speak Ruthenian.

I didn't get a chance to express myself more clearly, for Arnold stuck his head through the door and announced that he had brought Pastor Isopescu's two mules from Schadowa. That clergyman was a white-haired Greek Orthodox priest loyal to the kaiser. He had lent them the peasant costumes for this expedition as well. He and his three budding daughters had tearfully taken the colorful garments out of the clothes chest of his wife, who had died at a young age, and of his son, who had already fallen for Austria. I reflected that Father perhaps planned to tell the foreign invaders that Mother was his sister, for wasn't that what the Patriarch Abraham had done with his Sarah in order to make it easier for the lecherous Abimelech of Gerar to sin?[2] "No," I said to myself, banishing from my mind the thought of this ancient, unmanly behavior, "Father couldn't be intending such a fate for my mother!" Before I rolled onto my right side and went to sleep, I sent a hefty bundle of fresh prayers wending after the donkeyback riders on their dangerous paths, asking that they be protected and fortified in their devotion to us.

My parents had promised to be back for supper on the third day. But by the morning of the fourth day, they had still not returned to us, and as we drank our morning tea with caramels, I could see by the listless way Arnold stuck the sweet between his teeth that he was inwardly troubled by my parents' continued absence. Later, as I sat on a chest, swinging my legs back and forth, he struck me on the knees in annoyance, supposedly because these movements might bring the travelers bad luck. That was the first time in my life that anyone had struck me. Although I was astonished at being hit, I was much more preoccupied with Arnold's worry about our absent parents. At lunch, he shoved aside the bowl of thick soup the girls had served him first as the oldest man in the house, with a curl of his lip and darkened look on his pale face, a sure sign he was angry and planning some ineffectual demonstration of protest. Although I saw no reason for him to feel that way, it made me uneasy to see him look like that, and I didn't let him out of my sight.

In my concern, however, I seem not to have been unobtrusive enough, for that evening as we once again lay down to sleep next to each other on the bedding spread on the floor, he barked at me, "What do you think you're doing staring daggers at me all day as if I were a thief? You don't have to follow me around anymore. You're a big boy now. You can look after yourself. When I was your age, I was already driving to market all by myself with the milk and the butter and the eggs and selling them. Can't you get it into your head that I want to be rid of you? Are you going to stop following me?"

"When did I ever run after you?" I replied with cast-down eyes.

"OK, but don't do it anymore."

Then I knew that he was planning to do something terrible to himself. I mustn't leave him alone. But I knew how soundly I slept and how little I was capable of standing up to him. So I waited until I was convinced my poor brother was asleep beside me, then I took one of his shoes that lay at the foot of our bed and tied its lace to the toes of my left foot, which were always swollen and very tender in the wintertime. But Arnold seems to have noticed my ruse. After a short sleep, I awoke not from the shoelace jerking my toes, but from the cry of one of the girls sleeping next to us on the floor on whom Arnold had stepped on his way to the door. It was Relly. He quieted her down and told her he was just going out into the yard to relieve himself. I jumped up in a flash and went to slip into the clothes I always laid out neatly in a certain place on top of my shoes before going to bed. But they were not there. Arnold had put them on. Although he was older and much taller than I, his feet and hands were no larger than mine, perhaps even smaller. In this, too, he cut a more noble figure than I. So I forced my feet into his shoes, biting back the pain they caused my chilblains. Without stopping to tie the laces, I rushed to the door that Arnold had closed silently behind him. My only thought was to stick to my brother's heels, so I didn't even bother to put on my jacket when I couldn't find it right away. As I turned the corner of the house, I bumped into Arnold. He was expecting me.

"You're following me again!" he said with an angry grimace, just like Father did when he was in a rage. What could I reply? He was right. But I couldn't help it. I hung my head.

"I'm leaving now. If you follow me, I'll throw stones at you and drive you back like a dog."

"Why are you leaving? Nobody's done anything to you."

"Promise me you won't come after me, and I'll tell you why."

"Tell me."

"Promise me."

"Tell me first."

"OK. But woe to you if you follow me once I've told you. I'm going to look for Father and Mother."

"Take me with you."

"You'll get in the way."

"I'll go on my own."

"Suit yourself, but don't follow me."

"Arzin!"

"Don't start crying. You can go tell the girls."

And in long strides he moved off toward the narrow pass through the rock wall whose entrance gaped in the moonlight and seemed to me like the opening into a terrifying abyss.

"Arzin," I cupped my hands and called after him softly. "Arzin!" Unheeding, he continued on his way.

He feared for our parents, and I for him. I thought Father and Mother would always be safe, thanks to their caution and to God's mercy. Arnold, on the other hand, always seemed rash to me, nor did I see the hand of heaven protecting him. I must not, I could not, allow him to go on alone. Through my tears, I measured the distance between us as he disappeared into the cleft in the rocks. I had no choice but to run after him. I now believe that my fear of how I would suffer for his sake during his absence suppressed all other feelings and became the motor driving my great, hot, crazy speed. In the dark passageway through the wall, I paid no attention to the sharp points of rock that were scratching me bloody. Nor did I let the stones thrown by a fraternal hand and hitting me in the face deter me. I was running for the salvation of my soul, driven and borne forward by that organ schooled in terrible experiences. But the same organ seemed to be at work in the more nimble body of the runner ahead of me—and more strongly than in me, for I lost sight of him and he escaped me. Unable to think clearly or hold back, I tore past the little clustered village on the floor of the valley, sobbing loudly and crying out my brother's name, until a rifle shot, echoing a thousandfold around me, closed my mouth, and I threw myself into the snow. I heard a chorus of excited dogs and the mountains snarling back at them. Birds fluttered above me. I heard them cawing and imagined they were black. Then the mountains gave a whinnying laugh, and in a moment of silence between these tissues of sound in the winter night an anguished cry tore the air and carried my name. It was Relly's voice. She had called from the lower entrance to the passageway. I stood up and started toward her, but a huge dog appeared out of nowhere and landed in front of me with snarling mouth and glittering eyes, bringing me up short. In the next instant, the beast was called off in a language that sounded like Ruthenian, and the voice behind me ordered, *"Ruki naverkh!"* (Hands up!). I complied and obeyed the next order as well, turning in the direction of the commanding voice. I found myself standing before two horsemen in tight-fitting fur coats and shaggy caps cocked at jaunty angles. At their saddles were long, curved sabers. They burst out laughing at the sight of me, wiping the tears from their eyes; their torsos swayed in all directions while their ponies stood as stiff and still as if made of wood. Once this performance had finished, they sprang from their horses and approached me on their knees, coaxing me with calls and reassuring gestures as if I were a deer or some other skittish forest creature. They took turns hugging me to their mighty shoulders and kissing my forehead. After a comprehensive and sympathetic examination of the scrapes on my face and the bloodstains on my skimpy get-up, they consoled me with *"Nichevo, nichevo"* (It's all right). Remembering how my foresightful Mother had told us to act in such an event, I answered their questions in Ruthenian and said that I was from Upper Staneschti and the son of the family with whom we had rested on our flight. I led them to believe that they had found me in Costeschti in such a terrible state because I'd been running a race with an older friend and had fallen many times on the stones and cut myself. My companion and I had been higher up in the mountains with some woodcutters from our village, but he had run away at the Cossacks' approach, leaving me here in the lurch. To that they answered only that I would now get home faster than my disloyal comrade. They wrapped me in one of their fur coats, and the one who had lent it to me held me very comfortably on the saddle before him on the ride down to Upper Staneschti.

As we rode into the village where the two horsemen were quartered with their lieutenant in order to guard the road between Staneschti and Costeschti, the stars were just beginning to fade in the sky. The men brought me to their billet and invited me to stay with them until daybreak. I could rest and make myself presentable so I wouldn't frighten my mother when I returned home. They warmed up some water for me to wash in. While I was sitting in the tub and soaping and scrubbing myself at their insistence—although at home, even on wash days, I preferred to rub myself down with bran or sand—my hosts were mending my suit and shining my shoes. After they had bedded me on the pallet they shared with each other, they placed a sizzling wash pan under my nose in which they had roasted eggs, cheese, and bacon in grade-A butter; all three of us dug into it with wooden spoons and had white bread to go with it. Food has never tasted so good to me. After that, we drank hot rye whiskey with sugar, and before I dropped off to sleep, we kissed each other and wept. When I woke up again, it was not yet daylight. What I didn't realize was that it was actually the evening of the second day. Thinking that it would soon be light, I looked for my clothes and found them in the natural light of the winter night that fell through the whitish blue windowpanes into the room. I began to get dressed. I was squatting on the floor and just tying my shoes when my friends entered the room carrying candles. They explained my mistake to me, and I was sorry to have slept a whole day away. But it wasn't yet deep in the night, so I could still make it to the family who had sheltered us there in that village, and I had an irresistible urge to do so. Since I knew their name and people were still out on the narrow village street, I easily asked my way to their house. The good people welcomed me warmly, which I found particularly pleasant because they did it in Swabian dialect. I learned that five days ago Father and Mother had passed through on their way to Berbeschti, and Arnold had, too, that morning, and they'd all promised to stay there on their way back. Their invitation to spend the night and have something to eat was outweighed by the chance to stay with my horsemen, so they bid me farewell since it was their bedtime. These friends escorted me out to their gate, and only then did I tell them I'd given myself out to be their son when I was with the Cossacks. When I returned to my new friends, they sat me right down in front of a steaming platter of bacon and sauerkraut. It tasted as exquisite as the other food they had given me. The good fellows told me that they had bet three to one on my return; the horseman who doubted I would had bet only one. After the meal, they drank hot brandy again, but this time they wouldn't give me a swallow since it laid me out too quickly and they wanted to talk to me.

From them I heard good things about Russia. They spoke of the vast land and its big-hearted people, of the size of its mountains, rivers, and lakes. The younger one was voluble on the subject of the sweetness of Russian girls, while the much older, bearded horseman showed me a photograph of his lovely children, whose older brother I could have been, although I wasn't as beautiful as they. Then that warrior father kissed my hands and sobbed, saying, "*Nichevo,* little father," and he taught me—blowing his nose into his hand and flinging the snot against the wall—that familiar things were always nearest and dearest, even if the foreign was as lovely "as you are, little father." The things I heard and experienced for myself there utterly contradicted what I'd learned from my maternal grandfather, now in his grave, to say nothing of our lieutenants and Relly, who parroted what they said. I was deeply moved, agitated, and perplexed.

My hosts seemed to sense my confusion, for abruptly they said, "You've heard that we eat people, cut up women, steal watches. Admit it. Don't be ashamed. It's not your fault, and it's not ours either." The old man spoke calmly in his bass voice, with sadness on his white face beneath its beard. But the young one was loud and sharp, embittered. "Don't get all hot and bothered," said the old man to his companion. "Don't get excited. We're only talking to a child. Well, little fellow"—turning to me—"now you've seen the truth for yourself."

My blood ran hot and cold, and I heard a strange voice coming out of my mouth: "But there's another Russia, too."

"Your Austria isn't as angelic as you are, either!" fired back the younger one.

"Calm down, Kolya," said the older man and held out a glass to him. "Here, have another drink and go to bed."

"But I didn't mean to hurt him," I said in a tearful voice, for now Kolya reminded me of Arnold.

Once the two of us were alone together, the old man said as if to himself, "Of course, there's the Russia of those who bear malice and start wars. But they're also to be found in Austria and France and everywhere on God's blessed, wretched planet. If only we could throw them out!" He opened a mouth missing quite a few teeth and poured a teacup full of schnaps down his throat. After wiping off his mustache with his index finger and thumb, he leaned down to me and asked, "Heard of Vladimir Ilyich?"

"No."

"Nothing about him in school?"

"No."

"Not here either, then. *Nichevo.* A great scholar, little father, a genius, even though he's a Russian." He stood up from the table and strode off. When he returned, he poured a little schnaps into a cup for me. "To your health, my son! So, and now let's hit the sack."

Next morning this more gentle of my two hosts took me to his commander, a lieutenant who was the General Staff's eyes and ears on the thirty kilometers of road between Upper Staneschti and Costeschti. In carrying out his duties, he used my mounted friends like a croupier's rake on a martial gaming table, with their help sweeping in everything that moved and breathed on the road and giving it a good once-over. This officer was billeted with Braha, the head teacher of the village school, and had a carpeted room where he slept, ate, worked, and received visitors. My friend shoved me through the half-open door without entering himself. In the middle of the room stood a young, clean-shaven man with a fur cap pushed up at an angle on his high forehead and a black coat that hung down to his ankles, patent-leather boots gleaming beneath it.

"So you're the spy," he said in Ruthenian. I seemed to be in a bad dream.

"Don't frighten him, Vanya!" A warm female voice emerged from among rosy pillows on a bed behind him. I could see only a straw yellow head of hair beneath the featherbed and a quick movement of something that a pair of soft white arms, which now came into view, tried to hold onto. "Oy, Vanushka, the doggie! He's trying to run away again. Can't you help me?"

As the lieutenant turned toward the bed, Muschka was already coming toward me. Our Muschka! I thought I was dreaming. She came up as though she had been with me just a moment ago and was now coming back. She'd probably learned her walk from my mother: silent, light footed, and demure. Not until she reached the toes of my shoes did she raise to me her intelligent face with its curved brow above her soulful brown eyes. I was never exuberant in the expression of my emotional life. In general, not even joy or pain led me to those extravagant exertions of the face, throat, and extremities that so often result in exclamations, kisses, tears, and hugs—even in public. And it certainly never happened to me in the presence of anyone outside my emotional sphere. It's true that I'd been known to caress or hug a tree, even in the shadow of other neighboring trees, but they all had grown and stood within the horizon of my emotions, just like the love for them that led me to such action. I couldn't allow myself in all good conscience to do it with animals, however, and even feared the gaze of the cow Finni when I stepped back from giving her a quick kiss on her white wooly forehead. Muschka knew me, and the beloved little dog was no more surprised at my standing stock still at this unexpected reunion than my mother would have been. But I couldn't prevent my gaze from falling from beneath my lowered eyelids into the great pools of her eyes looking up at me, and when I saw my image in them, I felt that it filled her with pleasure. But she, too, stood motionless. Then I caught sight of a large burn wound in the silky, golden hair on her flank and felt a tear escape my eye when I saw her turn to bite at it. I realized that she had sat on our house until it sank into ashes beneath her. Her great soul had tried to spread out her helpless little body over the huge property and thus cover and protect it. And when the house collapsed, she sank with it and got burned in its ashes. Ship captains act the same way when the boundless sea has worked on their loneliness and their emotions to the point where they are capable of extraordinary, superhuman achievements. Who knows of their heroism? Who can measure it? But the water allows no monument. Everything is buried and decomposes beneath the waves. But here, in spirit, I want to hold my Muschka above them for a moment.

I didn't notice it at the time, but now in retrospect I see that the lieutenant and his wife were carrying out on me, as on everyone else, their assignment to keep the area under surveillance. I always found people's curiosity about my own person repugnant. Even Relly's questions usually went unanswered, regardless of whether she was trying to guess my mood, my intentions, or my physical health. The lieutenant and his wife had quickly realized this and hoped to have more success by pestering me with urgent questions about my family and friends. I doubt that I would have needed the lessons in concealment my older siblings had taught me with regard to my parents—or my parents had taught me with regard to neighbors, guests, and the state—to develop the carapace of silence that had become my indelible seal. But those lessons alone would have sufficed to so harden my antipathy to any kind of inquisitive questioning that ax blows aimed at breaking my silence would sooner have broken my physical breast than my psychological resolve. During their interrogation—for that's what it was—these two strangers often wove Father's name into their phrases while watching me surreptitiously. The young officer went so far as to become pejorative about that worthy man he'd never met: "That cur . . . " he began and then continued, "keeps his hand over all the mouths in this country." Enhanced by his hatred, the officer's high regard for Father's importance invalidated the insult "that cur." This struck me forcefully, even back then.

In fact, that enemy couple opened my eyes for the first time to my father's political and social importance. Based on his well-deserved fame as an agriculturalist—a fame that put down roots and blossomed anew with each year's sowing and harvesting of a potato variety named after him—it stood to reason that this hard-working man without public ambition, this honest businessman and level-headed patriot, would be an example to many of his rural neighbors and serve a useful function for the imperial administration of the dispassionately administered Austrian Empire, bent on holding itself together. This last function earned him the hatred of the Russophile Pan-Slavs, which explains the stones and perhaps also the incendiary torches thrown into our house, as well as the price clapped onto Father's head. Certain Jewish circles were opposed to him as an assimilator, but they discharged their hostility only in the form of evasive irony. In fact, Father, although he sprang from the loins of half-baptized, reconverted Jews, was by no means an assimilator. Nor was he at all anti-Slav. He was simply neither more nor less than the only thing he was able to be—namely, a human being and a citizen. This dual aspect of his civic reliability could thrive only while the Bucovina was on the map of the Dual Monarchy. Father's greatness and his tragedy were that he stood like an island against a stormy sea of amorphous radicalism advancing from all sides. It was not his fault, nor did he deserve any special credit for it. He neither sought nor received the Order of Maria Theresia.[3] It was unfair to reserve a spot for him in Siberia and set bounty hunters on his trail. The cunning attempts of these Pan-Slavic bloodhounds—risen from darkness and in its service—to discover from my mouth where Father was hiding (and who knows what else) didn't get them an inch further than they had been before I showed up. The fact that they had already tried their wretched luck to no avail on innumerable children and adults before me filled me with pride and gratitude for my Bucovina, loyally silent in all its many tongues, and with immeasurable awe for my father, so secure among his tight-lipped compatriots.

My visit to the bloodhounds ended when the lieutenant in his black janissary's coat, imprisoned by the bars of his own blindness, shook his fist at an invisible throng. "*Nichevo*, you corpses! I'll send you all to Siberia!" Then he bent down to me and said in broken German, "You whole country traitor country, boy!"

His lady apologized for this outburst: "Five thousand rubles are at stake, dear boy. Nothing to be sneezed at, what? But what would you know about that? Ha ha ha! The people we have to talk to!" She was shaking in a fit of mad laughter. When she calmed down, she took hold of my nose and drew me to her bosom. When I angrily pulled away, she gave me a gentle shove. "You may kiss my hand now, little one! If you promise to come back tomorrow, you can have the dog," for in the meantime Muschka had curled up in a corner of the room, and I hadn't been able to keep myself from looking at her. As often as our conversation allowed, I went over to her and pretended to get to know her. Finally, I picked my friend up and held her in my arms. "We've got to go, right, Vanya? So, until tomorrow, my little one. Take this along with you." She reached behind her and brought out a bar of chocolate that I eagerly accepted, despite misgivings. "Now you may go. And don't get angry at me. I was just having some fun."

"You're still too dumb to understand that," chimed in her husband. "Doesn't matter. You'll learn. Here's a man's farewell present for you," and he gave me a piece of bacon.

Now I returned to the Germans who had sheltered us and stayed there with Muschka until my next visit to the lieutenant and his wife. I gave the untouched piece of bacon to the woman of the house since she gave me all I wanted to eat, and Mother, who kept kosher, would neither have used it nor tolerated our eating it as long as we were still able to get Jewish food. I carefully broke the chocolate into eight pieces, one for each member of my family, including Muschka. I saved the biggest pieces for Mother, Arnold, and Relly. After careful consideration, I left Father out, for I didn't dare offer him anything so trivial. I left myself out as well so as not to diminish my pleasure at giving a gift to my nearest and dearest. After my release from the bloodhounds, I knocked together a sled for myself and had some fun sliding down the steep village street. I got up early the next day to go to the road outside the village where there was more scope for the pleasures of sledding. There I again encountered my two horsemen returning from their nocturnal patrol. Would I like a little ride? inquired the elder one and lifted me up onto his saddle. The younger one, barely returning my greeting, had ridden on ahead and called back to remind my friend that they had another patrol that afternoon. His intention was probably to admonish him to think of getting some sleep rather than talking to me. My friend spurred his horse to a trot through the village to escape the barking of the dogs, which is as annoying close up as it is inviting from a distance. Once out amid the fields, he allowed the animal to slow to a walk. Ravens sat on the osiers beside the road. They looked like black urns and always waited until we came near before moving to the next tree in sluggish complaint.

"How was it at the lieutenant's?"

"Mm."

"Really tried to pick your brain?"

"Yes. How come?"

"It's his job." A hare sprang across the road. "We don't have to bring *him* in, but everyone else. What did you tell him?"

"Mm."

"I hope you didn't tell him any more than that."

"I told him who I was."

"Who are you?"

"I told you already."

"You were lying."

"Put me down."

"This time you've got to stay."

"You're stronger than I am."

"So you shouldn't have let me pick you up."

"I thought you were my friend."

"The stronger one is never the friend of the weaker one."

I managed to jump off and run a few steps into the field. He came after me and brought me to a standstill. "Good for you, little fellow! But I know who you are. I also know where your dog came from and where she was headed. They could have let her go and then followed her. Pets don't lie. I took her into custody right here. I'm sure she greeted you at the lieutenant's like a loving dog would. Effusively. What did you say?"

"She didn't. We're from here."

"Hm. It's a strange world we live in. So you probably think that I'm on their side?"

"You ask a lot of questions, like them."

"You're right, little boy. Now let me take you back. Don't be afraid. I'm not stronger than you."

"You're making fun of me." I climbed up onto his saddle again. We rode in silence. He put me down by my sled. He dismounted as well.

"You won't see us anymore, but the lieutenant will call for you again, maybe. It would be smarter to go there voluntarily. I can count on you. I am counting on you. My name is Nikifor Petrovich Zimkin. My eldest is Nikifor Nikiforovich. From the village of Chernovka in the government of Perm. Maybe you'll visit us someday."

"You're a Cossack."

"As you can see." And he knelt down in the snow, took my face between his hands, and gave me a kiss on each cheek and on my forehead. Then he walked away, leading his horse. Such were the Cossacks.

Late that afternoon I went to the lieutenant's house. On his threshold, I remembered that I should have brought Muschka along, and I wanted to go back and get her. The couple were playing cards at a pedestal table, and both said at once that I was welcome even without the pup. They gave me permission to operate the old gramophone that was standing on a rolltop cabinet, its tone arm droning hoarsely on a dance record. A cuckoo clock on the wall clattered softly, and the green-shaded kerosine lantern hanging from the ceiling hissed. It was homey. The plump blonde, her hair nicely dressed, wore a hat with a saucy feather and made a pretty picture sitting in a fur collar whose light brown triangle framed her white neck and high bosom and left her long arms bare. From time to time, she exchanged melodious remarks with her opponent or told me how to work the talking machine. In the meantime, the curtainless windowpanes turned dark blue behind their blinding white frost patterns, and the noises from the street became less frequent. When I went to sit down and, glancing around, could discover no available chair, I saw that the bed was now concealed behind a screen, with only the footboard showing. I could push the screen aside a bit and sit on the bed. And there I fell asleep.

When I woke up, I found myself stretched out on the bed with my shoes removed and separated from the room by the screen that again concealed the entire bed. I heard the door open and the room fill with a babble of voices, from which emerged Mother's warm alto, amplified by anger.

"You're our liberators! But you don't let us move freely along the roads of our own country! And now you heathens intend to lay your un-Christian hands on our sacred altar silver! That's the thanks we get for being Orthodox believers and showing you the way and welcoming you with bread and salt! I'm here to demand justice from you, Herr Lieutenant! These two myrmidons here assaulted us on the public highway of God and the emperor of all true believers, Nikolai. They searched us and pointed their carbines at us and forced us to make this detour."

The lieutenant said something mollifying and sent my two Cossacks out of the room. I peered through a crack in the screen and saw Father and Mother looking just as they had when they set off from our hideout among the rocks five days earlier. And to my instant relief Arnold was there, too, dressed as a Ruthenian boy, with a half-empty sack on his back. The lieutenant put a couple questions to Father, which he answered in a clear, quiet voice.

"And this woman?" He pointed at Mother.

"My sister." So he was going to deny her after all, sell her out to protect himself. That dreadful bedouin tradition, prefigured in the Bible. We can't escape it: our blood flows through biblical veins. So she was no longer "Fanny, my wife," but rather the expendable "Sarah, my sister." Oh Father, Father! If only you had never uttered that word! If only I had been standing there in your shoes. Relly and I. "Relly," I would have said. "That is Relly, my wife! Don't touch her, you heathen!" Do you build your trust on God, Abraham? Then why don't you trust him with your own life instead of avoiding danger and pushing forward your wife, you cowardly desert hare, counting on God to protect the spouse who was counting on you? I hope and pray like you that He won't abandon that plucky woman as her back-stabbing husband has done. You think you're so clever, but you're already bereft of Him, for God abandons the man who denies his spouse.

Lieutenant Abimelech raised his eyebrows and said, "Brother and sister. Did I hear you right? Are you sure you're not mistaken? Or do you call your wives your sisters the same way you call a bed a *yebalnik*[4] around here? Think it over so you're not sorry afterwards, because I'm unmarried and lust after your sister." And so the white-armed woman was also being denied. They deserved each other, Lieutenant Abimelech and Father Abraham. A nice pair of brothers!

But now the fair Sarah-Fanny opened her own, truthful mouth. "Greatly edified as I am by the Herr Lieutenant's appetite, I must nevertheless protest that I am a married woman and the anxious mother of a trio of blooming daughters." What was she saying? Did she dare to expose this cowardly creature of God?

"And what lucky, enviable man is your husband, if I may ask?"

"The elderly pastor of Schadowa." It was Abraham who played this trump, his reinsurance policy. Then he lowered himself contentedly onto a chair.

Now that Sarah no longer wore the helmet of a rival, the lieutenant's white-armed wife hugged and kissed her repeatedly and urged her into the other armchair. "Just so you know, little sister, our union is consecrated as well. But my Kolya[5] violates the laws of heaven and won't stay within these arms." And glancing toward Abraham, she raised those very limbs, the loveliest part of her figure, into the lamplight in a gesture of recrimination and yearning. "I hope that you, little sister of my heart, are happier as the wife of a man of God." And full of sympathetic self-denial, she let her hands drop to her elastic thighs, where they bounced once and came to rest.

"Ah, Frau Lieutenant Abimelech . . . " Sarah wiped off her mouth with her thumb and forefinger and began anew. "Frau Abimelech, men of God feel they have heavenly permission to expend their seed the way the sky expends clouds or the sea sand. You just can't keep up with them, my dear, and one is not discontent—although not exactly happy—to see it be planted elsewhere from time to time."

"So even the holy men do it!"

"Even them, dear friend, even them."

"Especially them, Taniushka. Just be glad you have your lieutenant. But now bring some more chairs and the big table. Our guests will be hungry and thirsty. This boy—what did you say his name was, sir?—Akim. Akim can help you. Meanwhile, I'll just stick my imperial nose into these people's sack and that will be my last official act for today."

In the sack were, among other things, the aforementioned domestic silver implements of Jewish ritual observance. They were wrapped up in a stole to make more plausible the story that the priest of Schadowa had been ordered by the regional church authorities to salvage these remnants from a shot-up chapel in the Pruth Valley. He had assigned this sacred task to his wife. In fact, the stole, with gold ribbons in the shape of crosses appliquéd onto a silver background, seems to have tipped the scales of official suspicion in favor of the prevaricating couple. If a random scrap of evidence against an innocent person is often enough for a policeman to conjure up whole penitentiaries of guilt, the same policeman can with as little justification throw open the way to freedom and honor to a self-evidently guilty person. Not until the lieutenant had reverently returned the implements to their sack did he introduce himself to my parents, clicking his spurred heals together and kissing my mother's hand. Meanwhile, Arnold-Akim and Taniushka had brought in chairs and a table, on which I could make out several bottles, a platter with cold cuts, and one with slices of bread.

"At last we have cultured guests," said Kolya to begin the meal. But when he had uncorked the first bottle and was about to pour the wine, there were no glasses on the table. He leaned back in his chair, breathing heavily. Tanya looked pleadingly at him. "Oh well," sighed the host. "You see, my wife breaks every piece of glass in the house so our marriage will last. Don't you think," he continued, turning to the defendant, "this is getting a little too expensive?"

"Please, Kolya," she said with tears in her voice, "not in front of our first proper guests. . . . Madam Pastor, would you allow me to borrow a few of your cups?"

"Akim," said the priest's brother-in-law, "hop to it."

"The boy is your son, I presume?" said the lieutenant, instinctively sensing the ground of truth beneath his feet.

"Yes, he is," Father confirmed. "He certainly is," he repeated in confirmation, as if even that was no longer a certainty. And Arnold took the silver cups out of the sack, polished each one with his sleeve, filled them, and served the wine, just as he had learned to do in the prayer house in Stanislau and in Father's tavern. As a reward, he was allowed to pour himself a glass as well. My mouth began to feel dry, and when he drained his glass, I decided he didn't deserve my chocolate anymore. They drank several rounds, with all sorts of highfalutin and abstract toasts: to Victory, to Faith, to the Empire, the People, and finally, to the Women and Children.

At which point, Taniushka said, "But Kolya, darling, we've forgotten all about our little boy. We have a little boy here, you see, Madam Pastor. A charming little man, I can tell you, one of your people here whom we've adopted. We found him up along the road." And so the mendacious floodwaters of this farce reached out for me as well.

"I'll go get him, OK, Koliushka?"

"Not necessary."

But she was already pulling aside the screen, revealing me to the assembly. I stood there feeling exposed. They made me sit down, and while my adoptive parents tenderly put shoes on my feet, I saw Arnold's clenched fist, Father's grimly pursed lips, Mother's ironic and furious eyes.

In dreamlike apprehension, I turned my back to them and said to Taniushka in my best Ruthenian, "Mother, put the screen up again. I don't want to see these wicked people."

But do parents ever pay any attention to the feelings of their children? I was made to join the party, had to eat and drink, although, unfortunately, I no longer felt like it at all. And when the adults got up to dance, I had to run the talking machine. But by the second record Arnold-Akim was already pushing me aside, saying it was my fault that the tone arm was scratchy and curing it immediately like an experienced appliance doctor. As a reward, the white hands of our hostess took his handsome head and pressed it feelingly against her bosom. I guess he must have dived in there with more proficiency than the two men could stand or the beauty expected, for she blushed and watched with moist eyes as the two envious men grabbed him and threw him into a corner. This little scandal distracted our hosts and gave Mother a chance to quickly pull me out of the room and hide me under the hay in their sleigh, which was standing in front of the house. There I fell asleep again.

When I stuck my head out, I heard the jingling bells of the mules pulling the sleigh uphill. Father and Arnold were sitting on the coach box, Mother right near my face, with Muschka on her lap, and above them the stars were shining. I closed my eyes and burrowed back into the straw so as not to let this dream vision slip away. When they woke me up, our sleigh had halted on the sloping drive of a little summer palace with a pedestal-like ground floor, two upper stories, a roofed porch, pavilions projecting from the middle and the corners, pillars, pilasters, and tall windows beneath a green glass ceiling with a balustrade, all of which was shimmering, flashing, and sparkling in the morning sun between the glittering snow and the blue sky, as if made of diamonds. On the broad steps leading to the entrance stood a stooped patriarch with white locks on his head, holding in his trembling hands a round loaf of bread and a saltcellar. One step above him, three girls were holding hands. They looked like three trees in bloom and smiled at us like spring, summer, and fall. The old man said in a voice that carried despite its quaver, "Welcome! For it is written, 'Blessed are they that mourn, for they shall be comforted.'" It was the priest of Schadowa with his daughters.

We stayed two days in that Romanian rectory. Father had stopped there because he feared that the lieutenant would send spying eyes riding after us. Seen from the outside with sober eyes, it wasn't actually a palace, but inside it was like a fairy tale. However, that, too, applied only to what was seen by the eyes of the heart, to which rooms and furnishings can seem transfigured by the charm of the inhabitants. Despite the unobtrusively tasteful arrangement of rich carpets, chests, and benches alternating with writing stands along the walls, the suite of four paneled rooms the priest and his family occupied in one wing of the building would not have left me with a lifelong sense of marvel if the three slim sisters and the saintly old man had not moved through them, enveloped in the scent of lavender and the talismanic magic of silver icons. I am not unaware that my memory is also dictated by gratified vanity, for it was in that house that I became the representative object for a demonstration of virginal desire that mightily enhanced the small person I was. After having heard the call of sexuality in myself, I had the good fortune to see it there in those sisters in an ingenuous, compulsive, tragic form that I had experienced neither in Relly's school of timid pleasures nor, two years earlier, in the uninhibited whirlwind round dances of the Kalahura tomboys.

On the evening of our arrival, we all were lying on the benches along the walls of the guest room, about to fall asleep, when suddenly the door opened and the three seasons, the three trees—namely Aurora, Cornelia, and Pulcheria, the priest's daughters—entered in long nightgowns. They presented Mother with a little basket of fragrant winter fruits, which, to judge from the smell, contained rennets, dried pears and plums, and almonds. They asked Mother's permission "to abduct your little one." They literally said "abduct." Mother, who always had great compassion for the female sex and could never refuse anything to its younger representatives, granted the strange request without a second thought and, reaching her arm out from under her quilt to underscore her liberal generosity, gestured imperiously toward my bed. Frightened more by her permission than by the request that led to it, I pulled my blanket more tightly about me and pressed up against the wall, into which I would have gladly disappeared.

"You're afraid, eh?!" said Aurora triumphantly.

"The coward!" scoffed Cornelia.

"Grab him!" commanded Pulcheria.

"Take *me!*" Arnold interjected. "He'll just cry."

"Keep out of this, you skinny bum!" was their inexplicably nasty reply to my good brother.

They laid me on a mattress in the middle of their room, knotted red sashes around their waists, and, chanting some spell, circled me in a sort of dance. I felt as if the earth were opening beneath me and that I would fall into the abyss forever were it not that my eyes, glued to the eyes of the girls treading slowly around me, kept me up. After a considerable time, they said in exhausted yet nasty, threatening voices, "Now get out of here!" As I lay back down on my bench, delightfully woozy, I could feel my brother's eyes upon me.

At the beginning of March, we could hear the thunder of cannons higher up in the mountains. Shortly thereafter, shell casings fell like early raindrops into our rocky enclosure. One day we climbed a peak and saw a flood of Russians streaming downhill through the swales and passes below us. It was the same image of a beaten and retreating host that we had seen four months earlier when the Austrian troops, animals, and baggage trains had fled into the mountains. Now it was the Russians pouring out of the mountains and plunging downhill in a thousand streams like water from the spring melt. And one evening we saw the heights around us covered with Austrian fighters, as if with the harbingers of spring. They wore white camouflage coats or green riflemen's tunics. At a crossroads, we quickly set up a tea stand to which Mother conveyed her entire supply of caramels. The girls, having decided to kiss the first liberators they caught sight of, took the liberty of putting on Red Cross armbands and lay in wait for their victims. Father and Arnold put large nightshirts on over their clothes, procured rifles from the first troop that passed, and fell in beside them to go and liberate the Kalahura. The soldiers in white coats were young Poles who had been permitted to form their own units to drive the Russians from their land.

On the Kalahura, only the railroad inspector Venderéu's house—which he hadn't fled this time, either—had escaped damage. One entire side wall of the train station was missing, which made it seem somehow an even more generous invitation to travel. Only the bare, roofless walls of the post office remained standing. Stray cats and dogs had got in through the shrapnel holes and were congregating there. On the spot where our house had been was a large stain of gray ash from which the oak timbers that had not been completely consumed protruded at crazy angles. But the cellar had survived partially intact, and there we discovered a young Austrian from the Forty-first Infantry Regiment. He was sitting on a small keg in his spruce blue uniform, leaning his back against a larger keg, and he held a long rifle between his stretched-out feet. His face had fallen forward, and the rifle's fixed bayonet was buried in his lower jaw. Dried blood covered the shiny blade and seemed to have run out of the wound and over his Adam's apple. We also found a hole in the cap on his head, from which blood and brains had emerged with the bullet, fragments and drops of them having fallen back onto the blue cap and stained it black. We saw, too, that one of his feet was bare, and his big toe had pushed down the trigger of the rifle.

To assuage the pain this sight caused me, I wrote the following poem:

> I know not the tongues of the people,
> but their sufferings I know quite well.
> Let me write them down for You, Father:
> For You gave me the hand to do it.
> Greatly they fear each other,
> and what frightens them in their neighbor,
> many make the same of themselves:
> a sightless lifeless corpse-man.
> Sent down to earth by You,
> I feel no fear of them;
> But for the load of their pains
> I feel no muscles within me.
> So give me the word to help me,
> for what I say gets lighter:
> with almost no effort I lift the dead man
> up to You now, on this page.[6]

We stayed in the railroad inspector's house. In the daily presence of the inspector's lovely illegitimate daughter, Aurelzia, it wasn't easy for me to remain faithful to Relly. But I did stay true to her and even in my thoughts remained stronger than the allure of temptation. Arnold teased me anyway and called me Aurelzian. He was at that querulous age when love can be the object of ridicule. Our faithful hired man had rescued the most valuable things from our burning house, among them the horse and the two cows. All three of them had resolutely tried to go back into the fire, and when the man had prevented that, they were said to have danced around it for a long while in blind stubbornness. In the meantime, Father sold the big-eyed milk producers, whom our good neighbor Venderéu had taken in and put up in his stall. So every day at sunrise, I had to go to the village to fetch milk, cheese, and butter, our main nourishment along with bread and potatoes. Twice a week I strapped a rucksack on my back and hiked to the market towns of Staneschti and Waschkautz. I reached the first by going through our village and then up the slope beyond, the second through Czortoria Forest. At these markets, I had to shop mostly for flour, sugar, lemons, spices, and kosher meat. Sometimes I also brought along poultry we had purchased in our village to be slaughtered by the kosher butcher. Mother was now keeping strictly kosher and believed that the ritual required meat on the weekend.

Father wouldn't allow supplies to be stockpiled. He had no confidence in the reassurances of the lesser lords of war, who, mounted on their horses, sent divisions wading up to the line of fire through the morass of spring fields while promising over glasses of hot tea to throw the enemy back into the Volga and impose an iron-fisted peace. Father feared a new setback and lived from hand to mouth, his eye on the front and his feet set to flee. Nevertheless, he invested his entire liquid assets in war bonds. He set up and maintained with his own money a first-aid station and two tea stands for the passing troops. Our girls staffed the former, while Arnold and I dispensed tea. In return for a mug of hot tea and a piece of bread and butter, the stalwart men marching to their deaths amid hardship and deprivation gave us many heartfelt words of thanks as well as little souvenirs and quite a lot of loose change. Especially generous were the Bavarian regiments, who sang lusty songs that sounded melancholy to me as they bore their huge bodies into battle. Every night we returned from our patriotic endeavors with pockets full of nickels, medals, rings, and other rewards, and in the morning, before we went back to work, we donated half of it by weight to the war effort. The officials, for their part, however, fished out only the coins and gave us long cobbler's nails in return, which we were then permitted to push into predrilled holes in the wooden likenesses of our kaisers and commanders that stood steadfastly on the station platform.

It was about that time that we received, after long silence, a sign of life from our soldier brother Sigmund; it bore the stamp of the Russian Red Cross and gave us to understand that this fighter had been taken prisoner with a serious head wound, was at present in Siberia, and hoped to survive since life was long-suffering. At the same time, we also got word of the death of our maternal uncle Chaim, the humble brushmaker. He had risen to the rank of platoon commander of an imperial and royal artillery battery and was torn apart by a cannon when he placed himself in front of its barrel to prevent it from spitting at his native town, Stanislau.

A little sketch of a field of corpses that our cousin Habermann from Sniatin had drawn himself informed us of his own hero's death. Over one of the fallen, on whose breast his own picture lay, he had written the word *ich*. Without informing our Susi, my parents had chosen this young man—to whose young life and diploma in engineering the hard-pressed fatherland had now added this death—as her future husband. Shortly after the arrival of that sketch of death, whose envelope had also been addressed to us by the hand of its creator, Susi disappeared in stealth from our house, the village, the entire region. This pain, too, found a silent corner to inhabit in my parents' faces. They knew that the twenty-one-year-old, following the call of nature but not of love, had flown to the teacher Frunza, who had lured her to his grizzled breast behind the lines in Moravian Ostrau. The whole village knew it as well, and its Jewish residents strongly suggested to Father that he would find consolation from this blow in strict observance of Jewish precepts. In other words, Father and his wife and children should regard the runaway apostate as having died, and, as a sign of despair, we should remove the shoes from our feet, pull sackcloth over our shoulders, strew ashes on our heads, and in this state spend six days sitting on the floor. "Fortunately," said one of these well-meaning friends, "fortunately, you've got a fine board floor for the purpose at the railroad inspector's house." Father, however, was no longer the man to seek to drown his troubles in any way whatever. Even though in his youth he had shuffled the cards and drained the wine glass—perhaps from an excess of energy, but certainly also out of sorrow—now the storms in his breast were quickly quelled by Mother's civilizing hand, and we never saw him give way completely to his feelings, no matter what the cause, be it an excess of joy or sorrow. Like Mother in her woman's way, he wrestled earnestly in his mind with every pain. Mother was the more practiced of the two, and only rarely did sighs betray the difficulty of her silent struggle. Father, on the other hand, had a man's tendency to feel sorry for himself, and the veins at his temples would swell in his flushed face. But that was the extent of it. And so both of them declined the well-meant advice of their fellow Jews and did not pluck the plucky runaway entirely from their wounded hearts. Keeping it secret from each other, they even sent the needy young couple sums of money they could ill afford to give. I, who had been the couple's secret courier, welcomed the union of the two lovers—as I thought—Susi and Frunza, as a victory of emotion over the prohibitions of tradition.

On the heels of the combat troops whose armed might was driving the foreign invaders before them, there followed units with the authorization to forage. From the stalls, barns, and houses of the peasants they abducted cattle, grain, and doorknobs as well as the bells from the church towers. The third arm that the ancient imperial power laid upon its reconquered crown province was martial law. This appeared in the form of drumhead courts-martial accompanied by hangmen and bailiffs who took from the houses their only remaining inhabitants: old men and women. The landscape sprouted gallows like an oil field wellheads, except that the latter extract a precious fluid, whereas the former spill the most precious of all. It was not unusual that the arrestees were hanged on the very branches under whose blossoms they had been condemned to die. I saw such spring trees on my way to the market towns and heard the grownups say that there was also one standing in front of the rectory in Schadowa. From its blossom-bedecked limbs hung the four sublime figures who had brought it to life out of the soil in the first place. At the beginning of the war, only Ruthenians had fallen victim to the courts-martial. Germans and Jews were considered trustworthy. The Romanians were not, but were regarded merely with caution and even treated courteously as long as there was a possibility that their nearby motherland might become our comrade-in-arms. When that proved to be an illusion, the Austrians began to be suspicious of but not unjust to them, for they expected a complaisant neutrality from their smaller neighbor. After this hope was also dashed but before Romania's public declaration of war against the Dual Monarchy, our Walachian neighbors were eagerly persecuted, if not yet explicitly as Romanians, then under the pretext that they were the coreligionists of the Russians. Above all, the intellectuals and among them especially the most upright were hunted down and killed. It is the curse of every regime that resorts to terror to be served by criminals who naturally first of all go after their own enemies and not necessarily the enemies of their masters, unless their masters are criminals as well. And so the saintly priest of Schadowa and his four daughters had to have their necks snapped.

Meanwhile, all the sounds of war had been carried away from our country. Only now and then would we hear a rider galloping by in the night, and the late winter of 1915–1916 hung so white and still over the country that one thought one heard its last snowflakes falling. But the spring winds that melted the snow and broke the ice on the Pruth bore anew the voices of cannon fire, and shortly thereafter the barking machines themselves appeared. Two months later families not native to our region were forced to evacuate, and we, too, along with all the other inhabitants of the Kalahura, were invited to board boxcars. We carried with us our surviving possessions, consisting primarily of bed linens and kitchen utensils. Father and Arnold did not come with us. They had agreed to drive the cattle herds of some of the local estate owners across the Carpathians to safety in Hungary. The goal of our flight was unknown, but wherever we ended up, they were supposed to join us. Shortly before our train left, Mother counted the heads of her loved ones and discovered that Muschka was missing. The train was already signaling its departure when without Mother's permission I left the boxcar to look for the beloved creature. Whenever it was a question of making good some oversight that could lead to pangs of conscience later on, my courage and resolve took on almost the same irresistibility that I so admired in all of Arnold's actions. I found our Muschka in the middle of the road, not far from the train station, where she had been run over by a wagon, probably while trying to join us. As I brought the little lifeless body to the platform, all the Kalahura children came down from the boxcars, and we buried the earthly remains of our domestic guardian spirit, crying and sobbing in an emotional funeral procession. It was especially the girls who wept, the expression of their feeling springing from the deeper wells of feminine emotion.

With some delay, our train full of refugees started to roll. The official who was running it knew only what direction our journey was supposed to head. Its most important stations were

Lvov, Stry, and Kraków. We were passed by troop trains thundering along in the opposite direction, and we often had to wait on a siding while they passed, and then we always got forgotten there for hours. In the stations, members of patriotic-philanthropic ladies' clubs passed bread, tea, and soup up to us and from time to time a medic would ask if any of us were ill. By the time we disembarked at the Zaibusch station on the border of Galicia and Lower Silesia, we had spent eight days in the boxcar and had covered a distance it took a normal passenger train only sixteen hours to traverse. I had seen almost nothing of the country through which we passed. I didn't like watching the changing panorama of images gliding by, for they only excited my need to ponder things without satisfying it. And I abhorred the confinement in that big box, rolling and rattling through the countryside but always foreign to it. In short, I slept through the larger part of our journey and didn't even want to stay awake while the boxcar stood waiting on the sidings, for the railroad workers signaling with flags, lanterns, and whistles disturbed me, as did the grimy locomotives and the soot-covered rail yards.

At the Zaibusch station, we were called from the train by ladies of the local refugee aid committee, who read our names from a piece of paper. We followed two of these female officials into the little town, and they led us to Bahnhofstrasse 4, the house of the head rabbi Dr. Bau, who had cleared two rooms for us in the top story, next to his apartment. Behind the house was a little garden with an arbor surrounded by flower beds and lilac bushes. June had arrived in the meantime, and this slice of the vegetable world was in heady bloom. On the first Friday after our arrival, our rabbinical host invited us all to a festive evening meal. There I met his four-year-old son, Arthur, and his daughter, Anne, known as Andsja. If the broad-shouldered, olive-skinned boy with blue-black hair was a perfect miniature version of his father, the long-legged blonde daughter resembled her mother, the rabbi's stately wife, whose great blue eyes shone from a paper white face like two stars of longing above a snowy landscape. Andsja was thirteen years old and in the sixth grade of the local Polish-language gymnasium. I had already lived a dozen years and had nothing to show for them. The fact that I could milk a cow, harness and—in a pinch—ride a horse; could sow, mow, split wood, and carry water; could throw a stone with my hand or a sling and hit my target; could lead a band of warrior boys—none of that proved anything in this town of apparent leisure. There was no call for such things. I didn't possess or even know about the skills needed here: erudition, above all, and a quick tongue. Not that I thought any less of myself for all that. I carried my villages within me, and they lent even my silence weight and significance. At least, that's how it seemed to me. But, after all, I thought I needed more than that to be on an equal footing with Andsja. My feelings for her had not a thread of what had bound me to Relly, from whom I had meanwhile withdrawn physically without thinking about approaching another girl. I wasn't attracted to Andsja in the same way I had been to other girls before her, but rather as if she were a task to complete or a riddle whose solution I could hope to get only from her.

And then one afternoon she came to our rooms. She walked up to me and looked at me for a long time without a word. Then she turned around and went to the door. I followed her. In this way, we entered the garden and went into the arbor. There we sat silently and without moving until after sunset, then returned to the house only when it began to get dark and our mothers called us in to supper. The next afternoon Andsja called to me from downstairs. Never before had I heard my name spoken in such a compelling way. She didn't say "Munju" (the diminutive form of Edmund) like all the others, but Mun-ni-u, emphasizing the doubled dental and each of the three vowels. Several afternoons and evenings of sitting silently side by side passed before she uttered the first words, which were, "We must talk, too." I replied, "No," so we remained silent for several more days. One evening she picked a tulip. She handed it to me and told me to wait a while before following her into the arbor. She walked up to it more slowly than usual, and before sitting down on the bench, contrary to her usual custom, she pulled the wicket closed behind her. I thought this was some kind of game unfamiliar to me and watched each of her movements to try and guess from them my role. In fact, after she had rested her chin in her long white hand and waited a bit, she spoke.

"I'm ready. Now it's your turn." And so I went up to her and gave her back the tulip, which I regarded as her property. She pushed the red flower into her hair, precisely above the middle of her white forehead, and said, "You gave it to me."

"Why is she lying?" I wondered. "It belongs to her." But then I remembered that it was a game and said, "Yes."

Whereupon she deeply inhaled and then quickly exhaled the cool evening air several times, so that I could see her chest in the moonlight, heaving between her shoulders, and I asked if the game also required me to act so excited. She didn't answer, but stepped out of the arbor, hid behind a tree, and said, "Now catch me." As I stretched my hand out to her—for she was very close to me—she said, "It's not dark enough. I'll blindfold you." And she did so with the broad sash of her green dress, below whose hem her squarish kneecaps were visible. Blindfolded, I was afraid to bump into the trees or step on the flowers. I stood rooted to the spot and only bent forward and back from the hips, my outstretched hands searching the air in vain for my playmate, who circled me noiselessly, tweaking my nose with her long fingers. After that evening, our meetings in the garden became more animated, but neither loquacious nor sexual. Andsja, however, seemed to undergo a serene development from within, like flowers that imbibe the moonlight. Once I happened to overhear her father telling my mother that I was a blessing for the child, whom he described as having a hereditary tendency to melancholy. I don't know why, but when I overheard that, I thought of Andsja's passionate mother, into whose thoughts I imagined sinking every time her daughter lured my gaze into her own expansive eyes. When the school holidays began and Andsja had ten weeks of vacation in which to regain her strength, she refused to go to a spa (which was her annual custom), and her good and understanding parents let her have her way, after Mother—out of pride and lack of funds—had declined their offer to send me to the country with their daughter, for if she was not able to pay for me herself, she would not allow others to do so either.

In those days, my instinct for play, long suppressed by family cares and the need to work, began to reassert itself. Andsja, however, was incapable of satisfying it, so I sought out playmates of my own age from the neighborhood. Above all, I felt the urge for boisterous outdoor action, uninhibited pranks, and tests of courage and strength. I had a need to run and swim in races, get into fights, and play soccer. I also took part in raids on forbidden orchards and didn't shrink from acts of revenge on infamous enemies of youth. At home with Andsja, however, I was always quiet and contemplative, and when I went to bed, I was so fearful with concern for my family and the fate of my fatherland, both in tatters, that even my shrewdest prayers were of no avail, and I couldn't calm down until I had expressed my worries in verse. Since longhand was difficult for me, I didn't write down my poems, so I forgot them from one day to the next and had to put together new ones each night. I decided to use nothing but German for my poetry because it corresponded best to my thoughts. And because the other tongues incessantly abuzz around me always interrupted and distracted me, I began to expunge them mercilessly from my memory. Meanwhile, Andsja had gradually become talkative. She talked to me in just the way I needed—namely, quietly, slowly, without substance or coherence—for I was the sort of listener who lingered long over every sound and word, filled myself with the sense that inhabited each one of them, and so usually lost the gist of the whole sentence and surely would not have been able to grasp that of a paragraph. Did my companion know me so well that she spoke in such a pointilliste way for my benefit? If so, she was like water, which spans the globe but also adapts itself to the smallest container. Or was the narrow conch of my comprehension precisely and uniquely the right size to echo the short-lived wave of her spirit?

When the hot days of the wheat harvest arrived, I went out into the stubble fields every evening with a bag hanging around my neck to glean the leftover stalks, for we lived in great privation and had seen no bread on the table since our arrival. For the same reason, and not from the high spirits that motivated me later in the day among my friends, I invaded the orchards every morning to harvest the windfall. One day, when I'd made a particularly rich harvest in the lushest of the orchards, I was intercepted by two dogs. These inhuman watchmen kept me cornered until the owner arrived. He grabbed me by the ear (whose unfortunate jug-handle shape was probably too tempting to resist) and led me to a pigpen. He made me serve those grunting gluttons the precious contents of my basket and then look on as that container I had woven with my own hands from green willow branches lost its useful shape and purpose under the feet of the cruel man. I thought it an unnecessary wrong that the angry fellow also smeared my hand with a yellow substance that it took me days to get rid of. I hadn't changed the way he looked. What gave him the right to deface me? And if he wanted to brand me as a thief, as was plausibly explained to me, that was an insult that demanded retribution. I perceived right and wrong, like wealth and poverty, as problems of relative power within society. Weakness was perhaps unfortunate, but under no circumstances was it shameful. A slander, however, besmirched one's honor, one's societal garment, as it were, which must be kept clean at any price, in this case by means of revenge by whatever means possible so as to appear terrible, to make oneself feared, and in this circuitous way to compel respect and exclude the possibility of future insults. That's how I felt back then. And so one evening I snuck up to my enemy's house on the opposite bank of the San River and bombarded it with stones from my sling. Each one was wrapped in a piece of paper on whose inner side I had written in my best hand the words, "For the thief's color." Despite the hubbub that arose after the piteous crash of the first windowpanes, I kept up my cannonade until all the windows facing me, aglow whether with light from inside or with moonlight, were rendered blank.

And so my days were filled with privation and play, worries and high spirits. Like a tuft of flowers growing at the edge of a scree, our host, the head rabbi, and his family gleamed on the margin of my life, and my loving feelings embraced them in their five-headed totality. The parents, the two children, and their buxom Masurian[7] maid, all similar in temperament, lived together in peaceful harmony, moving under the influence of the gentle melancholy emanating from the stately lady of the house. How different from us! Just as we all differed in appearance, our inner feelings also drove us apart. Ruthlessly we transgressed the threshold and each other's hearts, fled the house and each other's company. Sigmund, Pepi, and Susi had already virtually elbowed their way out of the family circle to jump aboard the departing trains of their respective destinies. That was not Arnold's intention, but, like Father, he wanted to rule over family life rather than dwell within it. The nubile Tylka and Relly were going on clandestine outings with unknown young fellows and, in whispered nighttime conversations, were dreaming of happy flights without return tickets. For my part, I began to perceive my family as a crumbling shell and inwardly tried to struggle my way down toward my ancestors. I felt their vigorous presence deep within me and hoped it would accrue to me, cushioning the collapse of the world around me. In doing so, I had no more regard for my younger brothers than our older siblings had for me. That left only my mother, herself unable to leave and enfolding us all, for we were within her, while above us there was only Father. Mother called him our support and provider; I felt his presence like a divine shield, bound to us of his own free will and goodness. But our parents were so somber with worry about us that they were barely able to perceive us beneath them. At any rate, I never sensed them giving their full attention to me, and, as far as I know, Arnold felt only the weight of their concern.

The latter didn't return from Hungary until the twelfth week of our stay in Zaibusch. We were just eating our evening millet gruel when the door opened just a crack and the tall fellow stepped across the threshold. His blue pupils with their golden irises on a dark background with tiny red blood vessels were shining more brightly than usual from their wreath of long lashes, for his face was haggard, and a pallor shimmered through his windblown, weathered suntan. He also seemed to have grown taller and to have been forcibly matured in the sun of the half-Mongolian Puszta,[8] across which he had driven the herds. He seemed to be uncomfortable about entering a room, alone and loaded down with sacks and suitcases, and he forced his soft mouth into a crooked smile that seemed to beg our pardon. Or did he feel that he ought to be ashamed of the deeds beyond his years that he had performed in Hungary out of joyful overconfidence? As a young man not yet spoiled by success and praise, he still possessed a natural sense of proportion, and to overstep it, even in a positive direction, seemed shameful. Mother judged by this same criterion, although in her case it seemed to me disproportionate, at least as it applied to Arnold. Not only did she ask him nothing about the circumstances of his journey to Hungary, she also rebuked him for leaving Father alone and found words of praise only for Father's foresight when it transpired, once Arnold had opened his unwieldy sacks, that they contained precious foodstuffs. My stalwart brother had brought home cooking fat and egg noodles, honey and dried fruit, condensed milk and sugar.

In those days, such provisions were unavailable at any price to a mere mortal inhabitant of the imperial half of the monarchy.[9] Yet they were lying about in great piles under the jealous talons of the Hungarian eagle who had pushed his twin brother Austria into a world war, but then left him in the lurch. Once Father and Arnold had guided their herds, flanked by home-bred shepherd dogs, through the Carpathian passes, ferried them across the Tisza River, and driven them into the Puszta, Father had obtained pasturage for them on the southwest edge of the steppe and had pens built for them. Arnold had personally supervised and lent a hand with this task, which was carried out by two Hungarian herdsmen to whom Father was able to entrust our precious livestock until peace was concluded, a peace everyone was yearning for by then, although it was still impossible to discern through the smoke of battle. Father, before boarding a train to Vienna, where he had important business to conduct, had given Arnold money and the assignment to purchase the fruits of sun and earth that he had now brought home to us. It cannot have been easy for a Mosaic-Germanic lad to turn this tall order into living (and life-sustaining) reality in some village in anti-Semitic and Germanophobic Hungary. Under the burden of the shortages common at the time, it was an accomplishment that would have done honor to an adult. The difficulties began at the farmyard gate, where a boy of such reviled lineage would be turned away, or, once he was inside, resistance would become even more massive in the peasant mistrust of the currency of the tottering state. Even for a master of such negotiations, it would have been a test of doubtful outcome there on the border of the bloated monarchy, where a living sieve of sanguinary customs officials barely allowed even Hungarian air to pass into Austria. My fifteen-year-old brother overcame all these obstacles and laid at Mother's feet his weighty fulfillment of the paternal assignment in the form of overflowing sacks and suitcases whose transport alone should have deserved her praise. Mother, however, praised only the giver of the order and overlooked the agent who had carried it out. I was astonished by her lack of respect for the difficulty of the deed compared to the ease with which it had been ordered by Father, and I suspected my mother of intentionally disregarding her son in order to intimidate him.

Meanwhile, the Russians had penetrated deep into the province of Galicia, and we had lost touch with Grandmother and Pepi in Stanislau. My oldest sister, shortly after the wedding that took place before my grandfather was even cold in the ground, had in the meantime borne a little girl to the sitter for the photograph sent by the matchmaker (the photograph on which a mouth, between a moustache and a starched collar, connected two ears topped by the peaked cap of an Austrian official), namely the postal clerk Josef Trost, in response to his premature proofs of affection. We were introduced to the child by a typical photograph of the time showing her lying naked on her belly, like a fish out of water.

Two weeks after Arnold, Father returned. He did not enter the door festooned with bags and suitcases. His tall frame, however, seemed to be barely holding up under an even heavier burden. Strangely enough, I had this impression even before noticing my sister Pepi, whom he led in by the hand. She looked like herself, yet seemed to be someone else. A strange being was animating Pepi's familiar features, which were too capacious for it, so that it inhabited them with uncomfortable hesitation and a guilty conscience. When someone who has suffered a misfortune reencounters his loved ones, he feels guilty and therefore often lies in response to their solicitous questions. For the moment, Pepi was too drained to repeat the many lies she had been telling in her letters since the wedding. Before allowing them to be stamped and canceled, her postal clerk had censored them. Nor would it have made any sense to continue to conceal the ugly truth, for Father had seen them in bed. In the imperial capital, he had found out where they were living from a registry of refugees, and, since it happened to be in Vienna, he had gone there in the evening after taking care of his business affairs. After wending his way up five flights of back stairs in the tenement, he found himself in a dark, stinking vestibule. The light coming through a keyhole led him to what was presumably the door to their domicile, and as he approached it, his presumption received aural confirmation in the smack of blows and suppressed sobs. Overcoming his repugnance at the curiosity rising in his chest for the first time ever, he peered through the keyhole. One look was enough for him to grope for the door latch, but he found none. It took but a moment to discover that the door opened inwards, and he shoved against it with all his might. On the other side of the door, meanwhile, the blows were growing louder, and the sobbing turned into screams. The door yielded, and Father fell into the room. As he picked himself up, the woman he had seen through the keyhole lying naked on her stomach was now covered with a coarse wool blanket, and the man who had been whipping her with a wet rubber hose like a woodsman splitting logs was now stroking her head, buried between his hairy thighs. Father only wanted to know where the child was. It had been dead and buried for weeks. And then he wrapped his daughter in the blanket and carried her down to the street as if from a burning house. He hailed a hackney cab and took her to a first-aid station, where he obtained the physician's report needed to file for a divorce.

Pepi had entered marriage in utter ignorance. Mother had told her no more than that women are born to suffer in a man's world. Mother's own lot in life, well known to her sensitive daughter, only confirmed this view. Mother's ardor for married life had bled away in childbearing, through which she had also lost her powers of attraction, and her husband's attention had turned to other women. But she had to remain at his side, harnessed to the family. And while he shouldered the farm work, she had to look after the house and a horde of children as well by the sweat of her brow. And whereas he could cast off the traces and play the master among his friends or the lover with other women, she had to cook the meals, do the laundry, and scrub the floors. With such dismal preparation, my sister married her dismal Herr Trost and wasn't capable of complaining when soon after the marriage he asserted his rights to give her beatings instead of children. Their child, conceived before the wedding and liquidated soon thereafter, had been just the stamp of approval the postal clerk needed.

From Pepi we learned that Grandmother had died in a Stanislau charity hospital. The poetess without an audience had died of a stomach cancer that appeared unexpectedly a few days after her admission. She was in full possession of her faculties to the end. No copies existed of the manuscript poems in the immense account ledger, which she donated to the director of a prayer-house library. Probably intending to honor and comfort the dying woman, that worthy custodian had promised to keep the large volume with the Torah scrolls in the ark. She thanked him but said, "No, put it among the other books that are there for people to read. Perhaps someone will cast a glance at mine as well." I don't know whether this uncertain wish was ever fulfilled. But after hearing Pepi's story, I was determined to go and find Grandmother's book. Like so many other good intentions to be of service to my fellow man and also, no doubt, to benefit myself, this one was left lying along life's road, unfortunately unfulfilled. Grandmother lived to be sixty-seven years old and suffered through her last four years without her cheerful, feckless husband, who had gone to his eternal reward shortly before the first deaths of the world war.

Having lived a mere two dozen years, but already buried a child and returned home, our eldest sister made a quick recovery in our midst and to everyone's great satisfaction resumed the roles she had played before her marriage: she was Mother's lieutenant in the kitchen and, as she rolled out dough, the purveyor of German fairy tales as well. She was a good cook and a wonderful storyteller. Mother was even better at both things, but we were happy for her to get some relief from cooking, and we seldom got to hear her splendid stories, for she was taciturn by nature. But once she opened her small red lips to utter some edifying wisdom, it was a delight to the spirit. Her subject matter was only what had really happened in her life, and yet, in sentences nourished by humor and irony and so precisely constructed that each word fit like a brick in a wall, she conjured up images of life beyond which one's ear always caught the distant rustle of the landscape of eternity, the spirit of the Seven Days of Creation.

Not until vacation was over did Pepi get Father to agree to put Arnold and me up for school entrance examinations. At a time when the military situation prevented him from performing productive work, that restless man used the enforced period of inactivity to attend to his sons and give their progress a brief personal inspection. Without any preparation, Arnold passed the entrance examination for the middle school in Zaibusch with outstanding scores in all subjects and was admitted into the highest grade. Pepi took me to the German gymnasium in the Silesian border town of Bielitz, a two-hour train ride from Zaibusch. The results of my test, to which I submitted myself in considerable ignorance, were generally unsatisfactory. But as the examiner Professor Haar—without mincing his words despite my sharp-eared presence—explained to my sister, who stood holding my hand, my German essay showed quite an appealing talent, and the style of my oral responses had persuaded the strict board of examiners to overlook for the present my violation of every convention of grammar, spelling, and logic, and to allow my native talent to trump the rules. The friendly teacher took my chin between his long, slim fingers and spoke directly to me: "What you have, my lad, is water. Now you'll come to us, and we'll help you get a container to hold it. By that I mean education, without which it will just drain away into the sand." I felt

I had been accepted by Professor Haar, but not by the school. I granted this fine man a large place in my heart. Back at home, Pepi reported that I, too, had passed my examination with an excellent score. This annoyed me to the point that I contradicted her openly, in front of the whole family, which cost me quite an effort since I didn't like to embarrass her. But what right had she to conceal my deficiencies and encourage vain expectations of my success at the cost of the truth?

I was issued a peaked cap with a red ribbon and a silver stripe that constricted my thoughts. I felt much more capable of cogitation in an unassuming civilian hat. I left for school at 5:30 every morning on a train filled with laborers and schoolchildren. Every evening, Mother prepared my meals for the entire next day, for I never got back home before 6:00 P.M., and twice a week, when we had drawing class and gym, not until nine at night. The kindly Professor Haar was my homeroom teacher. He was tall, thin, and blond. I can also still remember what our teacher for geography and natural history looked like. He was no taller than I, but stocky. His head was a sphere of red and black—his face red, his eyes and curly hair black. His movements were abbreviated and vigorous. He wore suits that were too tight for him, and he always seemed ready to burst. I can't remember his name. I don't recall our other teachers at all. Our long classroom had two rows of benches, and we sat crowded so close together that when we wrote, we had to press our upper arms against our ribs. I didn't become friends with any of my classmates and was so exclusively immersed in my own preoccupations that I hardly noticed any attempts to establish contact and certainly didn't encourage them. I ate my breakfast on the train and my lunch in the station waiting room, where I also did my homework in the hours before the return train home. Sitting on poorly sprung seats in the filthy train cars with their boarded-up windows and toilet smells, my throat, nose, eyes, ears, and hair full of soot, I suffered constant headaches and nausea. The first thing I did when I got home was to wash myself. But I always had to attend school in this disgusting state, for the train never arrived in Bielitz much before eight, and I had to run to get to class on time.

In the evenings, I often sat in the arbor with Andsja—sometimes just to be polite—or with her and her brother in their nursery full of mechanical toys and erector sets, which left me cold. Even as a small child I liked only outdoor play with other living beings. In my free time in Zaibusch, I was above all attracted by the sight of handsome human faces and the sound of voices speaking calmly. That's why I spent less time with Andsja and my sisters and Relly than with our mothers. And that's why I felt compensated to some extent by Professor Haar for having to suffer through the irritating clamor of the school day, in which that good man was my guiding star. He taught German and Latin, and because I was a talented swimmer in the element of the living language, he didn't leave me to drown in the dead one. He had also taken notice of my inadequate eyes and weak hearing and had given me a note in an unsealed envelope to take home to my parents. But it got misplaced before they had a chance to read it, and when I repeated its contents from memory, Relly set the tone of mockery in which they accused me of wanting to lend myself airs of premature importance by wearing glasses and using an ear trumpet. My parents joined in the fun by reassuring me that I already looked enough like the picture of my Stanislau grandfather that hung over Mother's bed. Pepi didn't intervene because the question was not of importance to my education. And so the attempt to improve my two deficient organs of perception was dropped and never mentioned in our house again.

The drawing teacher brought me to the brink of despair. His classes were held in a dusky, unlit room, and he wouldn't allow me to sketch the models from close up, yet he called my cross-hatched attempts dilettantish because they lacked outlines. He didn't like my compositions in color, either. They were too dull for him, too flat, and, again, not contoured enough. I felt that my sheets were not as unsatisfactory as he said and asked my homeroom teacher for his opinion.

My dear Haar smiled with some satisfaction. "They remind me of your German. Where on earth did you get so much irrepressible artistic talent, little fellow? What does your father do?"

"He's a farmer."

"German Ruthenian, is he?"

"Jewish Austrian."

"We're all Austrians. So he's a Jew. And your mother?"

"The same."

"Curious. Are you like them?"

"I'm like my maternal grandfather."

"Maternal grandfather," he repeated several times, enjoying the sound of the words, "oh boy, oh boy!" He picked me up and hugged me tight to his breast. It felt very good. On my trimester report card, in place of the grade of "Unsatisfactory" threatened by the drawing teacher, stood "Good." My knowledge in the subjects of religion and mathematics was also rated as "Good" and "Satisfactory," although both teachers had sworn an oath to crush me pedagogically—and with just cause. But the unjust grades of "Satisfactory" and "Unsatisfactory" in geography and natural history, respectively, traduced my knowledge, for I was the best in the class in both.

In contrast to so many benevolent injustices, I can only explain what earned me the two hostile ones by recalling my first meeting with the aforementioned teacher of these subjects. He had entered the classroom silently. The moment he crossed the threshold, he began upbraiding us harshly because instead of jumping to simultaneous attention, we had risen from our seats like sleepy lambs and untuned organ pipes. He compared our posture with a grain field after a hail storm. Then he strode between the two rows of benches from the back of the room toward the podium.

I could hear his hand smacking the backs of heads and his repeated cry, "*Pfui!* You look like a Yid in a prayer house. Keep your head up!" To avoid this reprimand, I stood up as straight as I could. "Stiff as a Yid on parade!" I heard behind me and winced simultaneously under his slap. "Name!" the compact little man demanded and shoved his round face into mine.

I felt suddenly very tall, as if my head had separated from my shoulders and was high above the whole class. I heard my voice say, "Edmund . . . "

"A Pole?"

"A Jew."

"A Pole?"

"A Jew."

I heard a sound and the next instant was very small again, my burning head lolling on my chest. The little man had given me a slap in the face and now attacked me verbally. "A cowardly little creature. He pretends to look like a human being and disguises himself with a Christian name." He climbed onto the podium. "Any more Jews in the class?" A few boys stood up. "He's ashamed of your company, Edmund is. What do you say to that?"

"We don't need him," answered one, himself named Friedrich.

Then the red-and-black roundhead removed a picture from his lectern and hung it over the blackboard. A barnyard pig with skinny legs and blue eyes squinted down at us.

"Edmund!"

I didn't move.

"Edmund, to the blackboard!"

I didn't move. He came toward me with his pointer. "Stand up," he commanded threateningly. I remained seated. "Damned Jewboy!" he hissed and came at me with the pointer.

I rose and went to the door. He threw my schoolbag after me. "Don't show your face here again!" I went out and waited by the door of the teachers' room to lodge a complaint with my homeroom teacher. I didn't like having to do that. I would rather have fought my own battle for justice and respect from that bad man, perhaps even as I had with the orchard owner. But that would have cost me my place in the school, which I by no means wished to lose. From then on, that teacher called me to the board in every class. Every time we needled each other unmercifully. He with his tricky questions and I with answers that resulted either from my program of thorough preparation for his classes or from my inquiries about what things he had a right to quiz us about. This struggle lasted only thirty-six hours, for I left the school after nine weeks. I left very unwillingly and even shed tears onto the slender hand of my good Professor Haar, over which I had bent to kiss it in fervent gratitude. The eyes of that unforgettable man also teared up with regret, something I was not destined to see again soon in anyone's eyes.

◆ ◆ ◆

[*Prague, 1916–1917*]

AT THE TIME, the liberation of our homeland seemed very far away and the end of the war nowhere in sight. Father feared his means were too modest to be able to keep our heads above water much longer in that unfamiliar part of the empire. There were no opportunities for him to earn an honest living, and the refugee assistance he now decided to accept amounted in full to only a fourth of what was needed for all of us. So the foresightful man made an emergency plan to improve our circumstances. He decreed that the girls should contribute to the household income by working in an office or hospital, while Arnold and I were to disencumber the budget by agreeing to move to a free boarding school for refugee children in Prague. Our neighbor, the head rabbi, offered to take me into his house free of charge and look after my education, but when my parents declined, he sent his daughter to the country for a few days in tender paternal solicitude. I was so pained at having to part with Professor Haar that I was incapable of any other emotion attendant upon my departure. When I bid farewell to the rabbi's family, I was not conscious of any stronger feeling about Andsja's absence than about her brother's presence and was even surprised at the dreamlike ease with which I turned toward the door and away from the sight of her stately, melancholy mother.

Our train arrived in Prague—"Golden" Prague, as Father had told us—on November 22, 1916. Long black banners hung from the splendid, tall buildings. The streets stretched into the distance as if through a forest of black trees, for the telephone and streetlight poles on both sides were wrapped in black cloth and had long black banners hanging from them as well, rippling in the breeze. We walked past palaces and cathedrals all draped in black crepe. The streetcars and droshkies rolled along muffled in black. People on the street wore black ribbons on their hats, sleeves, or lapels and looked sad. It was like Pepi's fairy tales: when the dragon came for the eighteen virgins and youths, or a royal child had a fatal illness, or the old king had died, the fairy-tale cities looked just like this. Was Golden Prague with its palaces, domes, and towers a fairy-tale town? At that moment, certainly, for it was mourning a fairy-tale kaiser. The old man, increasingly silent toward the end, had lived 30,746 days and had held the throne for 24,038 of them. I say "days," "held," and "throne," for never did that monarch lift his eyes, his word, or his arm beyond each day. He never held a standpoint other than that of his inherited throne. And he never did anything but keep that rotting, golden chair afloat on the waves of contemporary events. His heart beat in that monstrous piece of furniture whose wooden arms and legs had become his. The fact that all around him the heads of his nearest and dearest were falling didn't touch him as long as he retained his seat. He didn't even go to their funerals. He knew no other heaven than the heaven of his throne and no other earth than the dais on which it stood, the dais borne by the peoples of the empire who had been subjugated for this purpose and now, like so many Atlases, must bear it without a murmur, for the slightest complaint was abhorrent, to be bloodily suppressed. As a consequence, the foundations of political order in the Dual Monarchy were silence, rigidity, and dust,[1] a political order that had not changed since Metternich and Gentz[2] and could be considered civilized only by comparison with the premedieval Slavic states on its northern and southeastern borders. Now the master of this empire was dead. Those who saw only the bloody chaos of that third year of the world war and the traitorous heads peering from dark corners, their forked tongues stretched out toward what remained of the empire, and saw no deeper or farther could not but attribute a legendary dimension to the past three-quarters of a century, a period of anemic peace under the man now lying in state in the Hofburg. They needed to attribute the awesome dignity of a fairy-tale kaiser to the old man who seemed not to have throned in reality and whose dream would now be buried along with him in the crypt of the Capuchins.[3]

Though not formulated so articulately, such were my thoughts about the events of those days. I had arrived at them with some effort, aided by adult conversations I overheard, newspaper editorials I read, and my own insights. I introduced myself in the Prague gymnasium for refugee children by writing down those thoughts in an essay for German class, whose assigned theme was "What I Know about the Late Kaiser." Professor Hayer taught German and Latin and was my new homeroom teacher, a sallow man with legs of unequal length and the expression of concentrated unsteadiness of someone always intent upon keeping his balance. A few days after I wrote the essay, he sat me down at his desk, gave me a fresh notebook, and bid me write another essay on the same theme, but without putting in my two cents, if I wouldn't mind. I didn't. I understood him the moment he set his sad eyes on me, and I wrote a variant in the prevailing tone about the late kaiser.

Father had dropped us off at the boardinghouse in the uliza Puchmajerowa ruled over by a certain Professor Wurzer. My first name caused him difficulties, as it also had when I registered for school. In the meantime, I had learned that neither my first name nor my date of birth were at all certain. The relevant information, first set down in writing in the Berbeschti elementary school, was the fruit of an imaginative collaboration between the school's old head teacher Kuschniruk and my sister Pepi. As the basis for their invention, they used my report card from the private school I had attended in Stanislau. That institution had been content to write down my nickname from home plus the number six: the sum of full years I had accumulated plus the one I had barely begun, which they extended to its end to make me the age required for admission. That document gave "Munju" as my name.

The worthy Kuschniruk, however, didn't dare sneak such an imprecise egg into the nest of the double eagle embellishing the cover of his register of pupils, a "K" balanced on each of its heads.[4] And so he and Pepi began counting together: 1909, when I had been six years old according to the Stanislau document; 1908, five; 1907, four; 1906, three; 1905, two; 1904, one. Once they had hit on the year, my brilliant sister was easily able to persuade the ancient teacher that the son of a loyal Austrian could not possibly have been born on any other day than the kaiser's birthday.

"Of course," the old patriot was said to have murmured, "of course, that makes sense. But on exactly the same day?" He was in favor of a little time lag. After all, even the field marshals in the Order of Maria Theresia always walked a few steps behind their ruler. Although Pepi wasn't particularly thrilled with the idea, she agreed that I should make my appearance two days after His Apostolic Majesty. And so, in September 1910, I was born on August 20, 1904. Now that I was a citizen of the state, I ought to have a name the state would recognize. Munju wasn't a proper name. Who has such a name, anyway?

"It wasn't just pulled out of thin air, Herr Teacher."

"No, but it's all air, *Panieczka,*[5] all air. Just listen to how it sounds: Munju!"

"Here, Herr Director!"

"*Na hui tebia!*[6] You little Tom Thumb; you gave me a scare! But tell us once what your name is."

"What you just called me."

"And what did the Polacks call you there in our downtrodden Haliczina?"[7]

"Mundek."

"Aha! Now you can go back outside, and don't listen at the window!"

"What if you need me again?"

"Then I'll give you a call."

"So then I have to wait outside the window."

"Mundek, Fräulein, is unmistakably short for Sigmund."

"The very idea! We call *him* Sigi!"

"Oh, I forgot about your older brother. . . . Well, at least the second syllable must be *mund*.[8] Now we just have to attach a first syllable to it."

"Liedermund."

"That adds up to three syllables and doesn't sound right. What do you think of Goldmund, Fräulein?"

"My brother has no gold in his mouth."

"But gold fillings are very fashionable."

"Healthy teeth are prettier, as long as they're clean. What do you say to Reinmund?"[9]

"Then why not Reimmund, which could mean he's a poet? Surely you'd like that?"

"We can't call him Poet."

"No, you're right. So let's call him Eduard."

"But his name is Munju or Mundek; the root is *mun,* we've got to keep that."

"Edmunju . . . "

"Edmunde . . . "

"Stop right there, Fräulein! Say it again."

"Edmund . . . "

"That's it! Edmund. Let's write it down in the register."

Thus had I been sentenced to a name and a birthday, and now I filed an appeal. I wanted to avoid at all costs a repetition of my encounter with the zoologist of Bielitz. And since I demanded that Father revise my name, I also broached the subject of my date of birth. Father recalled having given written notice of my birth to Weber, the mail-coach driver, two days after the event, and asked him to deliver it to the registry in Kotzmann, three hours from Berhometh. A few years later, when my parents requested a copy of my birth certificate, the official in charge of the registry claimed not to have received the notification and said he was unable to issue the document in question because he couldn't find any record of my birth in his files. And so at my own initiation, it was discovered in Prague that for the moment I, at the age of thirteen, had not yet officially been born. Father searched through the Bohemian capital and found two compatriots from the Bucovina who could recall the circumstances of my birth. They accompanied Father to the appropriate state office and had an affidavit drawn up, which they signed. According to this document, I was now named Moses and was born on July 25, 1904. Only during the eventful intermission between the two world wars did I myself discover the original entry of my birth in the lists of the aforementioned registry office in Kotzmann, as well as my birth certificate, the latter filled out not on the strength of a note from Father, but with the proper formalities, in the presence of solid witnesses still exuding wine fumes from the circumcision celebration. When Mother saw it, she smiled and conjectured that Herr Hitzig, the director of the registry, had withheld it because their request for it had not been accompanied by the promise of a present. As Father and his two witnesses in Prague accurately recalled, my first name on this unimpeachably authentic document was indeed Moses, in honor of my father's grandfather, but Mother had borne me not on July 25, but already on June 20, 1904. I never could bring myself to believe that the mail-coach driver, Herr Weber, who had chosen for himself a profession of such admirable trustworthiness, could have failed to deliver Father's note. But even the registry director, as greedy as he was for bribes, had not really suppressed, but merely withheld me, as if foreseeing that we, I and the times I lived in, were not really meant for each other.

The boardinghouse was a narrow, five-story building swarming with children from all the nations of the motley eastern part of the monarchy, but we Jews predominated. Everyone was in the upper grades of middle school. I was the youngest and the only one still in the lowest grade. Next came Arnold. He continued his studies in the last grade of middle school. I lived with four other boys in a room on the second floor. Each of us had a cot and an army blanket, and we all shared a table and two benches. Arnold's bed was above me, on the third floor. There were long tables in the dining hall, where the entire house was fed at 7:00 A.M., 2:00, and 7:00 P.M. Both the fare and the rules of the house had been copied from an army barracks, except that our rations were less, and, instead of drilling, we went to school. Our overseer as well as the placards on the walls unceasingly admonished us to be diligent and obedient. We were always hungry, bored, and sullen. We wore a uniform made of dark twill and linen shoes with wooden soles. Clattering home through the crepuscular city to the barracks from my semiweekly drawing class, I would often hear Czech voices jeering at me behind my back: "A patriot from the East! The kaiser's darling!" The mockers couldn't see me very well, for I kept to the darker streets, but the wooden soles gave me away.

I noticed nothing of Prague's gold except for the copper flashings on a museum roof and an equally shimmering exhibit in a glass case in one of its halls. On a field trip from school, I followed our geography teacher, Professor Wallner, to the Hradschin, where we climbed the Luginsland. Seen from up there, the city looked like the lace pattern from Brabant I had also seen in an exhibit in Prague. In the medieval robbers' caves beneath the royal vineyards, I was touched by the breath of those dark vital forces that always emanate from the depths to overthrow whatever glitters in glory in the world above. I thought I could discern the very features of the angry chieftains of the catacombs in the massive, contorted busts of twelve revolving old men, dressed as apostles and installed in the wall niche of some cathedral or other, who bowed lugubriously on the orders of a rooster.[10] I have the aforementioned Professor Wallner and his low-key tours through the city to thank for what I saw of Prague's list of attractions. With the exception of the city's air and light, whose local qualities were everywhere apparent, I would have noticed nothing, if left to myself, but the paving stones and the building facades in the streets through which I walked to school. And I noticed the street fronts only as a consequence of my uncontrollable obsession with counting windows. Left to myself, I would have dozed through my days there, conjuring up dream images of the meadow in Berhometh, for I was tortured by unspeakable melancholy and yearning for that primal landscape.

How different my brother! He returned to the boardinghouse only for the midday meal. In the evenings, he merely waited for the head count to be over that Director Wurzer was accustomed to take in the rooms at nine o'clock. Then Arnold would leave the building by way of a rope we would hang back out again for his return because the main entrance was locked and guarded all night long. The only other boys who did this were our oldest roommates, who went out to be with women. But while those other nocturnal pilgrims would congregate in the communal bathroom the next morning, whistling hit tunes through pallid lips, Arnold would be repeating passages from classic dramas. He seemed to be particularly moved by Kleist's[11] plays, for he declaimed most often from them and wanted to take me along to one. I couldn't imagine how the experience could be a pleasant one and didn't consider it or any other mass entertainment worth the trouble. In Prague, my spirited brother made more of an effort to talk to me than ever before. So little by little

I learned that there was not a single corner of the great city into which his exquisite eyes had not peered. One time he brought back a fragrant loaf of bread from the Otkolek Bakery, and we enjoyed it as if it were pastry and washed it down with water. He'd discovered that a woman who had once worked in our house was now living behind her bread shop in the suburb of Czischkow. We started going there on Sundays for the loaf of bread she generously gave us every week. We dispatched it right there beneath her gratified gaze rather than in the envious atmosphere of the boardinghouse, which turned positively threatening on such occasions. I liked eating in that little shop because I enjoyed the sight of our former maid now acting as our hostess.

One day, with averted eyes and in an offhand manner belied by the slight quaver in his voice, my dear brother told me that one of his comrades got into bed with him at night and behaved like that excited black stallion years ago, impatient for his mares. I didn't know what to make of this piece of news. It didn't sound like he was denouncing the other boy, but there was a tremulous note of complaint about it. Then I remembered Arnold's joke on the stallion and a similar game he had tried on me in Zaibusch and had to admit to myself that he might have done the same thing with a friend, who had then become importunate. Since I couldn't hold back my tears but didn't want to cry in front of him, I left the room. The boy who was harassing him was a charming blond who died in a tuberculosis sanatorium at the end of the school year.

Shortly before Christmas we received a package of food from Zaibusch. A letter lay on top of the heavier things underneath, but we laid it aside to devote ourselves to the latter. There was a large tin canister full of clarified butter, another with plum jam, and a third with goose fat. There was half a loaf of sugar and a little bag of rock candy; two large loaves of gingerbread and a *Königskuchen*,[12] each wrapped separately in waxed paper; and two bags of macaroons, cookies, and biscuits. The letter was in

Relly's hand. Her alphabet letters were tall, slanted, and pointy, genteel, demure, and fragile. Folded in the paper lay a brown postcard with a stamp and a return address. Arnold skimmed it and exclaimed in annoyance, "They've moved without us again!" The letter began: "Dictated by Mother. My precious children, we're all alive and well, thank the dear Lord. Hopefully our poor Sigmund as well, in prison in Siberia. Underneath this letter you'll find a few victuals to improve your diet. If you're frugal about spreading them on your bread and stirring them into your tea, they'll last you until Passover, when we plan to send another package. Knowing you as I do, you won't need my permission to share the baked goods with your friends. I hope you all enjoy them with my blessing. P.S., the head rabbi asks if you'd like to be his guests during New Year's vacation. Even if Arnold doesn't want to, you'd be welcome all by yourself, Munju. Relly is writing this down using our luggage as a desk. We're on the move again, this time to Hullein, near Kremsier in Moravia." There followed greetings from Pepi, Tylka, and Relly, who declared themselves the bakers of the cakes, the macaroons, and the biscuits and cookies, respectively. My parents, who had paid for everything, didn't emphasize their role. We recognized Mother's tone of voice; it was just the way she talked. At the top of the page, way over at the edge, Father had noted, "Agreed. F." The chances of persuading Arnold to exchange Prague for Podunk were smaller during a school vacation than at any other time of year. What did Zaibusch have to offer his soul, afire with the lust for life, in comparison to this capital? But far from wanting to win him over to a visit to Rabbi Bau's house, I myself had no ear for the invitation my Mother had conveyed. It didn't sound those chords in my depths that must respond to an external stimulus if I were to heed and follow it. It was not that Mother hadn't conveyed the wish of Andsja's anxious father emphatically enough. Even the sharpest emphasis would have penetrated no deeper, for I was filled from the soles of my shoes to the roots of my hair with a yearning for my first landscape: the cloud above the tree on the meadow by the river.

Arnold told me what to say in my reply. He knew exactly what he wanted but hadn't the patience to clothe it in sentences. So it fell to me to stitch together a written garment from his oral draft. I should convey to them his displeasure that they were moving again without him because he could have helped in the move. He declined Rabbi Bau's invitation and found it strange since that cleric had taken hardly any notice of him when they were living next door to each other. And finally he thanked them for the package that didn't need to have contained so much, e.g., the baked goods from the girls, whom he didn't greet individually by name—as he did Mother and Father—but collectively. I wrote, "Dear Mother, dear Father, dear Relly, Pepi, and Tylka, Hello from us. Many thanks for the letter and the package. We wish you luck in the new town and hope you stay well. Our life here is quiet. We spend the first half of normal weekdays in school. On Sunday afternoons we're with Marussja, who used to work for us. She sells Otkolek bread here and gives us some without taking ration cards or money in return. The end."

"I didn't need you for that," Arnold said after reading through this effort. He wasn't satisfied. Nevertheless, he set his name to it, leading with his elbow while his hand with the pen inscribed a succession of hairlines, shaded lines, and curlicues. My calligraphy followed his.

Christmas vacation was extended for two weeks because of a coal shortage. Our boardinghouse, too, was freezing for lack of fuel, and we with it. They seemed to be having a hot time of it at the front, however, for the mothers of Prague often congregated in noisy crowds before government buildings, demanding back their sons. One evening Arnold hid a matchbox full of bread-ration stamps in my schoolbag. Marussja had initiated him into the trafficking of these items. He used his profits to buy tickets to the theater, the movies, and the circus whenever he couldn't sneak past the ticket booth without paying. Since my honest brother had told me about his illegal activity and used me as his fence, he considered me a silent partner and shared part of his earnings with me by buying me goodies. He had more influence on me than I liked to admit, simply by urging me to accept or have a taste of one thing or another and to do so, if not for my own sake, then for his. And so I gobbled down carnival cakes decorated to look like the Russian czar and his generals, who, upon reaching my stomach, punished me terribly for my cannibalism.

Another time I went to the movies with him, but the frenzied sequence of moving pictures and the crashing of the piano made me think I was in a madhouse. No argument of Arnold's could persuade me to attend a dramatic performance, which, according to his description, showed people with swords drawn, in a fight to the finish with each other, and when the clever boy praised the theater in the ringing words of the poet as the "boards that represent the world,"[13] I answered in my know-it-all way that the poet couldn't have had this belligerent show in mind. I escaped from my seat next to Arnold at the circus when the ringmaster, in riding boots and top hat with a bullwhip in his hand, appeared among the somersaulting clowns in the menagerie and began to speak with that courteous brutality thought to be civilized by those cavaliers of the jungle. But then I became absorbed in the Punch and Judy show on the midway and lost track of the world around me. Arnold fetched me back to reality with a yawn. "To each his own," he declared philosophically and meant, "to children their dolls." But he couldn't get me to go back there a second time. I had thoroughly exhausted the wealth of insight the puppet stage provides by making the world bearable through caricature. I feared a repeat visit would have nothing more to offer and would only destroy the dream of my first encounter.

Meanwhile, the Passover festivities had arrived: the clear victory of the heavenly light, the redemption of the earth, where began "this day" that must be unto us "for a memorial"—a complete memorial in the sunken house of our grandfather in Stanislau, but only a partial one in the straighter-standing house of our father—and we "shall keep it as a feast to the Lord . . . for in this self-same day" our armies were "brought . . . out of the land of Egypt" and "journeyed from Rameses to Succoth, about six hundred thousand on foot that were men, beside children."[14] Clergymen were sent by every confession that had souls in our boardinghouse, and each assembled his children around him to celebrate the resurrection. First of all, our comrades of the Roman Catholic faith celebrated Easter together with those from its Romanian Orthodox branch since their holiday came first in the calendar. In the evening, their chaplain led them to the great cathedral in Vinohrady, the quarter of the royal vineyards, from which they returned after midnight. At noon on the following day, they were served their holiday meal of roasted lamb and red wine. Because of the dictates of the calendar, the last to celebrate were the Eastern Orthodox, who were given brightly colored hard-boiled eggs for supper before going to church. They also didn't return until past midnight. At breakfast, they greeted each other with, "Christ is risen," and answered, "He is in truth." Then they broke the shells of their colored eggs by striking them against each other. They also got mutton and red wine for dinner, but instead of the heart-shaped gingerbread on the Catholic tables, little bowls with grains of wheat in oil and sugar stood on theirs.

Our holiday fell in the middle, between the two Christian dates. The rabbi was preceded by a big box containing the unleavened bread. There followed a board with the "bitter herbs."[15] When the holy man himself arrived, like his Christian predecessors, for supper, a large *bocksbeutel* encased in straw and full of red wine was carried before him. Our clergyman was a skinny man whose long beard divided right beneath his chin, its two strands getting thinner the more they diverged. He sat down ceremoniously at the table; his feet were clad in shoes, and his loins were girded.[16] For our part, we all held staffs in our hands, for it was the Lord's Pesach. After the food had been brought in—the unleavened bread and the roasted flesh of the whole Passover lamb (with head, legs, and inner organs) and the bitter herbs to go with it and the glasses of red wine—it was my duty as the youngest present at that long table to turn to the envoy representing our ancestors and ask the four questions that would induce him to intone the history of this holiday. For this purpose, I was sitting next to the presiding rabbi, with Arnold on my other side as *souffleur,* for I hadn't had to ask these sacred questions for years and was feeling quite uncertain of myself. How did my brother, who had stopped having to voice the ceremonial curiosity long before me, still know the questions? Just because he knew and could remember everything better than I did.

"Why . . . ," I began, holding before me my bundle of sticks.

"Why . . . ," and my voice was shaking.

" . . . is this night," whispered Arnold.

" . . . this night . . . ," I repeated, certain of failure.

" . . . more sacred," hissed my brother.

" . . . more sacred . . . "

("Just 'different,'" corrected Forked Beard.)

" . . . than all other nights?" Arnold took over, for I was shaking with repressed sobs.

"But, my son," said the presiding envoy from atop a pile of cushions on his armchair, "it's a *happy* holiday we're gathered for. Just listen closely, and you'll find out and laugh for joy at what the Lord did for us when He brought us out of Egypt."

And without waiting for the second question Arnold was preparing to ask, he began to tell the Pesach story. While he narrated, he gave us the bitter herbs of the field and the tasty inner organs of the lamb to eat (although in our case it was the giblets of several geese), and I got my tears under control so they weren't spurting out of my eyes anymore. And when the great platter of meat with horseradish was followed by the wine, and I had drunk from my glass along with the others, my tears of embarrassment were dissolved by the sparkling wine, whose fire carried them down into my belly. This seems to have spread a broad grin on my face, for the kindly man presiding at the head of the table said in encouragement, "You see, my child, didn't I tell you? But the real fun is only just beginning." And since he had drunk more and had a professional responsibility to be more merry than we, he sang with great cheerfulness the parable of the journey through the stomachs, *chad gadya,* in which the smallest is eaten by the smaller, the smaller by the small, and so on until only the biggest remains. I can't remember anymore whether the biggest is an animal or the Creator himself, in whom everything finally comes to rest. Just as the lovely voices of the boys all round the table, including mine, flowed into the chorus, a neighboring church bell boomed midnight. As we rose from the table, only one silver cup full of red wine remained behind in the dining hall, probably to symbolize the blood that was once a sign to the Lord to spare this house as he went through the night, smiting the land of Egypt.

Almost every day during that Easter week between eleven o'clock and noon, we were lined up in the dining room to be inspected by the ladies from the committee of patrons of the house. Sometimes they dispensed home-baked goods from bags they had brought with them. In addition, I got a little book and a set of sturdy construction blocks. The book was a quarto with a dust jacket of glazed white paper, a light green sash, and blue letters. The linen binding was also light green with blue lettering. It covered the book like a little coat, and at the upper end of the spine a blue headband peeked out like the fancy top button on a shirt. The pages were edged in pure silver; the blank endpapers were a uniform light green, like hayfields in early spring. The flyleaf was white and silky soft, like a signpost to unimaginably tender delights. I would have had to crinkle it to lift it with my fingers, so I blew my warm breath under it, and it rose like a veil of fog from a meadow when the morning wind awakens the sleeping grass. I thought to harvest the first fruits directly from the title page. There my eyes caught the gleam of cherry red and cherry black words of great import, like solemn poetry, tall and slim as a tree. I was so impulsive I bit right into its crown and so rash I didn't perceive the poet's name on the page. Brought to an abrupt halt by my recklessness, I hesitated a moment, wondering whom I could ask for help, but then I just kept on reading: "The Tale . . . " (that was clear; firm ground underfoot for my understanding) " . . . of Gockel. . . . " The ground began to shift; I had stepped onto scree. But as it began to slip and slide, it sounded like crowing, like cock-a-doodle-doo. "Maybe it's a rooster," I thought and resumed reading. " . . . Hinkel . . . " Hinkel? Hinkel? I couldn't make sense of it, and I continued half-heartedly picking my way through this mysterious poem-tree, letter by letter, for the letters were so ornate that one probably had to be an artist to find one's way around. Perhaps the following word would illuminate its unintelligible predecessors. That was one of the lessons I had learned from my excursions through our textbook in German class. After "Hinkel," it said " . . . and . . . ," which didn't mean anything and was like walking on air. And so, my hands flailing helplessly, I reached " . . . Quackeleggia" and had to hang on if I didn't want to fall and break my neck.[17] My senses sharpened by desperation, I heard, "quack-quack, quack-quack." Could Quackeleggia be a duck? How it waddled! And wasn't that an egg toward the end? A quacking, waddling egg! So it was a duck named Quackeleggia. So far, so good. Cautiously optimistic, I now read backwards, " . . . and . . . Hinkel . . . " and forwards again: " . . . Hinkel and the Duck." But there was a comma, a blade of grass, and back behind it the Go-Go-Go-Gockel, the rooster, with its egg of an O coming out of its beak rather than at the end. Thus, I hopped around in my imaginary tree and finally suppressed the incomprehensible Hinkel, stretched the "and" across the gap, and joined together Gockel and Quackeleggia, the rooster and the duck, confident that the interior of the book would reveal the identity of Hinkel. It must be a barnyard bird in the company of two house birds since who else would be parading wing in wing with a duck and a rooster?

Beyond this title page stretched a dark, enchanted forest of language, eighty pages long. It began with red initials. In the very first sentences, I felt a spirit whose airy touch played such powerful music in the forest trees that it opened my mouth in song and set my legs to dancing. But I was not conscious of either and staggered from trunk to trunk, my mouth agape, until I fell to the ground and the music moved through me like water flowing with a metallic rush through hollowed rock. To be sure, I saw Gockel, Hinkel, and Quackeleggia walking through the forest hand in hand or single file, encountering all sorts of creatures large and small. But it was as if they were only dream figures, set against the great music, only one of those pretexts that poets understandably put into their works so as not to appear superior to the Creator, who—God only knows why—did the same thing himself. Clemens Brentano's fairy tale was the first German text I read that hadn't been predigested and regurgitated for me by some pedagogue. Since it hadn't been watered down, it intoxicated my brain, and that night, as I hugged the book I had just finished before falling asleep, I was like a drunk who has emptied a bottle without knowing exactly what was in it. I had grasped nothing of the meaning, the contents, the plot, the structure, the style, or the syntax of the fairy tale, but with my heart and through my blood I had absorbed it into the fiber of my being. When I awoke the next morning, I felt I was on the path to the fulfillment of my dreams, dreams that were all of creating works just like that. From the same fear that kept me from attending the puppet theater a second time, I never again read Brentano's story, even though I still feel its presence at work in my spirit today.

The package we'd been promised for Passover didn't arrive until the holidays were over. In the enclosed letter that Mother had dictated, she explained that she hadn't been able to assemble Passover provisions and so hadn't sent a package that would arrive during the week of the festival, so we wouldn't be tempted to violate the holiday dietary restrictions. She hoped that the people who ran the boarding house hadn't been guilty of serving us leavened bread to eat. She directed us to thank Marussja for her kindness and convey to her a choker of blue crystal beads that Mother had enclosed. She deemed it appropriate for a woman of any age, capable both of decorating a smooth neck and concealing a wrinkled one. But the good Marussja, despite the fact that she had a secure source of bread, had acquired a Basedowian neck[18] since Mother last saw her. A postscript reminded me that I must have by now received a personal invitation from Andsja Bau to spend the Passover holidays there, but had apparently left it unanswered. The letter closed with the news that Father had gone back home—the Kalahura having just been liberated again, for a change—to prepare for our return. On the margin of the letter, next to the reminder about Andsja, stood in Father's broad, clear hand, "Be a man. Don't get involved with womenfolk." It was too late: I already knew—and partly from my own experience—that being a man meant getting very much involved with womenfolk. But I had completely forgotten about Andsja's postcard, which had, in fact, arrived shortly before Passover. I'd stuck it unread into one of my schoolbooks and not pulled it out again. I had to rectify that immediately.

It was a sealed letter-card. On its front side, to the right, was my address. The other side was empty, a gray-green wasteland. Fighting an inner resistance, I tore off the perforated edge. What did the girl want? Can one still be together via letters? Not at all. You can call to each other, but then it aggravated me not to be able to join the other person immediately. So she had invited me . . . invited me for a visit. But why, when I'd just have to go away again? No, I wouldn't have gone even if I'd known about it in time. I saw her handwriting for the first time. What a vision! Her letters stood in rows like pearls and even seemed to shimmer. But they weren't connected to each other, nothing threaded them together. Every one of her letters stood by itself, helplessly, as if not knowing which way to turn. They also seemed rolled up in themselves like pearls. Suddenly I saw frozen pains, crystallized tears on the page. They were so small that I could barely gather them together into words. But the ones that were supposed to be most important stood on broad underlines, joined by their feet and thus well founded, so to speak. There were three such groups in all on this tablet of pearls and tears, and they formed the words, "Come here, quickly." As if to hold myself steady, I grabbed Mother's dictation in Relly's steeply slanting hand. But there I only sought out Father's advice and filled myself with his words, "Don't get involved with womenfolk." Now it had reached that point. I shoved Andsja's letter aside and began to reread Mother's dictation, from bottom to top. And there, squeezed against the lower edge of the page which had curled back, I caught the first sight of what Relly had written, in very small letters, as if in a whisper: "Andsja has lost her mind. They've put her into a madhouse." I ripped the edge off and tore it and Andsja's letter from Zaibusch into tiny shreds. I was going to throw them out the window, but no, men and animals would tread upon them. I went downstairs to drop them into the gutter, but no, there was rubbish in it. I slipped into the kitchen (which was against the rules) to throw them into the stove, but no . . . I wasn't sure why, but no, that wouldn't do either. And they were burning in my hand. So I put them into my mouth and swallowed them down with a glass of water.

Before we had a chance to return to our family, our boarding house in Prague caught fire. The fire had broken out during the night, and I would have surely slept through it with no chance for regret—everyone having forgotten me in their panic—if a piece of the ceiling of my room, where the fire had started, had not fallen onto my bed. As I opened my eyes, I saw that my clothes and schoolbag on the chair next to my bed were burning bright as a torch. Like flesh flayed from ribs, the ceiling sagged from the beams along which crept snakes of red, yellow, and blue. Afflicted by the flames, pieces of furniture were falling down. A chair was burning astride a beam that ran the length of the room. Swaths of smoke like storm clouds drifted through the room and out the window. I saw all this as I opened eyes still dewy from sleep, a dew immediately consumed by the smoke. My first impulse was to leave my bed and float out the window with the smoke. Then I remembered that Arnold slept a floor above me. The scream rising in my throat struggled with the smoke trying to get down it. Then I leapt from my bed and went to the window. It was open, and the moist coolness of the May night freed the cry from my mouth. It also took the sting from my eyes, and I could see people standing down below and hear their voices. In the loud hubbub, I could clearly distinguish my brother's voice calling, "Jump down! It isn't high!" In the meantime, a ladder appeared and came toward me with a helmeted man on its rungs. He took me around the waist and carried me down to the street beneath streams of water from the motor-driven pumps. Once on the ground, my rescuer promptly vanished. He thought he had only done his duty, but I could sense even then how much more it had been than that.

We moved into a new boarding house not far from the ruins of the old one, and I was supposed to share a room on the ground floor with Arnold. He protested and moved to the third floor. I remained on the ground floor, where I felt better. The higher floors were too unearthly for me. This building was solid. It had thick walls of brick and deep-set windows that made the rooms on the ground floor, which were also floored with flagstones, look like casemates. By comparison, our burned-out quarters seemed like cardboard, and one could guess from what remained standing of them that they hadn't been built of anything much more substantial than that. The school year ended in June, and on the same day as graduation we left to rejoin our family in their new refuge, Hullein near Kremsier. My report card contained only one grade of "Very Good"—for behavior. The rest were "Satisfactory" or "Sufficient" even though half of them should have been "Unsatisfactory." But the passing grades I had earned on the tests in history and natural history, geography and physics, sports and German must have been divided and distributed to compensate for my ignominious failures in religion, mathematics, drawing, and Latin so that I wouldn't have to stay back a grade, but could limp into the next-higher one. That was the doing of my homeroom teacher, a man who sought to balance things out. That well-meaning fellow even expected my thanks for his horse-trading and was surprised when I judged what he had done for what it was and pulled my normally round face into a long one. I wanted to see a clean differentiation between my talents and accomplishments and my failures, not a muddied mixture of the two. I didn't shine in my element, German, just so I could wrap myself in the fusty toga of Latin, which I didn't like. Why couldn't they let me lose the battle for the Capitoline but win Weimar? I didn't feel qualified to conquer the former, but the latter was of vital importance to me. Why did they grant me a bloodless victory in Latin at the cost of my passionate struggle for mastery in German? Latin was of complete indifference to me, but I came to hate it when it began to nourish itself on the object of my love. Today I know that rational considerations for my welfare swayed them to commit these injustices. Back then, I had no idea of that. I was unable to see through the sophistry, but even if I had had an eye for it, my love of honest directness would have revolted against it. At my side as I left Prague was Arnold, an expert on all its sights as well as a graduate of middle school with excellent grades in all subjects.

• • •

[*Hullein and Kremsier,* 1917–1918]

IN MY MEMORY, Hullein is a market town with a paved sidewalk surrounding a large grassy square in its center, from which streets radiated in all directions. The farmyards seem to date from the times of the robber barons, lying behind massive gates and high, interconnected defensive walls. They are evidence of hard-working farmers, these quadrangles containing stall, shed, and barn in addition to the farmhouse with its pump. At the end of the day, on the soft ground between the buildings, large four-legged farm animals with and without horns gambol among farm equipment and humans returning from their work, at their feet smaller beasts with rosy snouts or pecking beaks and clad in feathers. We lived in the quarters reserved for the retired grandfather on one of these farmyards in the center of the village. Father and Mother had hired on as farmhands and taken these lodgings. Our two younger brothers lived with them. Pepi, Tylka, and Relly were living and working an hour's train ride away in the small town of Kremsier, but came out to our parents' place for the weekends. At that time, Father was back in the Bucovina, so Arnold and I took his place as workers for our landlords. We were busy from sunrise until long after sunset because the work was not limited to the barnyard but included the farmer's fields, for his two sons as well as a son-in-law stood—or were already lying . . . no one could say, for there was no news—on other fields entirely. Sunday afternoons I played dominos or blackjack with my brothers, the latter to rob them of the allowance that Mother gave them but refused me since I always misplaced it.

Relly, on one of her weekend visits, brought along a book translated from the French and entitled *Indiana*.[1] She let me read it, and when she returned to Kremsier on Monday, she left it with me until the next weekend. I read it with eager pleasure, for it titillated me. It never occurred to me to compare it to the work by Brentano, recalled previously. But when I hold these two early reading experiences up to each other today and consider their effects on me, I would characterize those of the fairy tale as magical and spiritual, those of the novel as sensuous and erotic. For clarity's sake, I would say the fairy tale was contemplative in nature, the novel provocative. I will not comment on the banal mediating language of the translation, which did nothing more than dutifully convey the story and meant nothing to me. That I failed to comprehend the contents of this little book, as I had also of Brentano, was the fault of gaps in my intellect, through which blew the winds of creation. The only effect of the novel's story was on my now fully developed manhood, and it was comically peculiar to discover that the talented author's diverting eloquence was like fingers caressing my skin. In any event, the novel *Indiana* drew my thirteen-year-old attention to the supple calves and tempting hollows behind the knees of the farmer's pretty daughter, for up to then, despite all my premature, deeper experience, I had recognized beauty only in women's faces.

Then came the Saturday on which Pepi and Tylka arrived for a visit without Relly, who, according to their report, was stuck in bed with a sore throat. They needed eggs, butter, honey, and milk as quickly as possible, for the doctor had recommended heating this mixture and then giving it to Relly to swallow down. My poor little cousin couldn't be left there alone without anything to alleviate her pain. But since my sisters said they wanted to stay until Tuesday morning and Arnold on principle never rushed to the aid of "womenfolk," I was chosen to be the good Samaritan and departed immediately with containers full of the things the doctor had prescribed, which couldn't be obtained in town. I found her dressed, but in fact stretched out on her sofa and with her neck wrapped in a cloth. On a chair by the sofa sat a man whom she introduced as her doctor. Although I hadn't asked for any proof, the girl directed my attention with pointed finger toward her mouth. It was swollen, cracked, and bleeding, the symptoms of her infected throat. The doctor seemed to have the infection as well, for his mouth was similarly disfigured. I lowered my gaze in embarrassment and felt superfluous. The doctor told his patient to gargle with hydrogen peroxide and drink a heated mixture of the contents of the pots and jars I had brought along. After feeling her pulse, he stood up and was so tall he reminded me of the gigantic judges of the Bible. In any event, he had to be going. Before doing so, he bent down to me, took hold of and picked me up, gave me a penetrating look in the eye, and pronounced me, with a fiery glance toward the sofa, a genuine Cupid. But she was no Psyche, said Relly from her couch. Once I'd run a few errands for her, I'd be returning home by the night train since I was an obedient boy. Then the giant had to leave, while I stayed and was kept there overnight.

It's fruitless to press something upon us for which we're not ready. The more is offered, the less is taken, and if it's forced upon us, Nature locks shut the soul, and the offer remains only skin deep. Until that night, this had been my reaction to Relly's school of pleasure. She had taken hold of what was tangible about me without gaining the intangible, for whose sake she had fondled the former. I had liked following her lead in the foreplay to copulation but could neither love nor possess her as a woman, for I was not yet a man. Nor was she able to feel the soul in my premature embraces. Only its discharge could have justified her surrender. Lying beside her that night, I was able to make her such an offer for the first time. But when the surge of my soul was finally matched by the lust of my flesh, she closed herself off and dropped me, and I fell back to earth. Disappointed, ashamed, and embittered, I gathered my clothes together in the darkness, got dressed out in the hall, and went out into the night of the unknown town. A warm August wind was blowing. The streets were quiet, and the light of the gas lamps lay on the pavement like a green carpet. I followed my nose to a park with a pond surrounded by benches and tall trees. I got undressed and slowly descended a set of broad steps into the water, where I continued forward with outstretched hands, although at that age I would normally have leaped into the open water like a frog. I slept on a bench until sunrise. As I maundered through the park, it occurred to me that I had in fact reacted to the insult just as Arnold would have done. That annoyed me, so I hurried back to Relly to demonstrate my indifference. On her doorstep, which I approached on tiptoe so as not to wake the sleeping house, I had the hallucination that the doctor was with the girl. I was about to turn and leave when I heard his voice in the room. Now I had to go in. I wanted to witness it in her presence, and she would see that I didn't struggle or protest. She would see my indifference. I rapped on the door and was startled by the sound—for my knocking was much stormier than I had intended—but I didn't stop. Probably to silence my unintentional clatter, someone inside quickly yanked open the door. I entered and saw only the mounded-up feather bed on the sofa. Relly closed the door quietly behind me, and I heard her shivering. Seeing she was alone, I was going to beg her pardon and was just opening my mouth when the doctor emerged from under the feather bed and sat up. His laughing voice emerged from a chest covered with black hair, asking whether I was of the opinion that he ought to conceal himself from me. Now that he had apparently deemed it necessary to show himself, said Relly (not without sharpness), he could go ahead and lie back down again. I was like a grave, she continued, where much went in but nothing came back out. "Isn't that right, Muniku?" I had come to say good-bye, I said, and turned to leave. But they wouldn't hear of it. I was their guest, and they didn't have to go back to work until Tuesday, and I had to stay with them until then. And they would take me to the pastry shop, Relly said. I thought morosely that although she had known me for years, had tried to know me in a biblical sense for the past three years, she hadn't noticed that I didn't like sweets. That's how little she really knew me. Not that the other beauties of our house, Mother and my sisters, were any better. Did they even see me? Yes, when they needed me or wanted to tease me. How quick they were to rub my nose in the Andsja affair! Even Pepi was lying in wait for me as soon as I'd walked in the door. And I couldn't figure out why. Oh, women were all the same! Arnold was right. Father was right. You had to watch out for them; you shouldn't pay any attention to them.

Relly fixed a bed for me on one of the sofas where my two sisters slept. As I was getting undressed, I seemed to her so well put together that she told her lover to take a good look at me. "You're lucky he's not as big as you," she said from beneath the feather bed. "You're lucky I'm not as small as him," was his reply. They giggled. I went to sleep. When I awoke, the couple were no longer in the room. I read the note they left, written at one o'clock, as they had indicated. I could meet them until two in the Pension X in Y Street; until four they'd be by the pond in the park or rowing on it; until five I could find them in the N pastry shop in Z Street, or I could wait for them in the room, and they'd be back by six. I wrote on the same scrap of paper, "Gone home." Then I ate several raw eggs, washed them down with milk and honey, and choked down a piece of bread. It disgusted me to eat without being dressed and with sleep still in my mouth. At the same time, I felt a strange satisfaction in letting myself go and also had no objection to watching my right hand withdraw from my mouth and fall onto the upturned blade of the bread knife lying on the table. I pulled on my clothes with studied nonchalance. I didn't put on my sandals, for I wanted to confirm that the soles of my feet could still feel things. When I got to the station to buy a ticket, I had no travel money. I read on some sign or other that Hullein was only thirty-five kilometers away, and I set off on foot.

I walked along the crown of the trackbed from crosstie to crosstie. Imperceptibly, I had begun to be afraid and hastened my steps. Finally, I broke into a run, fear beating in my throat. I was shuddering with terror and had to summon all my strength to brake myself, stand still, and reflect, see clearly, take heart. But I had no success. The insult weighing upon me was too heavy; it pressed me down and made me small and ugly. Fear towered over me. I was conscious of it for the first time and, gripped by dread, leaped from tie to tie like a frightened hare. In avoiding an oncoming train, I lost my footing and fell into a ditch. There I lay without getting up. I closed my eyes and ran through what I had experienced at Relly's house, up and down, again and again, like a hot piston in my head. I hadn't noticed that day was dying and night approaching. So I was surprised to find myself bathed in dew and moonlight and hunched over from the cold. It pleased me to be in that condition. When I heard my teeth chattering, I was almost content. If I had had to howl and paw the ground, I might even have inwardly broken into an idiotic laugh. Had the betrayal struck me such a terrible blow because it was simultaneous with the moment I became a man? For only now was I finally able to appreciate and desire the prize of all those years of service to my beloved. And who else but I could have earned that prize with his loyalty to the frivolous female, who else burned like me in expectation of it? Who else besides me was so dependent on receiving the prize from just this person whom I clasped to my soul like no other—I, who could neither give up nor change, so deeply rooted was my love. For three years, I had prayed for maturity out of love for her, and now that I had offered it and never thought to withdraw it from her, she closed her mind to the fruit and took an ax to the tree she herself had planted. I don't think that the animalistic role played by the giant made my pain any sharper. He was just a symptom; his presence appalled me, but only made my illness clear without exacerbating it. I didn't feel myself to have been ripped out so that he could replace me; rather, he was able to occupy my place because I was already no longer there. That was the implication of their morning conversation beneath the featherbed, and it was confirmed by the girl's admission only a few weeks later that she had only pretended to have a sore throat so that I would come to visit and she could defend herself from the tall man's advances. But, unfortunately, I had simply proved to be inadequate. Unfortunately, for she had been in love with me.

In the wake of this defeat, the whole tangled flora of inhibitions and inferiority complexes began its rank growth within me. The most poisonous seedling was fear, which until then had been unknown to me. One consequence was the disruption of my straightforward aggressive male instinct at the moment of its birth. My psyche withdrew even more than before into an interior life, but now no longer confined itself to sailing in thought through actual and emotional space. Now my brain led my inner eye to believe conceptions of reality belied by the actuality of the world. And I often preferred the untruth. A prime example was my conception of my own body, which from one night to the next I began to think of as tall and with a correspondingly enlarged member. That was the first improvement on my own reality made by my compassionate imagination. Its function was surely to protect me from the bitter realization that my beloved had measured the adequacy of my spirit by the dimensions of my flesh. But how good an umbrella is a lie? It fooled me as long as I was standing under the eaves, but the rain soon revealed its holes. Or was it that my psyche conjured up this *parapluie* to get me accustomed to the precipitation I might not have dared to face without it? I was venturing into adolescence, that boggy plain of illusions, that training ground for the maneuvers of life—maneuvers that would lead to disappointments in the next phase of my existence so that I could finally taste the bitter sap of truth.

After the vacation, I was enrolled in the state German-language gymnasium in Kremsier, where I began sixth grade. And so twice a day I had to endure hours of jouncing in a filthy railway carriage between that little town and Hullein, as I had at the same time in the previous year between Bielitz and Zaibusch. But again this year I had to endure this torture for only three months. Mother moved us to Kremsier during the Christmas holidays, and when the school opened its doors again in the frosty January of 1918, I was able to reach them on foot, directly from our house, and at least outwardly in good form. I can't say whether that was the only reason I showed improvement in all subjects except for Latin. It was then that I began to study in earnest in order to escape my fruitless sexual obsessions. Probably for the same reason, I surrendered myself more willingly than before to the advances of the creative spirit and even began in secret to write down the products of our collaboration on little sheets of paper that could be easily hidden. For the sake of these spiritual offspring, I worked at improving my handwriting. To me, their appearance in clean and beautiful script was indissolubly connected to their linguistic form and inner movement, and I often judged the quality of a work in progress by its graphic beginnings on the page. Not infrequently I would give up writing down a poem if its first lines had gushed out in an unharmonious way, for it was my belief that perfect inspiration would of necessity control my hand right down to the tips of my fingers and the nib of my pen, creating correspondingly perfect script. Conversely, I was adamant in my conviction that repulsive handwriting might hinder or even prevent the emergence of a work of art. I felt evocative magic not just in how a poem sounded, but also in how it looked, magic whose power and character seemed to depend on the condition of the letters. In order to give the latter their hoped-for shape, I was always at pains while writing to keep my hand receptive, so to speak, to the oscillations of my spirit. And so my pages, which I stored unfolded between two little boards, gradually began to resemble prints whose nonverbal content touches our hearts through their visual rhythm.

Nevertheless, I also recall, running right through all of those creations, a flaw that periodically caused me to tear them up. Although their inner spiritual music was lofty, pure, and harmonious, their style, poetics, diction, and meter sounded like instruments strung either too tightly or too loosely, and the handwriting was alarmingly thick, with crowing ascenders and draggling descenders. Taken in isolation, the components of these little works—spirit on the one hand, expression and script on the other—made a harmonious impression, but taken together they yielded a mating concert in March, when the stag in rut, in one single moment of his life, pulls out all the contradictory stops of his existence: from the World Soul's call to love and battle, to his endocrine bass bellowing for his mate, down to the dance of mounting her. Although these registers may blend harmoniously in God's untrammeled reality, they seemed to pull in different directions within the circumscribed bounds of my civilized page, like the fractious stallions of a Sarmatian Boyar's troika,[2] whose combined strength nevertheless delivers their master to a rendezvous with his beloved.

As mentioned earlier, I was failing only Latin, and Professor Hubala, my fair-minded homeroom teacher whose job was to teach us the anatomy of that dead tongue as well as of the soulful and vibrantly living German, complained that I caused him no end of trouble by putting him in a great quandary. Of the two ponies pulling his bread cart, I attended only to the German one, which I cared for with the innate love I had once shown to the horses in our stall at home, while I let the Latin one languish along the wayside without a second thought. He found such cruelty unacceptable. He had no intention of belittling my accomplishments in German on that account, but that didn't help my Latin shine any brighter. He wanted to see each one looked after individually and according to regulations. So he kept an eye out for a tutor for me. That was the moment for a retiring classmate to step into the spotlight. Israel Laufer from Czernowitz, nicknamed Tuliu, was a model pupil. At that stage in the development of my judgment of him, that fact alone would have made him unsympathetic. I despised model pupils as uncollegial grinds and foolish promoters of the prevailing pedagogical system, which none of us liked. Their example enabled it to think of and declare itself to be excellent. Besides, Tuliu was dark complexioned and despite his blue eyes made a negroid impression that I found repugnant. And so he was the least likely of all my classmates to be able to win my friendship, although he had been attempting to do so from the very first day of school, with brilliant flanking maneuvers. So when Professor Hubala put out a call for an inexpensive Latin tutor for me, the rejected suitor volunteered. The professor knew that Mother couldn't pay very much. But Tuliu Laufer offered to do it for less than the cheapest and better than the most proficient of all other applicants, and moreover out of his liking for me. That tipped the scales in his favor, and his unwelcome presence in our house was forced upon me, for Mother and my sisters were of the same opinion as my teacher. I could defend myself against the intruder only if, under his tutelage, I ceased to make any more progress at all across the terrain of the dead language.

In the meantime, however, he had crossed our threshold, had become a friend of the family, and even after I fired him, he continued to visit me. Whenever he came, I couldn't think of anything else to do but to run off under some pretext. And one day this enabled him to seize the opportunity, rummage through the schoolbag I had carelessly left lying around, and stumble upon my secret poems. That happened in June 1918, two months after I had made the beautiful, perhaps twenty-year-old Hilde

Kampelmacher the queen of my heart. I knew her only by sight and at that time had never even once felt her Junoesque gaze fall upon me. Ever since I had first seen her, all the outpourings of my heart in verse and prose were dedicated to that young lady, the elegant daughter of one of the local nabobs. Although neither the girl's physical features nor her pull on my soul constituted my central inspiration, my works were nevertheless sanctified by being explicitly dedicated to her. I didn't realize what had happened until one day when Professor Hubala asked me a question in Latin class and I responded with silence, he remarked that it would be more profitable for me to study Cornelius Nepos than to sing the praises of Fräulein Kampelmacher. I gathered from my classmate's defiantly guilty look that there was a connection between him and this reproof. During recess, I forced him into a quiet corner, and, after some arm twisting, he admitted everything. Not content with the mere discovery of my secret, he had revealed it to our teacher and to my beloved herself in order to avenge himself and make me look ridiculous. He had made copies of a few of my shorter poems in his own ignoble hand, forged my name on them, and passed them on to the people in question. He'd given them to our teacher in person and slipped them under the girl's door along with a description of my appearance. Before his eyes, I ripped up and threw away the poems he had betrayed and compelled him to promise to go to both persons and declare them to be his own works. But it was too late to prevent the intended consequences of his misdeed, for Professor Hubala recognized my style, and Fräulein Kampelmacher was in possession of my description.

In fact, she recognized me a few days after I had been ambushed by the professor. I was just standing in the park on the shore of the pond, gazing into the water, which reflected my head and behind it the noonday sun and some little white clouds. I stood on the exact spot where I had walked into the water almost a year ago to free myself from a faithless female. In the green depths before me, I suddenly saw a lofty figure descending the steps behind me. My face flushed, not in hot waves, but rather in icy columns. In the pond, she slowly approached me. Her long legs grew shorter at each step; the stairs towered up behind her. Then her feet disappeared, leaving only the yellow silk dress and on it the contours of her full thighs and the narrow ring of her waist. Her elbows rested on her hips and, between her outstretched hands I saw the double swell of her bosom. Her chest supported her shoulders, from which . . . two wings came to rest on my eyes and I heard,

> Ich kenne dich nicht,
> und schaue dich innerlich nur:
> Was zählt ein Gesicht
> auf unserer seelischen Flur?[3]

Before this, I had heard her voice only in passing, and now she was reciting one of my purloined poems. Then she said, "But you're cold as ice! Are you all right? Come and sit on the bench." She took me by the hand as if I were a little child. And thus began my connection to the woman who had become my first reader, if Tuliu Laufer's assertion was to be believed that he had slid me under her door long before he betrayed me to Hubala (unless of course the honor of being my first reader should after all go to Tuliu himself). In the three months that followed this first meeting, I was permitted to visit my lady once a week in the paternal villa, join her when she went walking alone in the park, and from time to time seek to impress my verses upon her. I became convinced that she regarded me as an equal and even loved me a little.

In the meantime, I had completed the second year of gymnasium[4] in a generally satisfactory manner. Professor Hubala had given me an "Excellent" in German, turning a blind eye to the way my handwriting slanted backwards, for I placed my words more like a medieval poet than according to the 1917–1918 edition of

Duden.[5] When it came to Latin, that sympathetic man had needed two blind eyes to overlook my performance. But he shouldered this cross manfully, forgave me my sins, and allowed me to advance a grade, dragging the dead language behind me.

In June 1918, Father had sent for Arnold to join him in the Kalahura, where both were now creating a new foundation for our existence on the ruins of the old one. Our sights had been set on all returning home by the end of the year. By then, or so the newspapers hoped, the mantel of peace that Austrian generals and Russian revolutionaries had for months been stitching together in Brest-Litovsk would be ready.

Hilde and I were sitting in the summerhouse of the Kampelmachers' sumptuous flower garden. Hilde had her sewing box on the table in front of her and was embroidering intricate silk initials in the Austrian colors onto handkerchiefs. I was reading aloud from the manuscript of one of my new verbal compositions. The still, sleepy, golden air of an Indian summer afternoon shimmered around and between us. A few birch trees grew beside the little house; they stood motionless, weary and solemn. Wasps and butterflies flew past, looking like golden ships and white sailors on a golden sea. It was as if we were sitting on the ocean floor; only one silver cloud high in the blue seemed to be floating above us. The girl was much taller than I and half again as old. But the fact that she listened while I spoke gave me the feeling that she was subordinate to me. I had just reached a passage in my manuscript whose words, once I read them aloud, I wanted to replace with better ones. I reached for my eraser to clear the offenders from my path when a tall young man in a blue parade uniform rushed into our little house as if appearing out of thin air. My listener flew into his arms. As they stepped apart, she reprimanded him severely for sneaking up on us. He wanted to catch his rival in the act, answered the ensign, smiling at me. He was right, my listener said, she ought not to show me off to everyone, and I flushed.

Definitely not, he laughed, pointing out that the summerhouse offered no place to hide me.

"Oh yes it does," she cried in amusement. "I could have hidden him here in my sewing box." I felt my face burning and rose from my chair to leave. "But he's a great poet," she said sympathetically and looked at me in surprise.

I raised my pages in both hands, tore them in two, and threw them into the garden. Then I ran away. A few days later one of the Kampelmachers' servants brought my discarded verses. The torn pages had been glued back together. Accompanying the delivery was an envelope with a page of pale yellow stationery on which was written in large hand and without a signature, "I had them pasted together." But the pages were spoiled for me. Based on them, she declared her admiration of me as a poet to sugarcoat her rejection of me as a man. And I had hoped to be able to achieve the opposite with them. I did not aspire to the title of poet, thinking I had so little hand for it that being called one sounded like mockery. But I was full to bursting with eagerness to be thought a man. My sister Pepi took away the vexatious pages for safekeeping, and I never saw them again.

• • •

[*Return to Berbeschti*, 1918]

A FEW DAYS LATER we were unexpectedly boarding a train again for the journey home. As before, we traveled in a freight car. Unlike our flight from home, however, this time around we received no bread or soup in the stations along the way, and the Red Cross tea stands served only the soldiers returning in large numbers from the eastern front, where, in the meantime, peace had been concluded. Those who had picked the fight in the first place claimed to be the victors. Arriving back home on the Kalahura, we found everything just as we had left it the last time, except for the ruined post office. In the intervening time, our house had not risen from its ashes, which had gotten only blacker. Nor had the one shorter side of the station house been rebuilt, but its absence made the station somehow seem more inviting. Only the post office had been restored to its original condition before it got shot up. It was pleasing to find a building we had left in ruins two years ago whole and tidy once again. The sight of it filled one's heart with joy, like being greeted by a smiling, healthy friend whom one had left grievously wounded. This restoration had been carried out by Father and Arnold, who had installed there a new tavern and a dwelling for all of us. Meanwhile, since his return, my brother had worked side by side with Father, taking Mother's place to the extent that he looked after not just the bar, a new cow, and a freshly installed poultry yard, but also prepared a bag lunch and did the laundry for the head of the household, who was now often traveling on business. The youth had been completely alone on the Kalahura for days on end. The last evacuation had left it quite deserted, and I shuddered to think in what sort of mental state he had spent that time, especially at night, when I learned that the area had been rendered unsafe by deserters, who, divided into separate ethnic hordes of liberation, harried each other but also united to harry the peaceful civilian population. My brother didn't talk about it. But I could read in the paleness beneath eyes that seemed to open into an abyss the unfading mark of the horrors he had had to withstand. I sought to fathom why of us all it was always he who had to endure such terrible things.

With my limited experience, I was unable to perceive the destinies of my parents, of my siblings, much less of the world as a whole, for they were too far removed from me. When Arnold mentioned as if in passing that he had forced himself on a Ruthenian girl who had come to the tavern late one evening to buy schnaps for her father, it was just further, even more sinister, evidence of the hair-raising underworld atmosphere he had found and had to cope with on his return and that in the end had brutalized him. Rapes were nothing out of the ordinary in our villages even before the war; I myself had not infrequently seen boys in frenzy overtake girls walking along the highway, wrestle them to the ground, and rape them in broad daylight by the side of the road. But in those cases, a tacit agreement seemed to me to obtain. Weren't both the male and the female children of the same half-savage tribe of young Ruthenian peasantry? Moreover, the circumstance that in each case the female on the bottom, having been covered, shook herself off just like a hen released by a rooster reassured me that the violence with which this act of love began must be just the traditional practice, in keeping with the wildness of the landscape. But in a room! With a girl of a different people and class! To be sure, once the war began, foreigners had begun to claim the right to this abuse, but they were hostile intruders, not sent among us to generate good. But my brother! I refused to comprehend it and inwardly banished him from my sight. My eyes, by the way, were beginning to be completely occupied by Aurelzia, the beautiful daughter of the railroad inspector's wife, not without heartfelt reciprocation on her part.

Father, who was traveling to the big city of Czernowitz every week on business, always brought back for me installments from a series called *Once upon a Time,* published by a schoolteacher, containing tales from the collection of the brothers Grimm. Here at last were writings suited to the orientation and level of my intellectual capacities. As in Uhland's stanzas about the apple tree, I once again experienced in these elemental works, retold by the two robust masters, the happiness of complete comprehension in language. In the words of these stories, too, the real landscape and my place in it pulsated like a wave in a river, and this harmonious accommodation of reality within imagination, of nature within the spirit of art, delighted and enraptured me. It made more sense to me than anything had before. But the fantastic and laughable heroes were nearest and dearest to my heart. I considered us as alike as two drops of water.[1] I felt literally absorbed into these figures, the fulfillment of whose wishes fit the world of my own thoughts like a glove, a world I had created as a sanctuary amidst my impossibly crude environment. Thus, on walks through the woods, I would concentrate on my wish for an herb I could lay on my eyes to cure them, for a magic spring to clear my skin (because for quite a while now my complexion had been marred by pubescent pimples). After my encounters with Relly's doctor, Hilde's ensign, and Aurelzia's mental obduracy despite her physical openness, there could be no doubt that I would need to rescue the maiden meant for me from a monster or evil spell. I didn't think about Andsja Bau, languishing in a madhouse, although from time to time I sensed her presence deep within me, like someone buried alive or an indigestible scrap of food. I lost Aurelzia over the tale "Die zwei Brüder." But unlike in the dramas of separation with Relly and Hilde, in this case it was I who was regretfully leaving her, and she, the pretty child, was the jilted one. It so happened that for a long time after I became enchanted by fairy tales, we continued our evening walks, silent and hand in hand. One evening, however, when we sat down to rest in a thicket of tall cornstalks, I wanted to draw her even closer to me and knew no better means to that end than to repeat the story of the two brothers that filled me to bursting. For a while, my girlfriend seemed to listen compliantly. Then I noticed her growing impatient—at first covertly, then more and more openly—and since I nevertheless persisted, she finally pressed her crimson lips to my irrepressible mouth. But it was not to be gainsaid, so I lifted her from my lap and put her down on the grass within earshot, so as to continue unimpeded. From where she sat, her face, illuminated by the moon, sought to persuade me to relent, a wan smile on her rosy lips, her eyes sadly glowing. "The lion, in his great haste," I persisted undeterred, "in his great haste had set his master's head backwards on his shoulders. But the latter, lost in sad thoughts of the princess, failed to notice. Not until midday, as he was about to eat something, did he see that his head faced toward the back. He couldn't understand it and asked the animals what had befallen him while he slept. Then the lion told him that they, too, had all fallen asleep from exhaustion, and when they awoke, they had found him dead, his head cut off. The hare had fetched the life-restoring root, but in his haste he, the lion, had held the head backwards. But he would make good his error. Then he tore the hunter's head off again, turned it round, and the hare healed it back together with the root."[2] That was just for stupid children, said Aurelzia, in peevish boredom. But I couldn't let her deter me in my struggle to liberate her soul from its petrified spell.[3] How wonderfully different it would be one day when my beloved, freed from the evil enchantment of daily life on the Kalahura, would follow me through the spiritual totality of this fairy-tale world. But when I reached the passage where the lion emerges from the wine cellar into the daylight, staggering from side to side since he's a bit drunk after his extensive tastings down below, Aurelzia put her nose to my mouth and ordered me to exhale. After I had done so several times, she returned to her place and said pensively, "No, you're not drunk." Then she stood up angrily and said to my face, "But then you must be nuts, Munju. So just leave me be." And she went away, slowly at first, then faster and faster, without looking back. Once I completely lost sight of her, I heard her crying.

The fairy tales from my sister Pepi's lips had prepared me for the puppet theater in Prague, and that had prepared me for this collective product of the German folk spirit. At the Punch and Judy show, I had seen how the spirit can make use of mechanical devices to portray life. They enable it to present demonic and caricatured figures that transmit human destiny in all its permutations, just as the surface of the sea transmits the storms and calms of the air. But the parodistic play of the spirit reveals itself much more comprehensively in the characters of a fairy tale than in puppets of wood, wire, and cloth. In the fairy tale, their disposition is so subtle that it seems like nature, and the figures make their appearance as if directly from the hand of the Creator. How little Aurelzia understood in her disdainful contempt for them as stories fit only for the ignorant. "By no means, my precious lost love, by no means!" I cry out, now that I am able to rise up from my helpless silence of those days to protest against your peevish rejection of the fairy tale, and I present it not just to ignorant children, one of whom you once were, but to enlightened humanity everywhere as the most perfect parody of creation. But should you still think it foolish to have animals turn a backward head round right again, I'd like to remind you that when my successors to your favors turned your little head, they possessed neither the lion's surgical precision nor the hare's herbal lore. By which I mean to suggest that in many instances our reality strikes one as a bland parody compared to the imaginative world of the fairy tale.

For the same reason, I despised the wishy-washy terms of the dictated peace of St. Germain and Versailles, which we had begun to hear about, for they awarded, at least in our area, the fruits of victory to cowardly but impudent illegitimacy. As a consequence, those whose absurd claims had been justified by this injustice took possession of our possessions. It wasn't long before we, like foreigners, had to request the newcomers for residency permits in our own country. Even when we were issued the requisite official document after much hesitation and many furrowed brows, a simultaneous directive went out via the back door to make our lives as miserable as possible. Thus, Father and Arnold were forcefully hauled from their beds one night by the new gendarmes. For three days, we had no idea where they were. They showed up on the fourth in the bloodied remains of clothes that inadequately covered the barely congealed wounds and purple welts on their skin. Father signed over the newly rebuilt farm with the house and everything that went with it to our sister Susi, just returned with her husband and a child at her breast from Moravian Ostrau. Her husband, the teacher Frunza, was Romanian, like the new rulers of the country. He was permitted to remain without having to fear the methods by which the foreign newcomers sought to assert their rights.

◆ ◆ ◆

[Czernowitz, 1918–1919]

WE MOVED TO CZERNOWITZ. There Mother had already rented a cramped two-room apartment on the top story of the rear wing of Russische Gasse 18, at a time when it was becoming difficult to find anything better at a reasonable price. This was part of her plan to place Tylka and Relly, both long since of marriageable age, as well as the divorced Pepi, on the urban marriage market and to send me and my two younger brothers to school. Thus, the apartment was meant to serve as both a schoolboy hostel and a marriage-launching site, and until the girls got married, they were to keep house for us boys. At the time Mother rented the place, our land was still under the sway of the imperial and royal double eagle, which, though sadly bedraggled, nevertheless still seemed to guarantee the security of civilized behavior. But by now, the Great Entente[1] (great only in horse trading) had auctioned off our homeland to defeated hangers-on, and we got the feeling that in moving to the capital we were jumping from the frying pan into the fire. When even the cobblestones in the streets, shaken loose by the iron-clad passage of the world war, were hardly able to prevent the return of the prewar morass, the veneer of civilized public behavior from the days of the Austrian Empire already lay shattered in the mire of congenital negligence and mismanagement marked by corrupt, chauvinistic protectionism. Everything new was declared good, but goodness was not new and had already fled across the new border. Once the roiling swamp had calmed down and the school system (which had been privately run during the period of transition) seemed to be at least to some extent separated from the profit motive, I registered at the erstwhile State Gymnasium Number Three on the square formerly known as Austria Platz, now called Dacia Square.

In the meantime, we had settled tolerably well into the cramped apartment. However, in order to earn enough money to provide us with food, Father, Mother, and Arnold had again moved to a village, where I went every weekend with empty sacks, returning early Monday morning with full ones. These trips in overcrowded trains, whose looted cars carried passengers even on their roofs and running boards, led me more deeply into the events of that shattered era than had anything else up to then. There I overheard the conversations of soldiers returning from the front or from prisoner-of-war camps; of emigrants leaving the country; of Ukrainian partisans and Polish legionnaires;[2] of smugglers, profiteers, and food hoarders; of refugees from Russia and Hungary, expelled estate owners, and revolutionaries in handcuffs; of customs officials and gendarmes, priests and political agitators. These passenger trains were a kaleidoscope reverberating with the sounds of the life seething around me. What I heard was the chaos on the grave of the old order, where gray-faced grave diggers were coming to blows over their inheritance. The girls of our house, whose job it was to prepare our meals and keep our clothes clean, were also fulfilling their duties in only a slipshod and peevish way—even dishonestly, as far as their use of the groceries was concerned. Thus, we had to run off to school with grumbling stomachs and in grimy collars. And we did indeed have to run, for the girls awoke every morning impatient to receive the visits of their admirers and suitors, and we couldn't clear out of the apartment fast enough for them. These cavaliers were being served our fare. Whenever I saw them in the house, they were always chewing away while the girls watched eagerly, so I came to suspect a deep connection between food and sex and to understand why our young women had no qualms about increasing the potency of their beaus at the cost of their helpless younger brothers. But I despised them for it all the same. My young moral sensibility placed reason above nature, responsibility above desire, and honesty toward one's fellow man above everything else. Back then, I didn't yet know that women, as the animalistic fashioners of our lives, must obey a creative will that drives them to fulfill its aims even more relentlessly than it drives artists.

One morning I was lured to the window by a guttural whistling from the courtyard. A yellow-haired youth stood down below, playing with a brown dachshund. The boy's complexion had a white sheen. He wore a blue linen jacket over white knickers, from which calves massive as pillars emerged and ended in small feet clad in tennis shoes. It was Paul Konrad, the thirteen-year-old son of the Hönich family. Consisting of parents of differing religions and ethnic groups as well as two more children ten and eleven years older than Paul, the Hönichs inhabited an apartment in the front part of the building, facing the street, separated from our quarters by a vestibule with a lavatory between their kitchen and ours. Paul's father was a pediatrician in great demand at the time. This neighbor boy was in the second year of the erstwhile State Gymnasium Number One, where the more well-to-do families were accustomed to send their children. This educational institution was halfway along my own route to school, not far from the Town Hall (now called Primaria) in the Gymnasialgasse (now called Eminescu[3]). After a day troubled by the sight of Paul, followed by a sleepless night, I arranged it so that on the second morning after having seen him in the courtyard, I met him as if by chance on my way to school. Without my ever being conscious of it, the similarity of this boy's face to Andsja's had shaken me to the depths, gripping and stirring me passionately. Outwardly I betrayed barely a breath of my tumultuous attraction, especially to my beloved himself, but it quickly elicited the warmest response from his side, so that by the end of a week, overflowing with emotions, he led me down to the cellar of our building and, drawing a dagger, offered me blood brotherhood Indian style. As I now know, he got the idea from Karl May.[4] I, however, knew nothing about May and understood only that it was a sort of oath of loyalty unto death. I had to smile inwardly at that, for I loved him much too impetuously to be able to believe in his unfailing devotion. In this pact, I was satisfied just to have my feelings for him. Through the magic veil my heart had woven around him, I saw my friend in such sublime forms and colors that I didn't dare to break through them and grasp the adorable apparition with my own hands.

Paul lived in an atmosphere of scientific and aesthetic culture. His father belonged to a generation of doctors who regarded their profession as one that demanded universal education and intellectual commitment. Those physicians felt called upon to treat each patient holistically and not to lose sight of the human being behind the clinical symptoms. Their technical training seemed to them too narrow a base for the conscientious exercise of an office of such extreme responsibility. They made it their business to reinforce this training with fundamental knowledge of all the circumstances of human life, to which philosophy and the arts definitely belonged. And so Paul's father possessed not only a library of the classics of world literature, but also reproductions of fine artworks and a cabinet full of musical scores. He himself had a talented hand with both the fiddle bow and the paintbrush. In these arts, his two sons, Felix and Paul, were being trained to surpass him, although neither united both talents in one person. Paul sketched and painted and had already decided that art would be his life's work, but he was preparing himself for ascending its heights—surely with his father's preparation to be a doctor as a model—by acquiring a universal education. At the time I met him, he already bristled with erudition, and wherever

I touched him, he rang with knowledge. Not that he strutted or boasted about it; on the contrary: he was animated by the unimpeded directness of a child, more so than I had ever experienced before. Even the farmer boys in the village would show off their biceps since they thought they possessed nothing else that could excite envy. From time to time even Arnold, who had no need to prove how unmistakably superior he was to me, would point out one of his own virtues. Paul did nothing of the kind. But precisely that compelled me to feel his superiority. His virtues were intrinsic, after all, and not to be overlooked. He thought nothing of them, so he seemed to me like a god who finds nothing special about his heavenly raiments because they are his usual attire.

In the meantime, I had gotten immersed up to my eyebrows in the world of poetic imagination and, in its service, had become so practiced in the use of the German language that I saw no way out of either. In order to advance briskly and without turning back along this double path upon which I had unexpectedly embarked, I freed myself above all from the polyglot emergency ballast of my childhood and weeded Ruthenian, Polish, Yiddish, Hebrew, and Czech out of my memory. It didn't cost me much sweat to do so, for they were confined to small areas and had sent down only shallow roots. Nevertheless, they were interfering with my endeavors to encourage the growth of pure German within me. After that, I proceeded to jettison the excess baggage of Latin and mathematics with which school had loaded me down, for in my dream realm I saw no need for them. I refused to learn even the alphabet of ancient Greek, which, according to the school curriculum, was now to be added to my burden. An inner voice urgently advised me to learn from the trees, which stand close together and send down deep roots in order to grow tall, rather than to imitate the mosses, which spread out on the surface and get trampled. Having unburdened myself in the manner described, I envisioned my mind to be as agile as a mole and on my passage through the depths hoped to find only predecessors, masters, to help me acquire the craft and, thus armed, to reach the sources.

And so encountering Paul was a lucky coincidence, for he began to put the works of the classic authors into my hands. He started lending me expensive editions from his father's bookcases in such well-ordered sequence that as I moved from one to the next, I began to climb up out of the darkness of my ignorance, as if from one firm stair to the next. I believe that Paul sought the advice of his graceful mother in this endeavor. She came from a family of Bohemian nobility and had abandoned riches and prestige to follow the call of love that had chained her to Paul's inconstant father and made her unhappy. She was a ravishingly beautiful blonde, and whenever I glimpsed traces of the mother's melancholy smile in the paler face of her son, it awakened a yearning within me. One time, incidentally, she told me frankly that I was handsome. A moment later she felt extremely embarrassed by her remark and blushed to the roots of her golden curls. The first volume my friend gave me contained Wieland's tales in verse,[5] a gift so completely attuned to what I needed that it presupposed a fine sensitivity to my intellectual situation on the part of the giver. It was followed by Herder's *Stimmen der Völker* and *Ideen zur Geschichte der Menschheit.*[6] These works made me feel that my mind had been seized by the hands of a creator and molded into a universally comprehensive receptor.

Meanwhile, one day while Mother was at the flea market looking for silver tassels for her red sofa, she had found and brought home the works of Homer in two blue clothbound volumes, with an offset portrait of the translator Johann Heinrich Voß.[7] Mother had Pepi in mind when she gave in to the dealer's powers of persuasion and acquired the handsome little books. My tale-telling sister, however, had long since abandoned the resounding poetry of words for the unutterable sighs of lust. And besides, she had never progressed beyond that Mörike poem glorifying love's yearning. Relly and Tylka read novels whose quality led one to conclude that the beaux who slipped them to the girls were of a finer sensibility than the gallants of the divorced Frau Trost, who apparently consoled[8] her in quite an unliterary way. And so poor Homer lay untouched on the empty bookshelf where I could keep an eye on him while still winging my way between the peaks of Herder's *Reflections.* It was months before I was able to descend from them and make off with Homer. The others in the apartment didn't even notice that the little volumes were gone. It was my habit to keep the books I was reading hidden in my schoolbag by day and beneath my pillow at night. If the eyes or hands of others touched them while I was still reading them, they were of no further use to me. Voß's rhythms forced me to read his Homer aloud, so with these adamantine verses I spent half the night in the cellar by candlelight and my free daylight hours in secret corners of the forested outskirts of the city. I veiled these educational excursions in the same impenetrable secrecy as my own exercises in literary creativity. Nor did I talk to Paul about them, and if I happened to be reading a book that wasn't from him, he didn't find out about it. All the same, in the middle of my Homer period, which I hadn't told him about, he presented me a copy of Lessing's *Laokoon.*[9] I see this as yet more evidence of his emotional bond with me. At the time, I didn't notice this aspect of his splendid gift because I simply regarded all the books he gave me as acts of love. To Lessing's essay and the *Iliad,* which I proceeded to study in conjunction with each other, I owe the guidelines I was lucky enough to follow until, after concentrated hard work, I was launched into a developmental stream suited to my own native talents. Or, to vary one of Nietzsche's phrases, I was able to become what I was.

But one day after all, Paul came across one of the tall ledger books in which I exercised my verbal battalions, poetry and prose decked out in pedantic calligraphy: rhymed strophes and free verse, essays and stories. Among other things, there was my elegy in iambic pentameter on the destruction of the empire, with alternating masculine and feminine rhymes. I had portrayed it as a murdered mother whose orphaned children are carried off into slavery. My most passionate words were reserved for the second-youngest Crown province, the Bucovina, which I envisioned in the evil custody of a kidnapping stepmother, lost in the Sarmatian steppes[10] and beset by Tartar hordes. I accused the ethnic and nationalistic freedom fighters, in view of the rule of law and the higher civilization that had been shattered with their help, of being rebels, betrayers, and usurpers not only of their great victim, but also of the peoples they claimed to be freeing, but whom they had actually cast defenseless onto the road to an enslavement I saw threatening them from the northeast. For the lives of nations, I posited the norms of individual human lives and personalities and demanded the absolute brotherhood of all, but freedom only within the framework of law and according to the developmental stage of each nation. I absolutely refused to countenance the idea of equality. This section ended with the words

> You, brother still in the swamp, you want my rights,
> but do you live right, like me, to deserve them?
> If you live crookedly, you won't do well,
> when you emerge at last, completely grown.[11]

Having had a look into my spiritual and literary arsenal, much against my wishes, Paul changed his behavior toward me overnight. Up to then, he had been my childlike playmate and quiet sponsor of my education, but now he became a tyrant, glossing my brief utterances with ironic footnotes. And he stopped bringing me books. Instead, he now began to supply me with Seemann's reproductions[12] of old master paintings and showed me his own works as well, something he had never done before. To my chagrin, however, during one of our friendly tussles, a little notebook containing my attempts to express in words my impressions of some of the pictures in the Seemann portfolio fell out of my pocket. This accident cost me the opportunity to satisfy the need for art that my friend had awakened within me, for having cast a glance into the notebook, he brought me no more reproductions. Instead, he now began to read his own literary creations to me. Having experienced the unpleasant consequences of his seeing my manuscripts, I began to sift through them from week to week. Over a candle flame in the cellar, I burned most of the pages I had sown with poetry. I kept the few surviving pages in a small wooden box concealed in a hole behind a brick in the cellar wall. When my productions found favor with the resident rodents, I interpreted their perforation of my paper as a providential sign not to keep any of them. So after I had brought each of my experiments in form to the highest level I was capable of, I surrendered them to the appetite of the rats and mice, although I begrudged them my wooden box.

In the meantime, my parents and Arnold had also returned to live in the city, moving into the two rooms with us. They had left the countryside because the Romanian rulers were trying to ingratiate themselves in Ruthenian villages by inciting rabid anti-Semitism, making retail trade there a most perilous undertaking. Father was now preparing an extensive plan to divide up the large estates of the northern Bucovina and sell the parcels for profit while it was still opportune to do so. He hoped to be entrusted with carrying out this plan estate by estate since it shouldn't be difficult to convince the barons that the central government, having gained the support of the peasants by means of blatant persecution of the Jews, would soon proceed against the landowners with similar demagoguery.

My sister Pepi, meanwhile, having frivolously sampled the love of several suitors with the blind uninhibitedness of aroused desire, had decided in favor of the ogre among the aspirants. Father's warnings—he drew attention to the small bloodshot eyes, the receding forehead and chin in the mask of flesh that was the face of Pepi's chosen one—were in vain. His daughter was drunk, and her loving mother staggered under her child's intoxication. Again the unscrupulous young woman initiated her marriage with a lie by explaining to Father, who had no wish to put on a reception, that her bridegroom was already making plans to pay for one with his own means in the best hotel in the city. In fact, the expensive production was financed with a cash advance on Pepi's dowry, which the couple had wormed out of Mother before the wedding. I was not present at this party, which Father also shunned. When the couple upbraided me about it the next day, I surprised myself with my reply: "Now you will destroy not just your bed, but our whole house as well. Your party was the beginning. That's why I didn't wish to be there."

My unwished-for brother-in-law ground his lower jaw. I couldn't see his hands, but I had the impression he was balling them into fists.

"Pay no attention to him, dear," said my transformed sister. "Take a look at his hands," she continued spitefully, "they're just like his father's."

"Weaker, worse luck for him," said her husband, making his exit.

Father spent his hard-earned money to rent them a comfortable three-room apartment in a new building and have it furnished in up-to-date style, as if he had not heard or had already forgotten the premarital assertion of a degree in engineering, which now turned out to be false. He obtained for the swindler a responsible administrative post in a brewery and even stood surety for him. But after only a few weeks, Mother was already secretly covering an embezzlement, and at a flea market Relly discovered the brass samovar that Arnold had given his sister as a wedding present. But what did these outward signs of an unhealthy way of life matter, when at its center glowed the lustful heat of love, and the couple, like giant turkeys or besotted pigeons, billed and cooed? That's what the oily eyes in the spouses' pudgy bodies seemed to be asking. They were figures who perhaps belonged in a forest bacchanal, but who looked like madmen in the modern city.

I didn't ask myself if Tylka and Relly would have behaved with more morality than Pepi had they been in her shoes, but I perceived that those two splendid vessels of life were like live bombs, ready to explode with ruthless devastation at the slightest tremor, and I was relieved that their correspondence with distant lovers separated by borders, mountains, and steppes kept their excited, overheated feelings in check and prevented them from allowing the butterflies they attracted like orchids access to their pistils. I was happy about the separation and thought my happiness was for the sake of our poor parents, for whom the sexual excesses of my two oldest sisters seemed to be a heavy blow and whose spirits, I thought, were not in any condition to bear further assaults. But it may also be that my satisfaction at the two younger girls' rejection of the gallants swarming around them (and whom they apparently attracted for the sole purpose of repulsing them) was only the result of a jealousy thereby assuaged. The fact of my complete absorption by Paul at the time, however, argues against this conjecture because I couldn't bear to spend one day without him. I can't imagine myself—the little man cut from a single block that I was back then—being so conflicted, feeling love and jealousy simultaneously for two different people, and I see this opinion confirmed by the fact that when my soul's attraction to my friend became irresistible, my body was forced to follow suit. It was lucky for us that an unspoiled moral sense within both of us bounced us back every time our psychically enflamed libidos threw us together. Our temperaments were so vehement that neither of us could have resisted temptation by himself.

One day Paul asked me if I would pose for him without clothes. He wanted to draw an entire nude from the back. Not until many days later, when we were alone in the Hönichs' kitchen, did I declare myself willing, to my own astonishment.

While Paul dashed off to get his drawing implements, I removed my shirt, white knickers and underpants, my hands trembling as if I were trying to get ahead of myself. Since it was summer, that's all I had on, and I stared enviously at my feet, for they were still clad in their socks and sandals. Behind me, I heard my friend return, but didn't turn around to look at him. Then I felt his gaze on my back, like the beam of a flashlight, but heard no sound of drawing. I felt as though I had been posing for an eternity when I heard Paul whisper hoarsely, "Enough," but less than a minute had gone by. I leaped off into the lavatory between our two kitchens, and my friend shoved in through the cracked-open door the clothes I had left lying on the floor. Paul now no longer brought me either books or pictures. I didn't remind him or make a fuss about it. My attitude was that of a tree in the weather, standing patiently in the spring wind and enduring the denuding storms of fall with the same equanimity. Our relationship was thereby less impoverished than enriched, for now it also consumed the hours that we used to spend apart, absorbed in books. I didn't read, so my friend no longer did either, and we were together longer and more intimately since no intellectual experiences drew us apart. And sensual pleasure thus became more and more the object of our meetings, and neither of us lacked concrete evidence that it was going to our heads. Then one evening Paul made me a present of some clothes that he had worn but were still in good condition. I was certain that his quiet, graceful mother had also had something to do with this gift. I was happy to accept the proffered clothes, for my wardrobe consisted entirely of worn-out hand-me-downs from Arnold and was inadequate, to put it mildly. And just as my ugly pubescent pimples made me wish for clearer skin, so too did my aesthetic instinct cause me to fantasize about pleasing clothes with which to cover it. But I couldn't bear to accept the welcome gift without giving something in return. I pondered how to make a worthy response and discovered that I would need money to do so, for I possessed nothing worth offering to him. Then I realized that I was the only one in the family who never had any money. Mother gave the girls "going-out kreuzers" every time they had a date, and my two little brothers, because they were the youngest, got weekly "candy money" from Father. Arnold, who as Father's secretary was working with him on his plan to parcel out the estates, got a proper monthly salary.

I looked around for a way to earn money, and when I saw a little slate in a watchmaker's window saying that a Russian emigrant was seeking a German teacher, I grasped the opportunity with both hands. I met the Russian in need of German at his little workbench in the shop full of swinging pendulums, bent over a small clockwork he held between his white fingers, a loupe in his eye. He was a Jew by the name of Freifeld and was working there as a journeyman. He came from the other side of the Dnieser, where he'd owned his own shop. But the people there who were casting their country back into the era of the hourglass had smashed up his little up-to-date clock shop and driven him into exile. He wanted to learn German in order to "feel like a human being" and ordered four lessons a week from me, always held in his rooms in the evening. After a month had gone by, I had saved up enough money from my pupil to survey the windows of the downtown shops, which I otherwise never dignified with my notice, for a gift for Paul. While doing so, I caught sight of a color reproduction of Anders Zorn's[13] *Maja* in the window of a bookshop: a splendid blonde, seated and clothed, with a collar of light-brown fur. Her arms are bare and her hands folded in her lap. I fell in love with this magnificent woman and for a long time returned daily to the image, whose long, full arms I found especially captivating. I had decided to get Paul a dog collar and leash for his dachshund, whom he could never walk through town, however much he would have liked to, for want of this equipment. Shortly after I gave him this gift, he asked what I would like from him. "Books," slipped out of me, but I wanted to bite my tongue, for I didn't like to ask for things that people hadn't offered on their own initiative. "You can buy those for yourself," Paul said, thus opening up for me a path to infinity. This possibility hadn't occurred to me. The first thing I purchased were the complete works of Lessing in the Reclam editions.[14] The minuscule print of this series strained my eyes to the point of tears. This had not escaped Mother's notice, and I once overheard her asking Relly what kind of books I was reading that made me cry. Another time somebody said I must be crazy, laughing through my tears. Indeed, I always laughed when I read about the gulling of Polyphemus, which I often did, for I found nothing so riveting as the azure cheerfulness of the Homeric epics in the wiry style of Johann Voß, vibrating like a telephone line charged with the substantiality of Homer's visions.

Meanwhile, the government had decided to forego one of its diversionary demagogic games, at least as far as the letter of the law was concerned, and finally signed the Versailles provisions granting equal rights to the Jews. Now that the carpetbaggers couldn't throw the Jewish merchants to the restive peasant masses anymore, the estate owners felt that the sword of Damocles had been rehung above their heads. Thus, clairaudient members of that class, aware of Father's prescient plan, turned to him and began to sell off large tracts of their real estate to tenant farmers with the money to purchase them. My father's first clients were Baron Freitag from Czortoria, Baron Letzkowatski from Terebleschti, and Baron Flondor from Hlinitza, followed shortly by almost all their peers in the area because the expropriations in northern Siebenbürgen[15] had plainly confirmed the correctness of Father's foresight. And so the prophetic businessman had his hands full. He not only took Arnold, Relly, and Tylka along as hired clerks on his cross-country surveying expeditions, but also had to set up an office in town, although Mother failed to slip Pepi's second husband in as office manager, for Father had decided not to hold his protective hand over that untrustworthy fellow any longer. Every week our real-estate agents left on Monday and didn't return until Friday evening to gather at the festive weekend table. The four nights of their absence were for the four of us who remained at home a glorious period of undisturbed sleep since each was able to loll and stretch at will on one of the four beds without the otherwise inevitable bedmate. But the return of our main breadwinners was also a pleasure. They brought with them the smell and the fresh fruits of the fields without disturbing—at least in my case—the comfort of one's very own bed, for I then surrendered the entire sofa we shared to Arnold, my bedmate, and bedded down in the kitchen, where I pushed the table up to the stove for the purpose, or I stayed in the cellar all night, reading and writing, as was my custom. I don't know if Father hoped for children when he and Mother dreamed together, but, at any rate, he fed the ones who had resulted and, for as long as I knew him, simply took care of them. It was the natural thing to do, what the animals of the forest do for their young as well.

Did we then thank him any better than animals thank those who sire them? Is it natural for any creature to give thanks for what the inner laws of blood command to be done? Or is it only what is freely given, over and above those laws, that deserves noble reward? A dog will requite his master with exaggerated joy but ceases even to recognize his mother once she has prepared him for independence. And what is Jesus's denial of his mother but a rejection of that which is merely natural and is not sufficient to be called a creed, a profession of loyalty we prodigally lay at the feet of a voluntary benefactor, as the founder of Christianity did for his disciples. Our father, however, gave us nothing more than what nature called for. Or if he did, we were unable to recognize it at the time. It requires a great deal of maturity to realize that a gift has been given. And the wisdom of true humility gives thanks even for donations given in the natural course of things. In our behavior toward our father, we were very far removed from that ideal. Some of us, in fact, barely remained within the bounds of what is natural, finding it difficult even to accept the gifts of life and daily bread with mere indifference rather than outright hostility. Such was the case with Arnold and the two younger girls once they became Father's secretaries. They not only took advantage of Father's temporary dependence to force the overburdened man to the wall and extort exorbitant wages from him, but also rebelled against his paternal authority outside the work environment and at times even impudently disparaged him in front of the whole family. From the way their victim became softer and masked his defeats with laughter, I could see the pain and heartbreak within. But what sister Pepi did was still worse. She fired anonymous notes at him, saying that if he continued to deny his supportive arm to his lovely daughter and admirable son-in-law, he didn't deserve the name "Father" and only with reservations the title "human being." After his demise, we found these poisonous sheets folded up in his coat pocket. To the end, he had shown them to no one and swallowed them in solitude, as he did with so much that was unappetizing. Our youngest siblings, Milku and Duziu, were his last hope—not for his life on this earth, but for the afterlife of his soul. Only from them did he expect the observance of prayers for his soul once he had passed away. Only they had not yet disappointed him.

Since earliest childhood, my attitude toward him had not changed: it can be compared to that of primitive man to a benevolent domestic deity. Nevertheless, even I had lit into him once. I was nine years old, standing in front of our house in Berbeschti. I had become totally absorbed in watching a Ruthenian boy play: he was amusing himself by throwing stones against the wall of our house and catching them again like balls. Suddenly Father appeared behind him, reached out his hand, grabbed the boy by his tattered shirt collar, and belabored his back with his fist. "Leave him alone! Have you lost your mind!" I said, beside myself. The tall man gave me a dumbfounded look and let the boy go, who ran away crying. Following this incident, my father treated me with almost the same silent timidity as I did him, and only in a very good mood would he bestow upon me, with an apologetic smile, some benevolently ironic remark. Paul, who feared him, seemed to have learned this behavior from him.

My fifteenth birthday on June 20, 1919, two days before the end of the school year, was the first one of its kind that was taken notice of, at Father's behest, during the midday meal. It was a Friday, and Father had returned home with his staff of scribes a few hours earlier than usual because he had to leave again on Saturday evening to attend the wedding of Baron Flondor in Hlinitza. The baron was at long last going to lead his housekeeper—formerly one of his maids—to the altar after years in which Father, in his capacity as the inept nabob's advisor, had forestalled this event. Our meal that Friday consisted of dishes already prepared for Saturday's ceremonial board, and since Father also had wine brought out and I was to recite a school poem and receive a present of money from my jovial domestic deity, my birthday really turned into a family celebration, which up to then only the High Holy Days had been deemed worthy of. Paul, who had probably found out about this unprecedented event in our house from Relly, the favorite of his lonely mother, at long last brought me another book, but unfortunately as a gift rather than on loan, from which I sadly gathered that it would not be followed by others. And more books from the Hönich house would have been so welcome because of their larger type! My meager means permitted me to buy only Reclam paperbacks, whose nonpareil letters scattered like ants before my eyes or clumped together in hostile, gray, insoluble heaps. Paul's gift, entitled *Der Mensch,*[16] was an eighteenth-century anthropology by a certain Dr. Zimmermann, a powerful writer it seemed to me, and my imagination wallowed in his images (which even then I felt were quite unscientific) like a cow in clover.

In light of the fact that the most important people in my life had taken such notice of my birthday, I felt some obligation in my cellar that night to come to grips with this date myself. First, I must mention that in my poetic endeavors even then, I was intent upon gaining intellectual control over the river of time and everything it carries along. What I saw upon its waters at that moment were the bloody afterpains of the world war that lacked its fateful justification: revolutions, civil wars, interventions, pogroms, massacres in the name of freedom, and terror in the name of order. I hearkened to the voice of my soul:

"Now you have completed fifteen years!
The youthful half of life is all used up.
The world still keeps on murdering and burning,
and you have only dipped your pen in ink."

Oh my stern soul, what else could I have done,
when it was you who set my spirit's task:
to wed itself to words within my self—
and also sent the dreams to be my guests?

"But you have only frittered away your mission:
no chance for spirit in your hands to speak;
in brittle perfection of your chilly verses,
in adamantine rhymes its verve is withered."

Then should I let it loose, no rules to guide it,
to seize the word as mobs seize sticks and stones,
to rage in noble palaces of language,
the way a goat would in a flower bed?

"No time to heed the temple that is language,
where men stand speechless, mute beneath the sky;
the aged weeping spend the night in coffins,
and mothers enter labor in the grave."

So let me then embed them in my language
within whose ice they're indestructible.
It's only thus that I can save them here,
The mother in the grave, in her the child.[17]

My school in Czernowitz was the very image of the anachronism characteristic of the times in general. If the postwar world still found wars over redrawn borders acceptable in the midst of universal economic activity and with means of transportation that obscured all national colors, so also the school still promulgated ethnic prejudice and religious fanaticism despite the insights of philosophy that condemned the narrow-mindedness of the past in favor of an image of universal man. If, against better judgment, fortunes were still being wasted on the preservation of moribund institutions such as dynasties, monasteries, prisons, and barracks, so also in the school the best energies of youth were being frittered away on the cultivation of calcified subjects fit only for museums—such as ancient Greek, Latin, religion, and national history—for which libraries with the appropriate courses for specialists would have sufficed. The school's disciplinary code was also not a whit better than the blind Justicia on the covers of the rotting pandects that still dominated the market in our enlightened era. And what can I say about the teachers, those gray remnants of a collapsed multinational state? In this region, on the whole, the state had been out of step with the times, but only in the sense of being ahead of its time in its principles of order, public morality, and general tolerance—virtues that its successors never dreamed of. Ah yes, the teachers! First of all, they had to hit the books again themselves and be retrained. And those bearded Sugambrians[18] were forced to burn what they had worshipped and deify what they had deeply despised. So Professor Leschtscher, the one who bestowed the grade of "Unsatisfactory" on my German for the year-end report card, got the same himself in Romanian and a new subject called Fatherland Studies and got kicked out of the school, and I had to stay behind an extra year in the third grade of gymnasium because his decisive judgment upon my German, combined with negative verdicts in Greek and Latin, brought my cup to overflowing. This pedagogue's ire had been aroused by my predilection for complex syntax from which he was unable to extricate himself during his unthinking, official flights through my essays. Later, he worked as an editor at the Zsolnay-Verlag in Vienna. I'm convinced that the short-winded writers of that publishing house have fonder memories of him than I do.

Our poor teachers got paid irregularly and below the level of even the most basic necessities. Their necks were skinny and their collars greasy, their gait unsteady from weakness and fear of their superiors. They were bankrupt of truth and taught us lies: nationalism, worship of power, the cult of progress, politics, and propaganda. In terms of their background in imperial and royal Austria and their civilized hearts, they were both too late and much too early. In terms of their fate, they were still surviving beneath the leaky protection of an anachronistic humanism, an illusion, which the more up-to-date, medieval liquidators of the Habsburgs were hastening to correct with their red pencil, a pencil that wrote in blood. Ah, they were poor devils, our teachers, like dogs that had lost their masters and gotten new ones who kicked them in the belly. The best ones fled, the cowards wagged their tails, the witty ones became cynical. What could we learn from them? We flunked.

When the one-horse carriage Father had ordered arrived late Saturday afternoon to take him to the wedding of the estate owner in Hlinitza, Mother begged Arnold, Tylka, and Relly to accompany her life's consort on the forty-kilometer overland journey, for her afternoon nap had been troubled by a portentous dream of disaster. But the secretaries had planned to enjoy the weekend as they saw fit and were of the opinion that their boss would be able to hold up his end without their educated accompaniment because the wedding was only a country wedding and the hostess a former barnyard shiksa. Mother's dream-induced concern seems not to have included the country highways, which were still full of uncertainties for Jews despite the treaty provision granting them equality, for she had asked the girls as well to accompany Father, something that the practical woman would never have done if she had had a premonition of an ambush. However, she suddenly declared she was concerned about Father's health, based on absolutely no evidence whatever, and no one could take her seriously, not even that splendid man himself, who had never been sick and looked like a healthy forty-year-old although he was fifty-seven. The final argument the poor woman advanced in vain was that he needed someone to talk to on the trip. This met with uproarious laughter, and even Father smiled, for he prized contemplative solitude above all else. I stepped forward, however, and offered to accompany him. I had been more moved by the dream-spurred unease of Mother's feelings than I could possibly have been by more plausible, logical reasons. They all put me in my place and voted down my offer.

"Don't you go trying to get out of having to pick up your report card," said Relly (who had a sharp tongue), and then she explained to everyone, "Tomorrow morning at eight all the schools are issuing their year-end grades."

Whereupon my departing father suddenly said to me with great seriousness, "My son, may your prayers accompany me through all eternity once I'm gone." Then he said to Mother as he kissed her on the cheek, "He's got the only prayer mouth in the family." Only at fateful junctures did that gruff man take such elaborate leave of us. Mother's small face was contracted and gray with crying. Glancing at me, the "prayer mouth," she said disparagingly, "What good will his prayers do if they're not in Hebrew?"

In Mother's dream, a cat had risen up in front of Father's droshky in the middle of the road to Hlinitza. The animal had asked him not to run it over and then rolled up and gone to sleep on the spot. It took Mother a long time to get over this dream vision. She finally freed herself from it by telling the dream to Pepi, a proof of Mother's complete trust in her, for it was Mother who had taught me to spread a blanket of impenetrable silence over my dream life. The fact that she had even mentioned a dream as the catalyst for her unease before Father's departure was evidence enough that she had overcome her habitual reticence, something she could have done only because she was in despair and terrified for the safety of our provider.

At 9:00 A.M. on Monday, I received my flunking report card from Leschtscher, my homeroom teacher. I begrudged that smirking functionary his triumph and said, "Thanks. This should prove useful." In fact, I nourished the hope that the family forum would withdraw me from school in the wake of the injustice of my grade in German. But I had forgotten that they couldn't appreciate my German as I did because they had no idea of my literary accomplishments. I returned home by dilatory detours, thinking that in the end my utter failure in school would disappoint even Father. Back when we still had our fields to work, he had been against my attending school. But after we became refugees, he had relented and in Prague had even registered me himself. Now that the sustaining earth had been pulled out from under us forever, who knew? Perhaps after all he would be very much in favor of sharpening my wits, for apparently wits were the only appropriate tool for hunting one's bread on these sterile city streets. When I reached the Renner Pond at the rural end of our street, the Russische Gasse, whose new name was Romana, I stepped to the edge and peered into the water. I saw my beautiful hair, but not my pimples. I thought, Father will be gone a long time, he'll hardly be back before evening; and I began to take off my clothes, intending to spend the rest of the day in the water. The women could wait. I didn't owe them an explanation.

Then I saw my soccer teammate Stadler approaching from the direction of the city, hand in hand with his mother. She had a little house on the pond and sold duck eggs on the square in front of Town Hall. He called out to me but was unable to continue, for his mother, a resolute widow, gave his mouth a slap and spoke in his place: this was no weather for swimming; I should keep my clothes on and get on home. I wasn't in the habit of questioning such advice. I simply heeded it or didn't. In this case, suddenly filled with dark foreboding, although the sky was clear, I didn't dawdle but hurried home. I was surprised when neighbor families with all their children, out for a Sunday[19] stroll to the Horecza Woods beyond Renner Pond, either looked away when they caught sight of me or, without waiting for me to say hello, solemnly raised their hats. The grumpy little hunting enthusiast we called Tabaku because he ran the tobacco concession in our neighborhood leashed in his setter and bowed deeply to me. In front of the Eastern Orthodox peasant church not far from our house, they were holding an outdoor service. I was detained by the officiating priest, who knew me, and was entreated to have a swallow of wine. The tips of his white beard atremble, he encouraged me to go ahead and drink, just drink, it would do me good. But what was going on? What was the meaning of all this unusual, unexpected, solemn, portentous attention being paid to me? I had trouble keeping down the tears rising in my throat. Then I saw a neighbor lady at her window, wiping her nose with a red handkerchief, and I felt my tears obscure her image. The gate to our building, which was usually left open, was closed, and as if through a fog I spied Paul standing beside it. He seemed to be waiting there for me, but as soon as he saw me, he forsook the gate and took to his heels down the street without looking back. I watched him go and smiled involuntarily. Then I pushed open the little gate and was accosted by the howling Relly, who splashed me with her tears. I wrested myself from her arms and stepped into the courtyard. There stood a little hay cart hitched to a bay pony that was munching on the barley in his feedbag while his protruding ears twitched off the flies. Next to it a tall man was lying on a plank, my mother's arms around his waist and she lying next to him on the pavement, her face covering his beneath her loosened hair. "She has no tears left," said Arnold, who stood shivering next to her and looked through me like a zombie. What was lying on the board had been my father.

Only six hours ago the owner of the cart had spotted Father sitting in a ditch beside the road from Hlinitza. He had motioned for the cart driver to come over and asked him in a weak voice to drive him home to his family quickly. He'd been unable to tell him the address, but had held out a note he had tied to his hand. The farmer took the paper, and our address was written on it in unsteady capital letters. The farmer said that he had set the sick man on an opened hay bale with his back leaning against the seat box. Just before they reached town, his passenger had regained his strength enough to have him stop at an inn. Father asked him to fetch some water and alcohol and had him massage the left side of his chest with the spirits. After drinking some water, he asked him to drive his horse even faster. Not until they reached the tollgate at the edge of the city and were stopped by a customs official did the driver turn around to look at his passenger again. But the latter had slipped down from the box and was sleeping peacefully, so he had left him alone and asked his way to the address written on the paper. Not until arriving at our house did he discover he had transported a dead man, and that's all he could tell us.

The aforementioned notes from his eldest daughter were found in the jacket pockets of the deceased. The last one wasn't even anonymous, and Father had received it on the last day he spent with us. In addition to the shakedown notes, a large sum of money in banknotes was found on the body. This proof of the driver's honesty left no doubt as to the accuracy of his story. Our father had not died at his hand. The medical examiner whom

Tylka had sent for put a finger to the dead man's chest, took a look at his handsome face and short hair, and quickly decided that he had died a "natural death." His diagnosis was a heart attack, and he released the victim for burial. Father was laid out in one of our rooms, and in our stocking feet we sat down on the floor around him to mourn.

Around noon, the originator of the notes in his pockets arrived, pumped up fat and jolly with the high color of profane love. Unbecoming were the tears squeezed from the laughing eyes that belied them. The pomaded spouse at her side, incapable of producing even an artificial tear, begged her to calm herself, and I laughed out loud at the two of them, for they were just too comical. Whereupon my dear little sister declared that I had already gone crazy with grief and advised me to leave the mourning room. But I only rose and left when she said it wasn't fashionable nowadays to bury a person with their jewelry and instructed her gallant to remove the heavy watch chain from the dead man's vest, and Mother, crying genuine tears, yammered, "Take them, children, take them!" and "He doesn't need them anymore," and the couple stuck the ring from his finger as well his pearl stickpin into their pockets. Arnold followed on my heels, with Mother calling after him that he didn't need to follow my example, for I was an idiot. I called for Paul, and he led me silently into a garden. Beneath the tall trees, he pressed me to his chest and said, "I will stay by your side forever."

By the time I returned home in the evening, the Frunzas had arrived. They had brought their three-year-old son, Eugen, along, and my sister Susi was sniffing around in Father's closet, much to her husband's displeasure. For the burial two days later, Pepi's husband, whose ponderous body happened to have the same measurements as Father's, put on the frock coat of the deceased. Mother led the funeral procession, walking behind the hearse arm in arm with Pepi and her husband. Behind me, I could hear people expatiating on the course and grandeur of

Father's life. When we reached the grave, it was surrounded by a vast crowd of mourners. I was pleased that the officiating rabbi called some Ruthenian peasants and their wives to the front. My father had lived not just among us, but among them, too, and I think they caused him less disappointment than we had and, at any rate, no heartache.

The former barnyard maid and new Baroness Flondor, still warm from the oven, stood beside Pepi. I held the latter's final letter in her unmistakable hand, the last one Father had had to swallow before he died. And what had the arrivé maid given him to swallow? For I had no doubt that she had slipped him something. But why? To take revenge? Or like his daughter, for money? Among the papers we found on Father's person, there was an excerpt from the Hlinitza accounts, dated the day of the wedding. The document proved that the bundle of banknotes the honest cart driver had delivered with the body, large as it was, represented only an eighth of the money the baron's books credited to Father. The poisonous baroness wept on the bosom of the bitter daughter, both encircled by the greedy arms of the swindler who was playing the role of orphaned son-in-law.

As ropes lowered the coffin into the grave with a dull thud and handfuls of earth began drumming on its lid, we, the male seed of the deceased, were called upon to pray for his soul. We were eighteen, fifteen, twelve, and eleven years old, and we lined up by height, like organ pipes, on the plank next to the grave. Only Arnold, however, knew the old Hebrew text; we others watched his lips forming the words and forced our mouths to do the same. But inwardly I said the words I had composed at the first sight of his lifeless body and written down in definitive form during the next two days. The poem sought to assuage the anguish this death had burned into me for the rest of my life because Father had not been able to take leave before he departed from us. "Father in the hereafter," I said in my mind while my lips imitated Arnold's . . .

Father in the hereafter—for now you're there—
your going pains us, since without farewell
from your only treasure here, your loved ones,
you had to leave, go, as they say, to rest.

No consolation helps: not us, still stuck
in flesh, nor you, afloat in purity.
Perhaps forgetting covers this deep wound,
until reunion lifts it off at last.

Until we meet again, no tears of parting:
how good you've slipped away without good-bye!
So we must be yearning for each other,
till the Creator links us once again.[20]

I repeated this poem every day in memory of the departed instead of the suprapersonal words prescribed by the synagogue. I never tired of saying it; it expressed a changed relationship to Father that would now remain unchanged for the rest of my life, a change brought about by his dissolving into dust. When we returned home, we again took off our shoes and resumed the mourning that the burial had interrupted. Sister Pepi didn't join us in mourning, for she was in a good mood, compelled by her own base motives to busy herself with the division of the possessions left behind by the dead man. Nor did sister Susi join us. Like all the women in our family, she was a model homemaker and went rummaging through the kitchen cupboard and Mother's chest, even while its poor owner, although out of her mind with grief, was still among us. My brothers-in-law were not required to mourn. Nevertheless, it didn't seem right to me that one of them was filling his pockets with banknotes before our very eyes (the same banknotes Father's next-to-last coachman had declined to appropriate in stealth). My brother-in-law Frunza, however, went to a tavern, where he drowned his large grief in small beer.

He could get drunk with an easy mind, for however much Pepi and her spouse divided the spoils to Frunza's disadvantage, they still tossed more his way than he could have brought himself to ask for. He was an emotional dilettante and also an amateur in many arts and crafts. He did everything by halves and preferred a hangover to the realization of his own shortcomings.

After seven days, we arose from the floor, put our shoes back on, and went to the stonecutter to inspect Father's tombstone. Pepi had chosen the stone, and her husband had settled the bill. After her first marriage had ended and she returned to our midst, she had again arrogated to herself the scepter of culture and good taste in our house, even though she had never progressed beyond the servant girl doggerel of her adolescence. By this point, Relly had more intellectual maturity than Pepi. And yet it was Pepi who, as foreman of the jury consisting of herself, her husband, and Mother, chose the best inscription among the competing family suggestions. An eight-line stanza by Frunza was awarded first prize and the honor of being cut into the stone on Father's memorial. It spoke of a ship that has lost its helmsman and entreats his heavenly spirit to continue steering it. Since the competition was open, Relly, Tylka, Arnold, and even Milku had all chewed the ends of their pens over their entries, and I, too, entered with the following strophe:

> If you seek Father, come stand before my breast.
> Here lies but what of him was dust.
> That which he was, he still remains
> in me, and not within this hole,
> onto which I wrote his name
> for here his dusty coat remained.[21]

The reaction these lines elicited showed me that my teacher Leschtscher's "Unsatisfactory" in German would have had an echo of agreement from my next of kin. Which is why I decided to keep my report card secret from them for a good long time. Summer vacation was under way, so I could afford to do so. Paul, to whom Relly for some reason or other had showed my text, gave me a puzzled look, probably because I had exposed myself to the masses. But they had seen nothing, I thought, trying to wash away my bad conscience. Frunza apologized for beating me out and took me along to Geffner's Tavern. "For sure, Munju," he said after a few glasses, "for sure you're destined . . . " (I was startled: What did he know?) " . . . to become a great poet." OK. He'd left me some time to get there. "And someday I'll be ashamed of my victory today." He started to cry. "But I'm innocent, Brother. That Pepi, she twists everything around."

Arnold demanded the small amount of money that Pepi and her husband had left for Mother. But not for himself; he intended to do business with it and feed the family with his profits. This time Mother finally summoned the strength to resist Pepi's smooth tongue and caressing paws and provisionally handed the small capital over to my brother for a short time. That conscientious and able young man exceeded all expectations. After a short time, Mother was receiving from him not just her household money, but also the legal and soon even the prevailing usurious interest on her capital. Arnold thereby took Father's place as our selfless provider. The fairy-tale sources of his money were in the black market, whose publicly tolerated underhanded dealings stretched along the short Postgasse like a shadow of the legal stock exchange on which the full sun of official approval shone. Those who labored there were mainly Jews, driven from their small but honest businesses in Russia or in the countryside. Although the demagogic regime broke its word, kept persecuting these unfortunate fellows, and wouldn't license them to pursue legitimate commerce, it had nothing against their squeezing into the spaces between the laws to chase after their booty. This attitude of the eastern usurpers, far from conforming to the standards of Western jurisprudence, betrayed a medieval toleration of the Jew as a creature, while reserving the right to proceed against him arbitrarily at any time.

Arnold always returned home late in the evening and as if in a fever. Mother and my other siblings were usually already in bed. They hadn't given up their rural habit of going to bed with the chickens. When cold drove me from my cellar, I bedded down in the kitchen on the table near the stove and read beneath my blanket by the light of a flashlight because Mother couldn't stand the light that leaked into her room through the cracks in the door. On these nights, I put Arnold's supper on the countertop of the kitchen cabinet. Then when he came home and sat down to his food without turning on the light, I shone a light from under my blanket and watched as he consumed his meager meal without a sound. He ate like Father, who also had very proper manners. Every year Arnold looked more and more like the deceased except that his face and hands were pale, whereas I had inherited Father's healthy complexion. After his meal, when my black-marketing brother would pull a chair up to the stove, I held the light next to my cheek, and he totted up the banknotes he had accumulated in the course of the day. There were always tall blue stacks of them, for they had little value and came from the old Austro-Hungarian State Bank, which now lay in ruins. I was filled with disgust by Arnold's nightly counting of the cash. Every time, I would surrender the flashlight to him, withdraw to the foot of my improvised bed, and pull the blanket over my head. Whenever he held a longish stack in his deft hands and whispered numbers while the fingers of his right hand snapped the rustling blue bills from the left hand that held them, it felt to me as though he were handling poisonous vermin, counting hideous snakes. It was all well and good for me to feel disgusted. I took the liberty of condemning the actions of an impressionable young man who was without any doubt more sensitive than I, as had been his model, my father, who put up with so much abuse. And like Father before him, Arnold now did this for us—for me—so that it was easy to feel disgust for him, stick my head under the blanket, and daydream.

Once I began helping Mother, who was as busy as a bee, with the household chores—Tylka and Relly, constantly taking new courses in specialized skills and also constantly beleaguered by rejected suitors, had no time to help—even carrying home for her the full shopping bags from the morning market, she reverted to an opinion of me (especially once Pepi concurred) that she had long ago abandoned—namely, that I was a rough child, but a good child all the same. Moreover, once my sister Susi and Relly had told brother-in-law Frunza of the opinion voiced by Paul's mysterious, universally revered mother and even by her spouse, the doctor himself, that there was "something about" me that only further schooling could bring out, as well as in pious recollection of a remark of Father's about the "still waters" running deep within me, they turned down my petition to withdraw from school. But once I had set myself a goal, I couldn't help pursuing it with relentless consistency. If I ever tried to check myself by using my conscious powers of reasoning, the goal I had activated would flee into the depths and from there set in motion a thousand uncontrollable, irresistible appendages. I didn't want to hurt Mother's feelings, so I agreed to continue going to school. And in fact, the beginning of the new school year found me sitting at my desk and repeating the third grade of gymnasium. But despite the teachers' best efforts to attract my introverted attention to themselves and their subject matter, it was no use: I remained insensibly obdurate. Even the benevolent Professor Eidinger had no success when he used the whole of three of his German classes to read from one of my notebooks (which unbeknownst to me had somehow fallen into his hands). It brought the good man to the brink of exasperation when I answered with a shake of my head his inquiry whether I knew who had written it.

"But you like it?"

"Not the way you read it."

"Then please read it yourself."

"It's not in the syllabus."

I don't know how long it would have taken for my teachers' patience to wear thin. Mine had snapped by the tenth day of school in the last week of September. I wrote Mother a letter, whose gist was that what I needed was a craft and a master craftsman, and every now and again a taste of the country and some time to daydream. I asked her not to force me to go to school and submit myself to the teachers anymore. I called the former a machine for tickling ambition and the latter sublessees of the spirit. Full of foreboding, I sealed the envelope in such a way that I would notice if it had been opened and then resealed, and that night I stuck it into the mirror in front of which Mother combed out her raven black hair each morning before sunup.

The letter remained there several days, as if no one had noticed it. This proved to me that they all knew only too well it was there. I was ashamed of my Mother's diplomacy toward me, for I couldn't concede to her the same shyness I felt, and I hoped that she hadn't resealed the envelope, or that if she had, she had done so with disregard for my marks. I wished it as fervently as I had wished a decade ago that the knee bandage she recommended would ameliorate my headache. My marks on the envelope seemed intact, but only to the superficial eye. I could see upon closer inspection that they had been broken open and then very carefully restored. The letter had been opened. Using a loupe borrowed from my pupil the clockmaker, I could also see on the edge of the page various fingerprints that weren't mine, and I now knew for certain that my letter had been read. It had been read by several of them and probably by all of them. However, even if only one of them but not Mother had read it, she had certainly been informed of its contents. The message was addressed to her, and, besides, every scrape I got into was reported to her, even if she wasn't supposed to find out about it, especially the things that would annoy and turn her against me. But I needed no other proof that she knew what I intended to do than the united front of unbroken silence toward me in which they all without exception participated, from Pepi, the eldest, down to Duziu, the youngest. This unity could have proceeded only from the center binding them all together—namely, my mother. I was hurt and disgusted by my criminological game of persecution and deduction. It was like probing a festering wound. And what was I trying to prove, anyway? That Mother was deceiving me by not confronting me directly? Why did she avoid it? Wasn't it an admission of her weak position vis-à-vis my demand? When I discovered the deceit, a disarming sympathy for her rose within me. If anything could have moved me to abandon my purpose, it would have been this evasive behavior on her part, which revealed her opposition, but I, once launched on an endeavor, was unfortunately incapable of bringing it to a stop. I couldn't go to school anymore. But because Mother couldn't summon the strength to tell me yes or no to my face, I summoned the reptilian courage of all first-time rebels against weak governments and began to deceive her by playing hooky.

I thereby put distance between myself and everything represented by society, order, and law and embarked on an incalculable adventure in illegality. Thus, my day began with the pretense of getting ready for school and the lie that that was where I was going. I also lied to Paul, parting from him in front of his school and giving the appearance of continuing the rest of the ordained route to my own institution. By pretending to have a limp, I deceived my fellow pupils who hurried past, calling to me to run with them. If I caught sight of family acquaintances or teachers, however, I hid behind gates and in doorways, also stooping to retie my shoes and avoid the glances of passing inhabitants of the buildings. But I put myself through these embarrassing charades for only a few days. I quickly discovered that it was more advantageous to set off on my "way to school" before Paul and my younger brothers and to reach the forests and hills that ringed the city by way of the Jewish Quarter, a part of town forgotten by the angels of cleanliness, where the only awkward encounters were with stray dogs and rats.

Since I liked sticking to a routine, I regularly opened my "school day" by climbing the Weinberg, about a hundred meters high, from whose green summit I surveyed not my first-period class, but the panorama of the city spread out across the valley of the Pruth, its houses low as if stooping to climb the broad hills and its highest point, the flagpole on the Town Hall, looking like a needle. Behind it, sloping almost imperceptibly upwards, rose the well-to-do business district, separated from a lower-lying area of trees on its right by the walls of the prison and the school I was cutting, both located at the top of a slope. The two buildings stood on either side of a street that led downhill and formed the northwest corner of Dacia (formerly Austria) Square. If I raised to my eyes the field glasses that I had requested in lieu of money as prepayment for three months of lessons from my clockmaker shortly after he became my pupil, I thought I could still make out above the gate of the penal institution the dusty gold of the imperial and royal double eagle. I spent the second hour in a dell of soft grasses. My bad conscience made me fear the impossible—namely, being spotted from below. There I lay on my back and studied the sky, the slow progress of the clouds and the faster progress of the birds between them, flying in geometric formations. At ten o'clock, it occurred to me that my deskmate was now consuming his buttered roll and slices of brown sausage. Since I was usually a mere observer of the midmorning snack, anyway, I was not sensible of any important difference in simply regarding my mental image of it out here in the open. But I did get thirsty. So I made my way to a circular spring that lay by the path to the cemetery. This walk led me through a little wood running along the spine of the ridge or farther down along the terraced slope past an abandoned brickworks and along a narrow road between rows of poplars shading the ramshackle huts of cottagers. I studied the sky in the depths of the clear, more richly rewarding water, for here little fishes were flying through the clouds as well. And so the third hour passed. From eleven to twelve I wandered through the three-faithed city of the dead, the graveyards of the three official religions forming a single, large cemetery. Here all my senses were fully engaged: I studied the architecture of the monuments, the outward and inward form and meaning of the inscriptions, the names and dates of the interred, and the tributes of candles, flowers, and cakes that had been left for them. I was impressed when the period between birth and death had been a long one. A wide stream seemed to flow between the two dates. If less than five decades spanned the dates for a man, I was chagrined and looked away. I tarried longer, but sadly, at the graves of children and women. The obelisk on Father's grave was clad in brick red marble. I didn't really have anything against Frunza's inscription on it, but it started up too high and trailed down too low. It was in gilt letters, and the solemn stone seemed to have withdrawn behind the frippery. A good thing, I thought, that my dead father didn't have to stand in person behind it. He would have wanted no veil but silence, and now his stone had these garrulous, theatrical trappings imposed on it. It wasn't true after all that I had nothing against them.

At twelve o'clock, I scurried in a crouch past the Renner Pond, lying among trees above a meadow, where my soccer partner Stadler lived with his resolute mother, and stormed through the Neueweltgasse past the commercial school, traversed the Siebenbürgerstrasse past the infantry barracks, and entered the spacious public garden. From there, I continued through the Seufzerallee until I reached the Bieler Weg, then through it to the foot of the slope that seemed a continuation of the bastion-like playground wall of the school I had just circled halfway round. On the next day, I would complete the other half of the circle, through the Truthgasse, past the train station, along the foot of the Habsburgerhöhe and Schiller Park (from which our liberators had banished the monument to the poet of liberty) and through the aforementioned Bieler Weg, completing my clandestine circumambulation of the school. There I waited for the bell signaling the end of classes, then ran home, more relieved than I would have been after suffering through a day of instruction.

When I began this flimflam, I was sure that in a few days my homeroom teacher, Professor Eidinger, would investigate my absence and alarm my family. I promised myself that the result would be an open discussion of my request to be allowed to exchange my desk for an apprenticeship, the unending books for the quickly deployed tools of a trade. I didn't think my fellow pupils would tattle on me since we didn't even take note of each other's existence. But Professor Eidinger seemed not to have taken any action. He, too, had apparently allowed himself to be infected by the negligence of the newer teachers, who barely looked after their charges while they were in school, much less outside of it. In any event, I noticed nothing new at home. I didn't like to think that Mother would carry her shy, sly tactics of silence and evasion so far as to permit my guerrilla challenge to go unanswered, leaving me in the grip of my bad conscience. For that was my situation, not because I was stealing my days from school—on the contrary, I accused the school of stealing them from us—but rather because I was doing it secretly and indulging in idleness.

For forty-two days, I traced my constantly narrowing circles around that hated institution. The energetic progress of the year toward fall and winter ousted me from the forests and meadows with rain showers, fog, and storms and drove me back deeper into the city with each passing day. I found no protection from the weather in the suburbs, where people lived like villagers with fenced-in yards and watchdogs. For a while, I hung around in the waiting room of the train station and recalled my schooldays in Bielitz, where I also sat in the station, but with a clear conscience, unlike here. And how different that waiting room had been from this one, which looked like a beer joint. The one in Bielitz was airy and bright as a mirror. The tables and chairs stood in order as if for a banquet, and I could do my homework there. Here people's heads lay like dirty stones on the filthy floor tiles; I couldn't tell their bodies from one another, for they formed a dense mass. But Bielitz was the past, I continued in my sad recollections. And here there was anarchy pretending to be freedom, schoolboy rebelliousness with an urge to expand, the jungle with a token schoolbag. And now I was part of it. To what depths I had fallen! I slunk into stuffy Jewish prayer houses and drafty church naves as well, but was embarrassed when the worshippers regarded me as one of their own. So I could never stay very long in these places of refuge, and after the brief interval necessary for three slow repetitions of the text for my deceased father, I left them again, even if it was pouring outside. Finally, I found myself driven into such a corner that the only place left to hide was in the entryways of the Postgasse, swarming with usurers. There I observed Arnold in his own unlawful activities, which, in contrast to mine, were at least conscientious. Finally I'd had enough and, remorseful as I was, decided to emerge into the light again.

If I earlier asserted that it was all too easy for me to feel disgust at the financial dealings of my brother, who was taking responsibility for us in place of my father, I would have to add that it was perhaps the antipathy a rascal feels for a purposeful, responsible person . . . except that I, too, was acting from a sense of responsibility. In fact, that is what I was doing. The authority that compelled me to remove myself from the school's miseducation was my spirit. But I would be lying if I were to say that back then I was already rebelling against that institution out of a sense of intellectual duty. It happened because the spirit forced me to do it. I obeyed unconsciously, bearing the responsibility in the depths of my mind from which rose my contempt for Arnold's lower-order conscientiousness. I was ashamed of my inhuman arrogance, but at the same time I couldn't suppress it and was at pains to obscure it by being good-natured. In my essential self, I felt an obedience only to a higher authority, not to the concerns of the plains and lowlands where, in my eyes, everything—including my family—resided that comprehended life only as the fulfillment of material, nervous impulses. The fact that my illegality vis-à-vis that lower order still troubled my conscience and I suffered because of it was rooted in the mendacity of the procedure, a mendacity unworthy of the spirit. It was a morning in November. Snow and rain battled each other outside our windows, but the drops of rain still had the upper hand, devouring the first wintry blossoms on the glass. Only my eyes were occupied with this contest, while inwardly I was collecting myself for the struggle to come that day. I had had to abandon my makeshift bed in the kitchen, where the morning tea was being prepared, and had lain down on the sofa next to Arnold.

Now he was up and girding himself for his walk to the Postgasse. Tylka, Relly, and my little brothers were also preparing to leave and were already calling for their tea, which Mother served them with a piece of buttered bread. Before going out into the storm, the little ones came to my bed and looked at me a while, but I stared past them at the window.

"Munju is sick," they announced, tramping the length of our railroad flat. Arnold's sofa stood in the second room, next to the wall across from the door. Relly, never one to pass up a chance to take a swipe at me, came in too.

"Mother," she called into the kitchen, "he's really sick—sick of school."

"Hush, you tattle-tale," was the reply. I had closed my eyes and listened as Mother continued, quite near at hand. "He's a good student and has no reason to fear school. You're going to prove it to her right now, aren't you, Muniku? Hurry up and get dressed so you won't be late."

That's how they talked to me. I, who, having spent the whole night conscientiously weighing all the prerequisites, had just set myself the task of writing thirty deathless poems in German and making arrangements for them to be found by Relly after my demise. Once it was too late for the flesh, I intended that beauty not just to realize what she had lost in me through her mismeasurements, but also to have the consolation of an opportunity to make good her error by conveying to posterity the part of me that was immortal. In my narrow universe, she alone seemed capable of performing that function. For hadn't I seen Goethe and Hauptmann, Lichtenberg and Nietzsche, Ibsen and Sudermann, Schopenhauer and Stirner, Forel and Weininger and many other less-resounding names succeeding one another on the chair next to her bed beneath the night table lamp? One of her admirers by the name of Stephan Roll was in the habit of passing on to her the writings of these great minds. I didn't notice at the time that she behaved no better toward Roll's sensitive intellect and his books than Aurelzia had toward me and the "Zwei Brüder" in the forest of cornstalks. Unfortunately, Relly continued to mismeasure things, and the sensitive Stephan Roll probably had no idea that his legions of the spirit marched straight on past her and, via the chair, right into my soul. All the books that Relly brought into the house passed through my cellar before the girl, blind to things of the mind, returned them unread to the only intellectual among her admirers. After Relly had also left the house, Mother said, "You're already late for your first class. Now quick, get dressed and bring me two hundredweights of firewood. If you're nimble about it, you'll have time to split it and still not miss the second period. I'm stuck here without any wood and have to make dinner at noon." She put the money for the wood on the table and left me. I got dressed and went to dispose of the matter.

The firewood dealer was nearby. I split the few logs right there, taking off my jacket to do it, and brought the split wood home in our handcart, early enough to reach school before the second period, as Mother wished. But I had never been so determined as I was now, after the brief physical work in the sleet, not ever to tread that path again. I had swung the ax from my elbows, with all my might and sure aim, and as the logs sprang apart, I felt that all of life's complications could be split in this way. The cold rain cooled my skin, beneath which my heated blood rushed with the effort. I felt simultaneously cool-headed and burning, and it must have showed in my face, for as I brought the first load of wood into the kitchen, holding it against my chest between my chin and my outstretched arms, Mother said she had the impression that work with an ax did me more good than with a pen. "You're right," I replied and hurriedly continued with the confession that for that very reason I was no longer going to school. I did that to free myself from secrets and lies and to force her to abandon her elusive tactics. My confession was expressed in such a perniciously clever way that while admitting the fact that I was refusing to go to school, it omitted to locate the onset of that refusal in the frighteningly remote past. And so my declaration, supported by cowardice and combativeness, was both subtle and ambiguous. It was part catharsis and part preparation for battle. For it to be both in full measure, I would have had to present to my antagonist the full truth of forty-two days of playing hooky. And Mother parried my sortie just as half-heartedly as I had advanced it, by taking up only one of the possible meanings of my ambiguous declaration—namely, the easier one that I intended to stop going to school. Her avoidance of sharper conflict made me realize how much I was cut from her cloth as well as from Father's. I found it touching and amusing, and it led me to forego my woodchopper's resolution to achieve a decisive split. I spontaneously grasped the hand Mother extended: a compromise solution to the knotty problem. She waived the upper grades but insisted upon completion of the lower gymnasium, which would at least open more doors for a young man deciding on a profession than the presentation of a notice that I had failed the third year.

"But Mother, I don't care what profession I have."

"And how do you plan to support yourself?"

"That's what my hands are for."

"They're not enough by themselves."

"An ax doesn't cost much and a spade even less. And with them I can always find work and earn my bread in the forests and fields."

"And that will be enough for you?"

"Yes."

"But that's no kind of life."

"I don't expect it to be. I'll make a life within myself."

"You talk like your grandfather, and you know how he ended up."

"I don't know what you mean, Mother."

"In a charity hospital, like a beggar."

That was too much for me, not because of her words, but because of the meaning Mother attached to them. I didn't want to continue the conversation. "OK, Mother. I'll sacrifice myself for another year and a half."

"You're not doing it for me or the teachers. Only for yourself, for yourself alone. Will you finally take that to heart?"

"Yes."

I was ashamed of myself. I wanted to spit myself out. And as I had once wept five years ago because the gymnasium was still closed to me, so now I went down to the cellar to cry my eyes out because I had to return to it. The school accepted me again as if I had not missed a single day, and I felt like I was sinking into quicksand without even causing a ripple as my head went under. Professor Eidinger flushed when he caught sight of me, but he recovered quickly and observed rather than asked, "You were sick a long time." I found my old seat occupied, and one of the boys I sat next to in my new seat was also our neighbor at home. His name was Karl Rübner, and he lived across the street in Russische Gasse 17.

I had already noticed this boy earlier. His left leg was withered down to the bone and hung from his knee at an angle. This structural malformation caused him to limp, and when he walked, he always held his hands outstretched like wings to help him balance. The effort also informed his gaze, which was always straining forward. Once the season had covered the streets of our city with black ice and the municipal government seemed content to allow its citizens to negotiate these streets on their own, I began to walk with this neighbor on my way to school so he could take my arm and hold on to me as necessary. So began our acquaintance, but shortly thereafter it stumbled over an essay test in German. While we were writing, I looked over his shoulder at his test booklet because I was interested in his handwriting. He moved away. I shoved my chair closer, indulging my graphological curiosity. He moved farther away and held his left hand like a screen over his writing. I leaned down and continued to peer between his arm lying flat on the desk and the screen of his raised left hand, at his other hand writing on the paper. He hitched his chair away once more and bumped into his neighbor on the other side, who told him off. Finally, Rübner turned to me, blue sparks from his eyes making his pale face appear completely white, and said out loud, "You're not allowed to copy from me!" Aha, I thought, so that's what you're like, and on the way home that very day I abandoned him to the treacherously slippery streets, dangerous even to pedestrians whose legs were straight. If he had objected to my looking at his handwriting, I would have shrugged it off as stupidity, for the things that reveal us at our most exposed (such as our face, our hands, and our handwriting) exist precisely to be seen. Whoever conceals them has something to hide or is just as imprudent as a public speaker who conceals the truth. But the boy was instead refusing me collegial help vis-à-vis the authorities who passed judgment on us and had made known to the representative of those authorities and to the general public in the classroom my forbidden violation of the taboo, for he had protested out loud against my offense.

So he was a toady of the mighty and the majority and, to prove it, had kicked at a fellow pupil in need with his one good leg. So that's what he was like. Well, he'd just have to see how he got along on his withered leg if he used his sound one to kick a supposedly impotent fellow-sufferer in the belly. Did he hope that the mighty and the majority whom he served like a lackey would lend him an arm? I decided to put this to the test and followed him at a distance so I could gloat over his penance. The mighty did not stand by him. Might sits strapped on a revolving stool that it never leaves, for it must unceasingly administer kicks—to the right, to the left, in all directions. The backs and bellies receiving the kicks are brought forward by their possessors, their steps attended by the toadies. So the mighty didn't stand by him. Nor was the majority anywhere in sight. How could it have been? The majority was nothing but an assemblage herded together by authorities bellowing commands, and it flourished only between breakfast and lunch, in closed rooms behind chained-off entrances, and vanished into thin air like a soap bubble as soon as the doors were opened and the institutional police withdrew. Such were the mighty and the majority.

And so their inferior lackey, prompted by a healthy instinct to struggle against his fate and never carry a cane, waddled alone and endangered across the glare ice. He didn't walk on the sidewalk, where the ice glittered like a continuous mirror, offering no footholds, and the facades of the buildings threatened his head if he fell. Rather, he balanced himself on the cobblestones in the middle of the street, putting forward first the sound and then the withered leg and, though wobbling dangerously from stone to stone, still made relatively steady forward progress. In his struggle for balance, he had to use his head and his hands as well, which from the point of view of efficiency he always seemed to flail through the air in the right direction. At intersections, he stopped to look in both directions and wipe the sweat from his face. Sometimes he also stopped to rest. Then he peered far down the street to estimate how long he still had to struggle. And it was truly a grim battle the handicapped boy had to wage, not just a difficult piece of work. Watching his broad-shouldered back, I not only saw that this struggle of the lame boy to carry himself like a sound one, to make his crooked walk straight, to gain the security denied him, involved every fiber of his flexible neck, torso, and limbs, but also felt he was throwing the wisdom of all his senses, all his intellectual circumspection, all his soul's desire to live into this fiery dance on the ice. What courage, what energy, what stern obedience to the sacred gift of life were required to wage this uneven battle against the hostile forces of space. My classmate was a hero. Engaged as he was in an unending effort to stand his ground above the morass of his disability, his solidarity with the mighty and with the mass of the majority took on a different significance: it meant rest from the battle and from the uniqueness of disability, both so exhausting. Like every invalid, moreover, he already inhabited the realm of the spirit because of his bodily disability. As has already been remarked, one's only duty in this realm is to higher things, but in this case its particular object was above all the bodily well-being of the person. Such were the perceptions, feelings, and thoughts that besieged me as I followed my slippery path of revenge behind my icily endangered classmate. They may not as yet have had the clear physiognomy of the present sentences, but they were definite enough to make me understand what I had to do. I caught up with him and walked beside him to the entrance of his building. Not once did he make use of my arm, not even of my sleeve. But he redoubled his effort to tread firmly. We didn't exchange a word.

At about that time, I was studying August Forel's book on the sexual question.[22] It had become my habit to confront fully anything that claimed my attention, and in those days it was what that researcher calls *Urninge*.[23] The word itself made a stronger impression on me than the description that followed and would have been enough to frighten me off all the perverted acts comprehended by that concept. In Forel, I saw for the first time a scientific presentation of homosexual love. I had no difficulty in confirming early signs of it in myself. They were unmistakably present, from tender glances at my friend to the first kiss. Paul's influence on me was entirely one of attraction. It emanated from him with no effort on his part, and when I was in his presence, I could hardly resist it. So I began to distance myself from him and draw nearer to the physically unappealing Karl Rübner. The separation from my beloved cost me terrible effort. There were afternoons in which I had Relly lock me in the cellar so I couldn't go to Paul's, under the pretext that I had to force myself to study. In my narrow basement room, I ran back and forth from one wall to the other, like a rat in a trap, and thought I would go crazy with longing. If I heard Paul calling our customary password from the courtyard, I would sometimes begin to hammer on the door like a maniac and scream in desperation to be released, which I had to do to be heard because my cell lay in the middle of the dark, vaulted space with no outside wall. After such an outburst, Paul had to bargain with my jailor for a long time before she peevishly released me, contemptuously calling us Castor and Pollux.

I would have continued to suffer for a long time and in the end, perhaps even in vain, had not my friend himself involuntarily come to my aid. I always found it annoying to have someone present me with an image of myself. If anyone really wanted to antagonize me, however, he had only to misrepresent me, and it made no difference whether I thereby appeared worse or better than I really was. And Paul was beginning to enjoy riling me in just this way. For instance, he pursued me for weeks with a strophe of mine I had already discarded. One of its lines ended unrhymed with the auxiliary verb *haben*,[24] and to make it rhyme he substituted the dialect form *han*, insisting that's what I had written in the first place. He was able to do so because the strophe in question was unfortunately no longer around to contradict him with its living voice, in red and white. (For the sake of greater visibility, I had been writing with red ink.) Similarly, when I paid him a visit, he began to postpone the predetermined time when I'd said I would leave again, yet asserting that he had not changed anything. But the last straw was an act of presumptuousness that I, as his equal in years but his inferior in culture and reading, was unable to excuse as the result of ignorance. Actually, it had nothing to do with my oversensitive ego, like the two previous examples, but its blow to our friendship had a more devastating effect, for it struck my intellectual sensibility. My friend's extravagant ambition is an essential part of my memory of the break with him, which otherwise could not have been accomplished so quickly. The more desperately I resisted the perverse desire that I could now look squarely in the face thanks to Forel, the more powerfully it drove me toward my beloved, and I was already weighing liberation through capitulation. Moreover, the long list of great minds who, as I in the meantime discovered, had served this barren God, was more of a temptation than a warning, for it seemed almost as if, statistically speaking, pederasty was the intellectual's form of love. But one evening I came upon the assiduous boy bent over his writing, and when I asked what it was, he answered that he was working on a Faust tragedy. If any other human being had said that to me, I would have thought, "Good heavens! May the heavens forgive him, for he knows not what he says." If it had been Rübner, who was apparently also trying his luck in the intellectual sphere, I would have laid a hand upon his prominent forehead and recommended a cold shower. But Paul! Paul, the only person in my world whose elevated place in the solemn realm of the spirit I envied, whose words I kept numbered and cataloged in my memory. He spoke of important things, and what he said in all earnestness I could not help but take seriously. But what was I to think of an angel with the audacity to talk of creating the world after God had already created it? *He* was sent to hell, I believe. And satanic is what Paul now struck me as being, daring to create a Faust after Goethe had already done so. I left without bidding him farewell and went out into the spring night. I went to the cemetery, where great emotional storms always drove me, and there I slew and interred everything that had bound me to my friend, in my eyes a fallen angel. My love for him put up the most terrible resistance. It came as a great relief when the Hönich family left the apartment next to ours and moved to another street in the fall of 1920.

In the meantime, the confused state of the continent's affairs had been cleared up to the extent that central Europe, under the pressure of Western civilization, was lowered into its grave, and the eastern swamp and its fauna, against which the German lands had provided a defense for a millennium, flooded across the marches of culture. In the train carrying those who had come to plunder the corpse rode the diplomats of succession. They had been sent to make sure that those to be buried alive perished quickly, totally, and according to the schedule set by treaty. On the seats across from them sat the gardeners of revolution who were to sow the seeds of future gallows trees in the soil of the dying culture. The specialists for estate sales, however, were stretched out on their empty crates calculating the worth of the Belvedere Gallery.[25] Their poorer colleagues, with their sights set on bankrupt firms, were snoring in the luggage racks so they would be rested for their dash from the train to the stock market; among them were many idlers from the Postgasse. A fifth species, against whom even the countries whose demise had been dictated were permitted to defend themselves, would be beneath my mention were it not that in the midst of their swarm, standing in the corridor between his wife, Pepi, and my cousin, Relly, my brother-in-law was also riding to Vienna—a member of the species swindler.

Father had helped many estate owners sell excess acreage, threatened by the demagogic agrarian reform, to abutting tenant farmers, to their mutual satisfaction. When he was unexpectedly carried off in the midst of this business, his personal accounts among the buyers and sellers he had brought together remained partly unclear and partly unpaid. Mother, who had not been privy to his affairs, was especially ignorant of the largest deals, for they were not recorded in Father's books. For obscure reasons, they had been concluded on the basis of intimate personal trust and kept secret. The excerpt from the account of Baron Flondor that we had found on the dead man was an exception, and as its date proved, Father had requested it only at the moment when the maid whom he didn't trust had become the baroness. However, it turned out that rural honesty had not been condemned to death as quickly as the security that had perished with the demise of the Habsburgs. Almost every week Mother received visitors from the villages. But the majority of these guests were tenant farmers who had purchased small plots and were now paying back what they owed Father with the products of their farms: textiles, poultry, eggs, butter, honey, and fruit, but also grain from their fields and fuel from their woodlands. Their sheepskin caps weighed heavily enough on their guileless heads without having to bear the additional burden of a debt owed the dead man and his widow and orphans. By contrast, the indebted estate owners had hard skulls beneath their lightweight shooting hats, and however many corpses, widows, and orphans lay upon these hats, they hardly felt them at all.

Depending on what Arnold and Relly, Father's assistants in these dealings, could remember and whether other witnesses could be found, legal proceedings were initiated against the estate owners. At great cost to Mother, they were prosecuted by a relative and accomplice of Pepi's husband whom my sister had recommended as our lawyer. However, Mother's failure to gain anything from the legal battle against the young widow of Baron Flondor (the latter having passed away shortly after his wedding and the death of my father) could not really be blamed on our stalwart legal strategist. The defendant had called perjurious witnesses and had perjured herself as well, so our lawyer, who prosecuted Mother's other cases successfully—just not to Mother's benefit—in fact lost this one. Could this defeat have awakened in the mind of Pepi's husband doubts about the continuing productivity of Mother's tangled claims? Or had things begun to get too hot for him in our town? Or had his risk-free and effortless successes with us so completely turned his lopsided head that he was ambitious for greater things? Who knows the laws that govern instinctual actions like the migrations of fish and birds? I must include my brother-in-law's departure for Vienna in the same category, as an instance of the general exodus of adventurers from the East, for in setting off, drawn irresistibly to the streets of the metropolis, he was leaving behind in Czernowitz a forest full of prey. The libidinal motives of his wife and Relly were visible: in the case of the former, it was the animalistic masculinity of her husband's person; in the case of the latter, as I knew, it was her desire for the long extremities of her doctor from Kremsier, who had in the meantime moved to Vienna, a fact that had been kept secret from Mother. Profane love, when it is serious, not only blinds the lover, but also blindfolds others. When it is more frivolous, it just throws sand in others' eyes, as it did with me, to whom this man was introduced as a doctor when in reality he was a middle-school teacher.

I assume that Pepi and Relly understood little about the business plans of their lead goose. Of course, they were unscrupulous women, but also foolish ones, totally devoted to the god who ruled them from below. Himself a slave to his instincts, the adventurer must have succeeded in harnessing their drives to his thief's cart. And one fine evening, this threesome appeared before Mother, who sat herself down between me and Arnold, across the table from them. With time, she had become a bit mistrustful after all. She had already heard about their new plans, but knew herself incapable of withstanding the siren song of her girls and had brought in Arnold and me to stop her ears with objections. But her son-in-law began his preamble by saying he had not come on his own account. A sense of duty and deference to his dear wife's devotion to her family had guided his steps. Now he had come to submit a proposal that, if accepted, would relieve Mother and her minor children of all their worries, but, if rejected, would relieve him of lots of trouble and absolve him from any further responsibility. "Toward you as well, dear," he said, bowing toward my sister.

"But, sweetheart, why be so cruel? Mutti didn't say she would turn you down."

"I wish she would."

"I know. You've got all you need already."

Relly was less delicate. "Why beat around the bush? If you want to help us, do so. But don't expect us to beg. We have our pride, too, even though we're broke." Mother wasn't prepared for this tactic, and the artful construction of the triple colloquy bewitched her. And when a Danube-blue panorama of the *Kaiserstadt* was rolled out for her to feast her eyes upon, with a little X in the Second District to mark the site of their future four-room apartment, and their proposal was about to follow, Arnold and I were asked to leave the conference because we, as subjects, didn't have the right to know what our government had in store for us. We might have raised objections. Only when the whole miserable business was concluded did we learn what Mother had agreed to.

Supported by his Romanian connections, her son-in-law was to open a livestock-importing business. Mother's contribution would be 49 percent of the seed capital in the form of guarantees for loans that she authorized her entrepreneurial son-in-law to take, backed by the claims still under litigation by her lawyer. As watchdog to make sure this capital was used according to contract, Relly was appointed as Mother's representative and would go with them to Vienna. Mother was to pay for her trip and lodgings in Vienna until the first astronomical profits from their fantastic business started to roll in. At the latest, by then, but more likely already by the end of the first quarter, Relly would be living like royalty on the firm's earnings, while Mother herself would be showered with gold. Austria, gnawed by hunger amidst her magnificent antiquities, would surely purchase each Bucovina goose and every eastern ox with its weight in art treasures, which, converted to dollars by way of America and placed into Arnold's hands in the Postgasse, would be transformed into bullion. Mother fulfilled this clause of their contract, and right down to reserving a window seat in a second-class compartment for our fair-weather traveler Relly, Pepi used up almost half the savings resulting from Arnold's stock-market deals and the honorable payments from the small clients of our deceased father. As one of the directors of a large Viennese import firm, Relly had to be equipped with a wardrobe for public appearances, including an expensive pearl necklace. Mother's extra contributions for Relly, however, were supposed to last for only six months. I had never seen Pepi and Relly on such intimate terms with each other as after the conference with Mother.

It was touching to see how Mother put her whole caring heart and soul into her hands as her nimble fingers stuffed the poultry necks, braided the *Kolatschen,*[26] looped the *Kranzkuchen,*[27] and prepared a hundred other delicacies to fill the adventurers' food baskets. She had already given them everything, but said, "At least they should have enough to eat," in response to Arnold's annoyance at this foolishness. What she had retained of the entire mendacious business conference was that her dear children were going to a country where people were starving. As my sister and Relly took their leave, they asked each of us what we would like as a present. They would be able to fulfill our wishes by tomorrow at the latest; what was certain today was their good intentions. Arnold, his brows knit and in a low voice, required only that they fulfill their obligations. He didn't need any presents.

“Don’t take the last crust of bread from her mouth,” he said almost pleadingly, and I was shocked to hear him speak of Mother as “her,” as if she were some random female, since it had never been our custom to use pronouns to refer to our parents—except for Pepi since her first marriage, that is, and perhaps for that reason alone I no longer considered her to be one of us.

I was no rationalist like my brother and lacked the mental muscle for a quarrel with fate, which I felt his admonitions to the travelers amounted to. I had a wish that I conveyed to them on a piece of paper. It was for an edition of Nietzsche’s collected works, which I asked them to send me. In my choice of authors at that time, I was guided by their portraits and the reproductions of their handwriting in Eduard Engel’s two-volume history of literature.[28] After Goethe, Nietzsche made the deepest impression upon me. His small, separated letters seemed to me like pearls of light, and his intense head struck me as that of a prophet. It may also be that I was captivated by his Polish physiognomy, for I loved the Poles.

Meanwhile, I was able to obey my inner imperative and leave school in full public view and for good. In my final report card for the trimester of the third year I had had to repeat, the inevitable “Unsatisfactories” in Greek and Latin had been joined by another in Romanian, the new official language of the state, to which I refused to lend my ear, regarding it as the usurper of my homeland. Before I left school, I had discovered a dentist looking for an apprentice and had already negotiated with him. He was prepared to take me, but wanted to talk to Mother about it first. My wish to learn the techniques of dentistry foundered on this condition, for Mother could find no spare time for such an interview. After a few more failed attempts to learn some trade that was in demand, I gave up trying to prepare to enter society and earn my living in the future by means of a trade. Among the Russian emigrants, I sought and found students of the German language and earned enough, working eight hours a day, to reimburse Mother for my keep. But my main occupation was self-instruction in German and the craft of poetry. In the former, I confined myself to an unhurried and intense reading of the classics; in the latter to my own experiments in all forms and genres. In reading, I strove for clarity, concision, and honesty of comprehension; in writing, of expression. I subjected the results to severe inspection: I took notes on what I read and then compared them with the original texts, and I studied my own products and compared them with what I had intended. In both cases, I was more apt to accept inadequacies that could be enlarged upon than exaggerations that struck me as counterfeit. The linguistic or theoretical literary categories of what emerged from this organic process didn't concern me. I was aiming for the whole figure, not its skeleton; the garden, not its botany. I wanted to see and create, not unravel and construct.

Letters arrived from Vienna, written in Pepi's steep, cramped, and sharp hand on the letterhead of a world-famous hotel. The hands of her husband and Relly were present only in greetings along the edge. All was going according to plan, of course. When Arnold was skeptical, Mother showed him the passages that the letter writer had underlined on the sturdy sheets. After six months, the enterprise began to bear its first fruits as expected, and although it may be that Relly (as Pepi reported) was living like a queen, it was still (as we could see) at our expense. The sums that Arnold had to smuggle across the border for this purpose contained not just his and my pocket money, but also our thin breakfast butter, which was now replaced by margarine. Mother had no more objections to even her youngest sons' leaving school, and she stuck them into paid apprenticeships in tailoring supply shops where they were to become salesmen. Me alone she continued to upbraid for refusing to continue my studies. She seemed to have had fond hopes for me in that regard and treated me as a disappointment, with bitterness and reserve. My temperament was as steadfast as Arnold's, but softer. It's possible that she had hoped to lean her old age upon me. I bore that in mind and therefore thought no more about girls—although it cost me a struggle to stay away from them—and promised myself that the books I would publish would furnish the tangible means to support her now that I had failed to learn a trade. Mother just had to be patient with me. But her patience had been exhausted by her father and by ours, and she had none left for Arnold and me, we who so resembled the deceased. And so one morning even the margarine ceased to appear on my bread, and Mother said that if you weren't working, you didn't really need anything to eat either. And yet I was paying for my food and my part of the rent; my underwear and clothes were hand-me-downs from Arnold. And I was working quite a bit and helping out around the house. From Arnold she demanded larger and larger contributions, even though his yields were less since the government had converted from Austrian paper money, and our working capital had become a fiction. On the other hand, she felt sorry for our younger brothers, who had to drudge at such a tender age, "and not one word of complaint," as she tenderly pointed out. On the other hand, she sent packages of food to Vienna every chance she got and promptly paid Relly's emolument, which ate up almost all of Arnold's profits. In fact, we survived only because the purchasers of little parcels of land continued to pay off in kind their debts to Father, whom they remembered with even more gratitude once they saw that the currency conversion would have cost them half of the amounts they had already paid off for their real-estate acquisitions. However, even this source began to dry up, flowing more slowly from week to week.

Then came a time when we rose from the table still hungry, nor did it help much when, at Mother's behest, I went to the corner grocery and returned with more margarine instead of butter, more ocher powder instead of eggs, more sugar instead of honey. And one evening, two subletters moved into our apartment. They took possession of the second room, where Arnold and I had been sleeping like kings, each in his own bed, although not as sumptuously as Relly in the Hotel Kaiserhof in Vienna. That was all over now, and the two who displaced us were young themselves: a flaxen-haired Russian photographer and a black-haired Romanian journalist. They also boarded with us and got the best plates at table. I helped them write love letters in German to nubile neighbor girls, and in exchange they told me of the lands they came from.[29]

Published Works of Moses Rosenkranz

◆ ◆ ◆

Notes

◆ ◆ ◆

Published Works of Moses Rosenkranz

1930 *Leben in Versen*. Czernowitz: Pardini.

1936 *Gemalte Fensterscheiben*. Czernowitz: Körner.

1940 *Die Tafeln*. Czernowitz: Literaria, 1940.

1947 Martin Brant (alias). *Gedichte*. Edited by Herman Roth and Immanuel Weißglas. Bucharest: private printing.[1]

1971 *27 Gedichte*. Edited by Paul Schuster. *Neue Literatur* (Bucharest) 1.[2]

1986 *Im Untergang: Ein Jahrhundertbuch*. Munich: Südostdeutsches Kulturwerk.

1988 *Im Untergang II: Ein Jahrhundertbuch*. Innsbruck: Wort und Welt.

1998 *Bukowina: Ausgewählte Gedichte 1920–1997*. Aachen: Rimbaud Verlag.

2003 *Kindheit: Fragment einer Autobiographie*. Aachen: Rimbaud Verlag.

2007 *Visionen: Gedichte*. Aachen: Rimbaud Verlag.

◆ ◆ ◆

Notes

"I Carried My Villages Within Me . . . ": Reflections on Moses Rosenkranz's Autobiographical Fragment *Childhood*

1. Maria of Romania, *Traum und Leben einer Königin* (Leipzig: List Verlag, 1935).

2. The original German text follows:

Der Erledigte

Zu mir kommt niemand zu Besuch
und mich erwartet niemand mehr:
Gestrichenem im Lebensbuch
versagt die Welt die Wiederkehr.

Sie hat auf mir schon ausgeweint
und letztes Wort auf mich gelegt;
wer sieht schon gern wenn Sonne scheint
dass sich ein Toter herbewegt?

Und das bin ich. Sie will es nicht
dass ich entstiegen bin dem Grab
und nahm verflossnes Angesicht
und wiederkomm den Berg herab.

Gestrichenem im Lebensbuch
versagt die Welt die Wiederkehr:

Zu mir kommt niemand zu Besuch
und mich erwartet niemand mehr.

In Moses Rosenkranz, *Bukowina: Gedichte 1920–1997* (Aachen: Rimbaud Verlag, 1998), p. 117.

3. The original German text follows:

Der Kuss

Das weiße Licht vom Wächterturm
fließt über die da hocken
auf dem Brett im Schwarzen Sturm
und fallen lassen Brocken

Die Wachen nah daneben stehn
im Anschlag ihre Flinten
sie können so auch dienstlich sehn
wohl die Verrichtung hinten

Dass zwei Gesichter unbedacht
sich zu einander trauen
veranlasst einen von der Wacht
von vorne hinzuschauen

Und als er löste seinen Schuss
ein Mundpaar zu erzielen
blieb lange noch im Frost der Kuss
nur die Gesichter fielen

In Moses Rosenkranz, *Im Untergang: Ein Jahrhundertbuch* (Munich: Südostdeutsches Kulturwerk, 1986), p. 96; and Moses Rosenkranz, *Visionen* (Aachen: Rimbaud Verlag, p. 60.

4. *Im Untergang*, p. 32.

5. The original German text follows:

Arktische Landschaft

Ich gehe auf Sibiriens weißer Karte
wo es im Norden an das Eismeer grenzt

hier steht der Mond im Pfauenrad des Nordlichts
das knisternd auf die Tundra niederglänzt

Aus kaltem Rachen blasen Schöpfungsstürme
Gebirg kristallnen Urschnees vor sich her
nur große Flüsse kommen an die Küste
vermählend unterm Eise sich dem Meer

Hier würgt der Eiszeitgletscher noch die Scholle
in reiner Härte glitzert hier der Schnee
auf ihm erscheint wie aus ihm selbst geschnitten
der weiße Bär und als ein Traum das Reh

Am schwarzen Himmel klirrt ein weißer Wimpel
von unsichtbarer Geisterhand geschwenkt
es ist ein Gänsedreieck es bedeutet
dass Helios nun auch dieses Lands gedenkt

Im Untergang, p. 94; *Visionen*, p. 63.

6. In 1981, Rosenkranz wrote a second version of *Kindheit*, of similar length but with quite different emphasis given to the narrated events. In 1982, he wrote a fifty-page version and then a section entitled "Youth." Then he abandoned the drafts and considered the autobiographical project a failure. "The reality of my life resists every attempt to portray it," he said in an interview (*Bukowina*, p. 162).

7. The original German text follows:

Einklang

Im Untergang der Dichtung
das Ohr am Schulterblatt
fand ich meine Richtung
indem ich rückwärts trat.

Im eignen Erbe ging ich
drin auch ein deutsches Teil
deutsch an zu summen fing ich
gespaltner Brust zum Heil

Der Schmerzen Glut entwand ich
des Worts durchdringend Licht
und so gerüstet fand ich
ja fand ich zum Gedicht

Im Untergang, p. 7.

8. The original German text follows:

Gleichnis

Tiefes Dach und enge Wände
grausam seinen Wuchs beschränken
zwingen seine grünen Hände
künstlich sich herabzusenken

Doch die ihn gebar die Scholle
hält nicht still zu diesen Leiden
spendet tief das Maß das volle
ihres Reichtums ihn zu weiden

Soll er einmal doch zerstoßen
was ihn zwingt und mit Gebärde
streuen was ihm zugeflossen
aus der Heimlichkeit der Erde

Im Untergang, p. 20.

9. The original German text follows:

Ein Buch von Menschheitswirklichkeiten,
nicht Offenbarung, nur Bericht:
von Schweiß gehärtet seine Seiten,
in welche Blut die Bilder flicht

In "Der rote Strom" (Bucharest, 1959), unpublished.

10. Interview by Matthias Huff in 1993, broadcast on April 1, 1994, in *Schönes Deutschland in der Ferne: Moses Rosenkranz, der Dichter aus der Bukowina,* Deutschlandradio Berlin. The translation of all interview material is by David Dollenmayer.

11. The original German text follows:

Schule

Wissen lehrten sie sei Macht
das zog ich näher in Betracht
und verließ die Schule

Im Untergang, p. 19.

12. Interview by Matthias Huff, 1993.

13. "At that time, I attended the second year of gymnasium barefoot. Nobody else did that. Everyone had a midmorning snack; not me. The children—I was attending a public school, a state school—were more or less well prepared. Most of them were petit-bourgeois Jewish children and therefore well dressed and well prepared, although poor. The Ruthenians and Romanians, although children of peasants and therefore badly prepared and wearing their traditional outfits, were at least clothed. The teachers called on all of them with a certain friendliness, but on me with a certain condescension, if they called on me at all: 'You little fellow there, *ja ja ja*, you in the last row.'" Interview by Matthias Huff, 1993.

14. The original German text follows:

Das Dorf

Zuerst die Krust
gebrannt aus schwarzem Moore
mit seinem Wust
und tönend schrill im Rohre

Die Körper dann
geheimnisvoll entwachsen
als Weib und Mann
dem Sumpf mit seinen Faxen

Die spielen auch
keck auf den listig-schüchtern
in Pfeifenrauch
sich bergenden Gesichtern

Und im Getu
der Pflicht beseßnen Frauen
die einen Nu
sich auch zu lieben trauen

’s ist eben Torf
mit seinen Vorweltresten
was sich im Dorf
dem Leben gibt zum besten

Im Untergang, p. 9.

15. Interview by Matthias Huff, 1995, parts of it broadcast March 27, 1998, on *Aspekte,* Zweites Deutsches Fernsehen.

16. The original German text follows:

Buchenländlers Vision vom kaiserlichen Deutschland

Durchs Gerücht mir nur bekannt
und durch Werke deiner Hände
mir durch Nebel leuchtend Land
wahr bestehende Legende

Herbstlich wenn der Reiher Flug
hoch sich dreht in deine Richtung
folgt mein Blick dem graden Zug
aus dem Herzen Reich der Dichtung

Mag dich nur von Weitem sehn
schönes Deutschland in der Ferne
schrecklich heißt es sei was schön

Im Untergang, p. 21.

17. *Im Untergang,* pp. 81–83; *Visionen,* p. 77.

18. The original German text follows:

An der deutschen Grenze

Mein Volk hängt am Strange
mein Dorf ist verbrannt
ich komme am Klange

des Worts vor dein Land

Ich hielts in den Zähnen
ich hab es bewahrt
in trotzigen Tränen
für heut aufgespart

Es ist deines Stammes
ich hielt es als Pfand
so wirst du mir öffnen
das Tor in dein Land

. . . zu bleibt die Pforte
ich find nicht Gehör;
sind hier deutsche Worte
in Umlauf nicht mehr?

Bukowina, p. 125; *Visionen*, p. 110.

19. The original German text follows:

Das Spiegelbild

Lug in den Bodensee
guck in den Rhein
in deine Träume späh
Deutschland hinein

Findest dich nirgends nicht
siehst überall
wirr ein fremdes Gesicht
mit Kainsmal

Kein Wasser heilt dies Weh
kein Traum die Pein
auch nicht der Bodensee
auch nicht der Rhein

Im Untergang, p. 104.

20. Interview by Matthias Huff, 1993.

21. In a 1930 open letter to Rosenkranz upon the publication of his first book, Alfred Margul-Sperber called the appearance of these poems a "miracle." *Czernowitzer Morgenblatt,* December 21, 1930.

22. From a 1993 interview by Stefan Sienerth in *Bukowina,* pp. 147–48.

23. "It's unfortunate, for at home I'm a simple man who hankers after domesticity and children and yearns for the land of milk and honey. I'm not ambitious, have to force myself to work, and because of my mental makeup I find it uncomfortable to have to live against my nature. The special happiness, obviously a potent feeling within me, has up to now not been able to keep me from dreaming that the respectable and neighborly existence of the majority might also be possible for me." Letter to Alfred Margul-Sperber, January 21, 1931, in "Ein Jahrhundertdichter: Moses Rosenkranz [geb. 1904]," edited by George Guţu, *Zeitschrift der Germanisten Rumäniens* 1–2 (1995), p. 165.

24. *Bukowina,* p. 44.

25. Rosenkranz observed about his poem "Einklang," "and then I suddenly say, 'I started humming German.' All my poems began as some sort of faint melody. That too is part of my heritage. For the Jews, even on their way to work, in the middle of work, were always humming melodies, always . . . when they were studying the Talmud, they would be humming songs." Interview by Matthias Huff, 1993.

26. From the poem "Rettung" (Rescued), in *Visionen,* p. 65.

27. "I write from personal necessity. You see, I found myself mostly in situations where I was alone. If I hadn't had the ability to write, I would have suffocated in my misery." Interview by Matthias Huff, 1993.

28. "I'm still a peasant, even today. Although people have been telling me since I was fifteen years old that my poems were fit to be printed, I never thought of myself as a writer. And whenever I wrote lyric poetry, I was embarrassed and threw most of it away or burned it. Now in my old age, I'm weak enough to think of myself as a poet." Interview by Doris Demandt, broadcast October 24, 1993, in the series *Zeitgenossen,* S2 Kultur (SWR 2). "When people talk about my work, I find it embarrassing. It's not a work; it's a smashed-up affair." Interview by Matthias Huff, 1995.

29. The original German text follows:

Meine Dörfer

Meine Dörfer gleichend scheuen Hunden
liegen blind in ihren schwarzen Mooren
liegen krank und lecken sich die Wunden

liegen abseits von der Welt . . . verloren

Unbeachtet gehen hin die Jahre
kommt der Tod mit seiner Knochenbahre

Kommt der Winter mit den weißen Stürmen
drosselt sie in seinen langen Nächten
und verschließt in seinen kalten Türmen
wo sie bleiben als in Sühneschächten

Ihre Seelen nur mit Dunkel füllend
sich zum Schlafe eng in Kälte hüllend

Kommt der Frühling bricht des Frostes Schlösser
und die ausgelaßnen Wasser tragen
weg die Hütten die wie lecke Fässer
Hohl an die zerbrochnen Ufer schlagen

Kommt der Sommer trocknet sie in Feuern
Herbst verbirgt sie hinter Regenschleiern

Meine Dörfer gleichend scheuen Hunden
liegen blind in ihren schwarzen Mooren
liegen krank und lecken sich die Wunden
liegen abseits von der Welt . . verloren

Unbeachtet gehen hin die Jahre
kommt der Tod mit seiner Knochenbahre

Bukowina, p. 115.

30. "Der Außenseiter" (The outsider), in *Das poetische Werk in acht Bänden,* vol. 4, unpublished ms., p. 48.

31. The memoir provides an entire moral philosophy in one sentence: "My young moral sensibility placed reason above nature, responsibility above desire, and honesty toward one's fellow man above everything else" (p. 153).

32. The original German text follows:

Hinweis

Wir versuchen uns hinaufzustehlen
dringen zu den Sternen zu den Engeln vor

Toren wir an unsern Sohlen unsern Seelen
klebt das Moor . . .

Visionen, p. 145.

33. The original German text follows:

Der Kentaur in der Stadt

Ein Zorn hat ihn aus Schlucht und hohem Wald
von Göttern einst bewohnt zu uns verweht
den Bart in Locken wunderlich gedreht
trabt er verloren über den Asphalt

Von Einsamkeit und Licht der Ampeln blind
tritt unsern Wäglein er aufs Käferdach
und trägt sich Schuld los und gemach
durch Straßensperren wie ein Frühlingswind

Er findet nicht in seinen Hain zurück
und unser Tag nimmt seinem Huf den Tanz
dem Bart die Ringel und dem Aug den Glanz
und legt ihm um den Hals den Klepperstrick

Im Untergang, p. 44; *Visionen,* p. 27.

Stanislau, 1909–1910

1. German *Doppelmonarchie:* Austria-Hungary. The Habsburg monarch was both the Austrian kaiser and the king of Hungary.

Tlumacz and Berbeschti, 1910–1913

1. A sweet Austrian yeast bread.

2. "At dawn, when the roosters crow": the first line of the poem "Das verlassene Mädlein" (The forsaken maiden) by Eduard Mörike (1804–1875).

3. Hugo von Hofmannsthal (1874–1929), poet and playwright, best known as the librettist for Richard Strauss's operas *Die Frau ohne Schatten* and *Der Rosenkavalier;* Rainer Maria Rilke (1875–1926), one of the greatest poets

of the twentieth century; Georg Trakl (1887–1914), expressionist poet who committed suicide as a medical orderly during the First World War.

4. "An innkeeper, wondrous mild / lately was my host; / a golden apple was his sign, / a branch served as its post": the first strophe of the poem "Einkehr" (Stopping at an inn) from the cycle *Wanderlieder* (Songs of wayfaring, 1813) by Ludwig Uhland (1787–1862). The "innkeeper" of the poem is an apple tree beneath which the wayfarer spends the night.

5. Here Rosenkranz alludes to Uhland's best-known poem "Der gute Kamerad" (The good comrade, 1812), in which a soldier's comrade-in-arms falls at his side:

> Eine Kugel kam geflogen,
> Gilt's mir oder gilt es dir?
> Ihn hat es weggerissen,
> Er liegt mir vor den Füßen,
> Als wär's ein Stück von mir.
>
> A bullet came flying,
> Is it for me or you?
> Him it snatched away,
> He lies at my feet,
> As though a part of me.

6. In 1503, the sculptor, engraver, and painter Veit Stoss (c. 1450–1533) forged a document in an attempt to recoup money he regarded as misappropriated from him. He was branded through both cheeks for his crime.

7. "Oy, young man, young man, I'm calling you; come right on in."

The Advent of War, 1913–1914

1. "To My Peoples": Kaiser Franz Joseph's announcement of the declaration of war against Serbia.

2. Eugene of Savoy (1663–1736), Habsburg general in wars against Turkey and France and an Austrian national hero.

3. In German, k. u. k., *kaiserlich und königlich*, "imperial and royal," was the designation for all state institutions of the Habsburg Empire. See note 1 in the "Stanislau" chapter.

4. Secondary school leading to university study.

5. Walachia is the historic name for the region of southern Romania whose principal city is Bucharest.

Flight, 1914–1916

1. Schönbrunn Palace on the outskirts of Vienna was the imperial summer residence.

2. Cf. Genesis 26:1–7. Rosenkranz is in error here: it is Isaac who denies his wife, Rebekah, rather than Abraham who denies Sarah.

3. Founded in 1757 by the Empress Maria Theresia after the Austrian victory over the Prussians in the battle of Kolin, this award was the highest decoration for bravery in the Austro-Hungarian Empire.

4. Ruthenian: "lover," actually "fucker."

5. Rosenkranz appears to have conflated the name of the lieutenant (Vanya) and the name of the younger Cossack patrolman (Kolya).

6. The original German text follows:

> Ich kann nicht die Sprachen der Leute,
> aber recht gut ihre Leiden.
> Dir, Vater, laß mich sie schreiben:
> Gabst Du dazu doch die Hand mir.
> Sehr fürchten sie voreinander,
> und was ihn im Ebenbild ängstigt,
> so mancher machts aus sich selber:
> den blicklosen leblosen Leichmann.
> Von Dir herniedergesendet,
> empfinde ich Angst nicht vor ihnen;
> aber der Last ihrer Schmerzen
> fühl ich in mir keine Muskeln.
> So gib mir das Wort, mir zu helfen;
> denn was ich sage, wird leichter:
> Fast mühelos heb ich den Toten
> zu Dir nun auf diesem Blatt.

"Beim Anblick eines Selbstmöders in Uniform, 1918" (On seeing a suicide in uniform, 1918), written in 1920, first published in the journal Neue Literatur (Bucharest) (1971). Now in Bukowina, p. 13.

7. Masuria, today in northeastern Poland, but in 1914–1916 in East Prussia.

8. Arid grasslands in eastern Hungary.

9. See note 1 in the "Stanislau" chapter and note 3 in the "Advent of War" chapter.

Prague, 1916–1917

1. In the original alliteration: "Stille, Starre und Staub."

2. Prince Clemens von Metternich (1773–1859), Austrian foreign minister and architect of the repressive post-Napoleonic European order; Friedrich von Gentz (1764–1832), political theorist and Metternich's secretary.

3. The imperial crypt beneath the Kapuzinerkirche in Vienna, containing the remains of 138 Habsburgs.

4. See note 3 in the chapter "Advent of War."

5. Ruthenian: "miss," "young lady."

6. Ruthenian expression of surprise: literally, "Prick onto you!"

7. "Haliczina" is the Polish name for the Austrian crownland Galicia, in which the town of Stanislau was located.

8. German *Mund,* "mouth."

9. German *rein,* "clean, pure."

10. Rosenkranz is describing the Orloj, the elaborate fifteenth-century mechanical clock in a tower on the Old-Town Square in Prague.

11. Heinrich von Kleist (1777–1811), dramatist and author of novellas.

12. A fruit cake containing currants, almonds, and lemon peel.

13. "Bretter, die die Welt bedeuten." A quote from Friedrich von Schiller's (1759–1805) poem "An die Freunde" (To my friends).

14. Exodus 12:14, 17, 37.

15. Exodus 12:8.

16. Cf. Exodus 12:11.

17. The book is Clemens Brentano's late-romantic fairy tale "Das Märchen von Gockel und Hinkel" (The tale of Gockel and Hinkel, 1838), in Rosenkranz's edition apparently entitled "Das Märchen vom Gockel, Hinkel und der Gackeleia." Gockel and Hinkel, the names of an elderly couple who are the protagonists, are German dialect alternatives to the standard *Hahn* and *Huhn* (rooster and hen). Their daughter is named Gackeleia, from the verb *gackeln* (to cluck, cackle). Ironically, the villains of the tale are three greedy Jews who get transformed into donkeys at the end.

18. Basedow's syndrome, also called Grave's disease, is characterized by hyperthyroidism, bulging eyeballs, and a goiter.

Hullein and Kremsier, 1917–1918

1. Novel by George Sand (1804–1876), published in 1832.

2. The Boyars were aristocratic estate owners in czarist Russia and old Romania. Sarmatia was the ancient name for the region between the Vistula and the Volga.

3. The translation follows:

> I know you not,
> and see you but inwardly:
> What does a face matter
> on the lea of our soul?

4. The equivalent of sixth grade in U.S. schools.

5. Publisher of dictionaries and standard reference works on German orthography and grammar.

Return to Berbeschti, 1918

1. A phrase from the Grimms' tale "Die zwei Brüder" (The two brothers).

2. This passage is quoted verbatim from the Grimms' story.

3. One of the twin hunters in the tale is turned to stone by a witch, then liberated by his brother.

Czernowitz, 1918–1919

1. That is, the Triple Entente among France, Great Britain, and Russia.

2. Pilsudski recruited the Polish legions as units of the Austro-Hungarian army at the beginning of the First World War to fight against the Russians. They were supposed to form the core of a future Polish army.

3. After Mihai Eminescu (1850–1889), national poet of Romania.

4. Karl May (1842–1912), prolific author of adventure and Wild West novels.

5. Christoph Martin Wieland (1733–1813).

6. Johann Gottfried Herder (1744–1803), *Stimmen der Völker in Liedern* (Voices of the peoples in song, 1778) and *Ideen zur Philosophie der Geschichte der Menschheit* (Reflections on the philosophy of the history of mankind, 1784–1791).

7. Johann Heinrich Voß (1751–1826) translated the *Odyssey* (1781) and the *Iliad* (1793) into German hexameters.

8. There is an untranslatable pun here, for *Trost* means "consolation."

9. Gotthold Ephraim Lessing (1729–1781), *Laokoon; oder, Über die Grenzen der Malerei und Poesie* (Laocoön: An essay on the limits of painting and poetry, 1766).

10. See note 2 in the chapter "Hullein and Kremsier."

11. The original German text follows:

> Du Bruder, noch im Sumpfe, willst mein Recht:
> Doch lebst du recht, wie ich, es zu verdienen?
> Denn lebst du krumm, so machst du's grade schlecht,
> wenn du herauskommst aus den Wachstumsschienen.

12. E. A. Seemann Verlag was a Leipzig publisher of books on the fine arts.

13. Anders Zorn (1860–1920), Swedish painter and etcher.

14. The Leipzig publishing house Philipp Reclam issued the classic works of German and world literature in cheap paperback editions.

15. Region on the border between Hungary and Romania, colonized by Germans in the Middle Ages and claimed by Romania at the end of the First World War.

16. German *der Mensch*, "human being; mankind."

17. The original German text follows:

> "Nun bist du fünfzehn Jahre alt geworden!
> Des Daseins Jugendhälfte ist verbraucht.
> Die Welt fährt fort, zu brennen und zu morden:
> Du hast in Tinte Federn bloß getaucht."
>
> Was konnt ich anders tun, gestrenge Seele,
> wenn du den Geist mir aufgegeben hast,
> daß er in mir dem Worte sich vermähle—
> Und sendetest die Träume noch zu Gast.
>
> "Vertändelt aber hast du nur die Sendung:
> Geist kommt in deinen Händen nicht zum Wort;
> In kalter Verse klirrender Vollendung
> Durch erzne Reime sein Elan verdorrt."

So soll ich ihn gesetzlos walten lassen,
das Wort ergreifend, wie der Mob den Stock,
zu wüten in den edlen Sprachgelassen,
so wie im Blumenhaus der Ziegenbock?

"'s ist nicht die Zeit, des Doms der Sprach zu achten,
wo Menschen sprachlos unterm Himmel stehn;
in Särgen weinend Greise übernachten,
in Gräbern Mütter hoch zu Kinde gehn."

So laß mich sie in meiner Sprache betten,
in deren Eis sie unzerstörbar sind!
Nur so vermag ich sie noch hier zu retten,
im Grab die Mutter und in ihr das Kind.

18. A Germanic tribe along the middle Rhine (in Latin, the Sugambri) conquered by the Romans in 8 B.C. Germanicus destroyed the shrine of their goddess Tanfana in A.D. 14.

19. An inconsistency in the manuscript. On Saturday, Relly says he will get his grades the next day, and at the beginning of the previous paragraph, Rosenkranz says it is Monday.

20. The original German text follows:

Vater im Jenseits: Denn nun bist du drüben.
Dein Scheiden schmerzt, weil ohne Abschied du,
von deinem einzigen Gute hier, den Lieben,
verziehen mußtest, wie man sagt: zur Ruh.

Da hilft kein Trost: Nicht uns, im Fleisch noch steckend,
und auch nicht dir, der schon im Reinen schwebt;
vielleicht: Vergessen, diese Wund bedeckend,
bis Wiedersehn es von der tiefen hebt.

Auf Wiedersehen, ohne Abschiedstränen:
Wie gut, daß du, nicht scheidend, uns entschlüpft!
So müssen wir uns nach einander sehnen,
bis uns der Schöpfer wiederum verknüpft.

21. The original German text follows:

Wer Vatern sucht, tritt mir vor Brust.
Hier liegt nur, was an ihm war Dust.
Was er gewesen, ist er noch
In mir, und nicht in diesem Loch,
worauf ich seinen Namen schrieb
weil hier sein staubiger Mantel blieb.

22. Auguste-Henri Forel (1848—1931), Swiss neuroanatomist and psychiatrist. *La question sexuelle* (Paris, 1905), translated as *Die sexuelle Frage* (Munich, 1905) and *The Sexual Question* (New York, 1909).

23. Also, *Uranist,* "homosexual." From Urania, an epithet of Aphrodite, engendered by her father, Uranos, without a woman.

24. German *haben,* "to have."

25. A palace complex in Vienna built for Prince Eugene of Savoy in the early eighteenth century. It houses a famous art collection.

26. See note 1 in the chapter "Tlumacz and Berbeschti."

27. A cake in the form of a wreath.

28. *Geschichte der deutschen Literatur von den Anfängen bis in die Gegenwart* (History of German literature from its beginnings up to the present day, Leipzig, 1906).

29. The first version of *Kindheit,* written in 1958, breaks off at this point. Subsequent versions of 1981 and 1982 were also abandoned. Moses Rosenkranz's mother died in the 1930s. His brother Arnold also died between the wars, of tuberculosis. All the other siblings survived the Second World War in eastern Europe, France, or Israel.

Published Works of Moses Rosenkranz

1. An alias was necessary because Moses Rosenkranz had already been arrested by the Russians and sent to the Gulag.

2. Printing these poems in the first issue of *Neue Literatur,* a Romanian German-language literary journal, was an act of courage because Moses Rosenkranz had already fled to the Federal Republic of Germany.